CARIB-SPEAKING INDIANS

ANTHROPOLOGICAL PAPERS OF
THE UNIVERSITY OF ARIZONA
NUMBER 28

CARIB-SPEAKING INDIANS
Culture, Society and Language

ELLEN B. BASSO, editor

Contributors

Nelly Arvelo-Jimenez   Marshall Durbin
Ellen B. Basso   Peter Kloos
Audrey Butt Colson   Peter G. Rivière
Lee Drummond   Helmut Schindler
Jean-Paul Dumont

THE UNIVERSITY OF ARIZONA PRESS
TUCSON, ARIZONA 1977

About the Editor...

ELLEN B. BASSO's field research, focusing upon language, cultural symbols, and social relations, has been among the Indians of South America and Northern Canada. She has written a book, *The Kalapalo Indians of Central Brazil,* as well as several articles on social organization, language contact, and cosmology. As of 1977 she was working on a book about Northern Athapaskan oral tradition. She attended Hunter College in New York City and received the Ph.D. degree in anthropology from the University of Chicago in 1968, joining the faculty at the University of Arizona in 1971.

THE UNIVERSITY OF ARIZONA PRESS

CONTENTS

Preface   5

Guide to Pronunciation   7

1. Introduction: The Status of Carib Ethnography   9
   Ellen B. Basso

2. A Survey of the Carib Language Family   23
   Marshall Durbin

3. Some Problems in the Comparative Study of Carib Societies   39
   Peter G. Rivière

4. The Akawaio Shaman   43
   Audrey Butt Colson

5. Carijona and Manakïnï: An Opposition in the Mythology of a Carib Tribe   66
   Helmut Schindler

6. On Being Carib   76
   Lee Drummond

7. From Dogs to Stars: The Phatic Function of Naming Among the Panare   89
   Jean-Paul Dumont

8. The Kalapalo Dietary System   98
   Ellen B. Basso

9. A Study of the Process of Village Formation in Ye'cuana Society   106
   Nelly Arvelo-Jimenez

10. The Akuriyo Way of Death   114
    Peter Kloos

TABLES

1.1 Extant Carib-speaking tribes: location, population, and ethnographic studies 10–11

2.1 Major subdivisions of Carib languages for which linguistic material is available 27

2.2 Internal relations among the Carib languages 35

5.1 Carijona clan names 66

6.1 Parental affiliation and legitimacy of 100 children born on Upper Pomeroon River, 1969-70 85

8.1 Partial taxonomy of "living things" important in the Kalapalo dietary system 99

8.2 Paradigm of Kalapalo cosmological terms 101

10.1 Akuriyo mortality and causes of death 117

10.2 Akuriyo age classification 117

MAPS

1.1 Location of Carib-speaking tribes 8

2.1 Carib tribes of Colombia and northern Venezuela, and possible migration routes 29

2.2 Carib languages south of the Amazon 32

2.3 Carib languages of the Guiana land mass 33

6.1 Settlement patterns on upper Pomeroon River 80

10.1 Akuriyo territory in southeast Surinam 115

PHOTOGRAPHS

Trio boy 12

Kalapalo man 12

Carijona man 12

Trio man planting manioc 12

Ye'cuana women returning from manioc fields 13

Ye'cuana women grating manioc 14

Ye'cuana woman making a manioc grater 14

Kalapalo girl grating manioc 14

Kalapalo woman preparing manioc bread 14

Trio woman sieving manioc flour 14

Ye'cuana communal house 15

Traditional Trio house 15

Members of a Pomeroon River Carib household cluster 16

Members of a Kalapalo communal household 16

Panare man in tobacco field 17

Kalapalo men entering a house to dance 17

Trio hosts assembled in plaza, awaiting visitors 18

Carijona men preparing a bark trumpet 19

Akawaio shaman pupil 48

Shaman with equipment for seance 50

The shaman's bird, the swallow-tailed kite 55

Ceremonial armbands of the Akawaio shaman 56

Shaman wearing ear pendants of bird down 57

Carijona men at dance festival 67

Carijona man preparing a roof covering 67

Carijona itutarï mask 68

Carijona iwo mask 70

Carijona woman 73

Timber crew on the Pomeroon River 81

Carib family on the Issororo River 84

Young Carib woman 84

Panare man building a house 90

Panare man collecting honey 91

Panare women preparing food 93

Panare men's communal meal 93

Panare man painting blowgun darts with curare 95

Kalapalo men dancing with Kuikuru women 101

Kalapalo women singing in the village plaza 104

Kalapalo women preparing piqui and manioc soup 105

Sketch of a Ye'cuana village 107

Carrying basket woven by Ye'cuana women 108

Ye'cuana man dressed up for a festival 111

Ye'cuana woman weaving a bead apron 113

Akuriyo children 116

Young Akuriyo man 118

PREFACE

This book is one outgrowth of a meeting of Carib specialists that was held at the Fortieth International Congress of Americanists in Rome, Italy, during September of 1972. Anthropologists from six countries, all of whom had extensive field experience with Carib-speaking groups, participated in a symposium on the ethnology of tribes speaking dialects of this widespread and numerically important South American linguistic family. The original papers, published in the *Atti del XL Congresso Internazionale degli Americanisti*, Volume II, reflected the inevitable range of interests and theoretical perspectives that appear at sessions focusing upon "areal" rather than "analytical" topics. The data that were presented, often collected among tribes as yet unrepresented by major monographs, provoked a great deal of discussion among South Americanists who were present. The success of this symposium encouraged the participants to think in terms of a publication that would include focused, topical essays about as many extant Carib-speaking groups as possible. Four of the papers originally given at the Rome meetings (those by Arvelo-Jimenez, Dumont, Basso, and Rivière) have been revised for publication in this volume. We were fortunate in being able to add five new papers (by Durbin, Drummond, Colson, Kloos, and Schindler).

Three general papers whose perspectives are comparative and classificatory open the book. My introduction is a survey both of the present condition of Carib-speaking tribes, including their location and estimated population, and of the state of Carib anthropological research. Marshall Durbin, who together with Haydée Seijas has been working on the classification of Carib languages for several years, presents their tentative findings together with an interesting summary of the history of Carib linguistic studies. Peter Rivière, in a paper on Carib social structure, is concerned with specifying some general structural principles that can be derived from Carib systems of kinship classification and rules for the selection of spouses.

Following the general essays are several papers that focus upon specific ethnographic aspects of individual tribes. Four of these are concerned with Carib culture, in that they deal with systems of classification and meaning, or "world view." Audrey Butt Colson presents a detailed interpretation of the symbolic content of Akawaio shamanism. Helmut Schindler discusses a selected group of myths from the Carijona tribe in the northwest Amazon area; Lee Drummond asks the question, just what does "Carib" mean to the Indian population of Guyana; and Jean-Paul Dumont writes about naming among the Venezuelan Panare and how this system reflects broader structural categories. My own paper deals with the relationships between Kalapalo dietary categories and Kalapalo cosmology.

Concluding the volume are two essays that focus upon problems of social organization and adaptive strategy. Nelly Arvelo-Jimenez discusses the cyclical processes that result in the fission and fusion of Ye'cuana villages in Venezuela. Peter Kloos is interested in the relation of certain Akuriyo social attitudes to their life as tropical forest hunter-gatherers in Surinam. Despite the specific topics of these papers, their authors manifest an interest in conceptual matters as well.

Indeed, there is in general a conspicuous trend in contemporary South American research towards an emphasis on conceptual systems; this is apparent in the choice of topics for papers submitted both to the symposium and to this book. Since it is precisely in this area of human phenomena that South American Indians are most poorly understood, the fact that ethnographers have begun to take this interest is of special importance.

The preparation of an anthology must inevitably involve the cooperative efforts of a number of persons, beyond their written contributions. I wish to express my great appreciation for the dedication both of the participants in the symposium on Carib culture and social structure and of the contributors to this volume. All cheerfully persevered in the face of difficulties and delays resulting from language differences, international political boundaries, and (for many) the disadvantage of having to communicate from isolated field situations. I am particularly grateful to those contributors who graciously translated their papers into English, although this was an added burden and inconvenience to them. At the University of Arizona, Professors Raymond H. Thompson and Keith H. Basso of the Department of Anthropology generously gave help, advice, and encouragement. My thanks are also due Charles Sternberg of the Arizona State Museum for his skillful preparation of the maps. Finally, I wish to express my gratitude to Gail Hershberger for her expert editorial assistance, to Barbara Fregoso for typing the manuscript, and to the University of Arizona Press for their help in publishing this volume.

The donation of photographs has enabled readers of this volume to benefit from a visual comparison of Carib peoples. I should therefore like to thank the following persons for their contributions: Peter Rivière (Trio), Helmut Schindler (Carijona), Audrey Butt Colson (Akawaio), Lee Drummond (Caribs), Jean-Paul Dumont (Panare), Nelly Arvelo-Jimenez (Ye'cuana), and Peter Kloos (Akuriyo). In addition, Mr. Ray O. Green kindly permitted reproduction of his photograph of *Elanoides forficatus,* the swallow-tailed kite.

ELLEN B. BASSO

GUIDE TO PRONUNCIATION

The following phonetic symbols are used to write terms in Carib dialects in this volume. Stress is not indicated.

Vowels

a	low central open
e	mid front open
ĕ	mid central open
i	high front close
ï	high back open
o	mid central close
ü	high central close

Diphthongs

ei as in s*ay*

ao as in h*ow*

ai as in t*i*me

au as in *ou*ch

Vowel nasalization is indicated by a tilde, as in *ã*.

Vowel length is indicated by repetition of the symbol, as in *aa*.

Consonants

p	voiced bilabial stop
t	voiced alveolar stop
k	voiced velar stop
b	unvoiced bilabial stop
d	unvoiced alveolar stop
g	unvoiced velar stop
ʼ	glottal stop
ts	voiced dental affricate
z	voiced alveolar fricative
č	voiced alveopalatal fricative
f	unvoiced bilabial fricative
s	unvoiced alveopalatal fricative
š	voiced palatal fricative
x	unvoiced dorso-velar fricative
h	unvoiced glottal fricative
m	voiced bilabial nasal
n	voiced alveolar nasal
ñ	voiced palatal nasal
ŋ	voiced velar nasal
l	voiced alveolar lateral
r	alveolar flap
w	voiced bilabial semivowel
y	voiced alveolar semivowel
j	unvoiced palatal semivowel

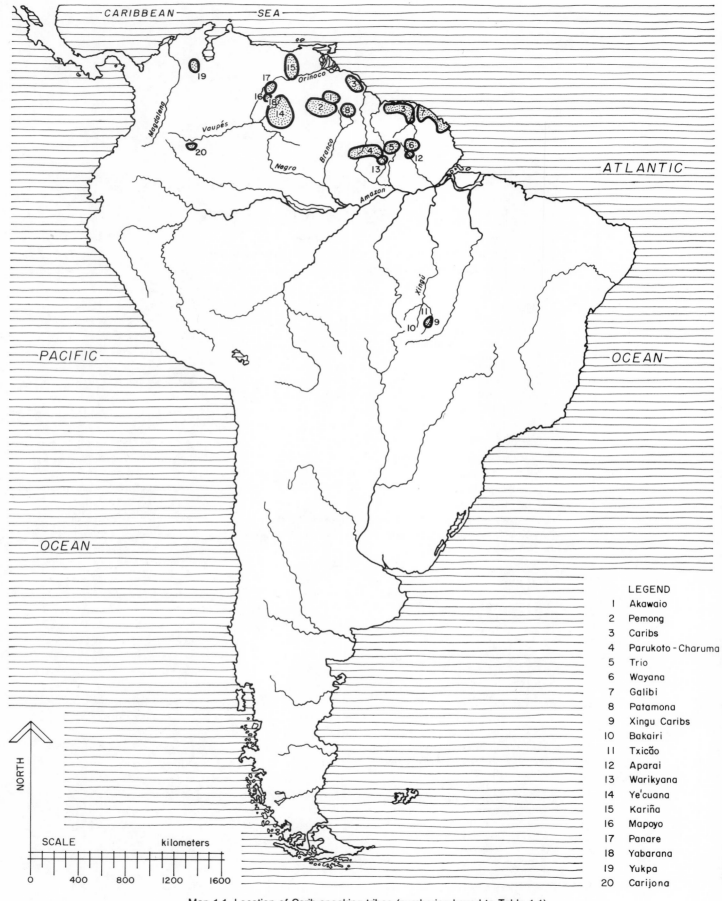

CARIBBEAN — SEA

ATLANTIC

PACIFIC

OCEAN

OCEAN

NORTH

SCALE   kilometers

0   400   800   1200   1600

LEGEND
1   Akawaio
2   Pemong
3   Caribs
4   Parukoto - Charuma
5   Trio
6   Wayana
7   Galibi
8   Patamona
9   Xingu Caribs
10 Bakairi
11 Txicão
12 Aparai
13 Warikyana
14 Ye'cuana
15 Kariña
16 Mapoyo
17 Panare
18 Yabarana
19 Yukpa
20 Carijona

Map 1.1. Location of Carib-speaking tribes (numbering keyed to Table 1.1)

1. INTRODUCTION:
THE STATUS OF CARIB ETHNOLOGY

Ellen B. Basso
Department of Anthropology, University of Arizona

The universal American process of cultural homogenization is nowhere more apparent today than in lowland South America. There, the ubiquitous forces of deculturation—epidemic disease, discrimination, forced acculturation, and exploitation—continue to undermine the identity and autonomy of the last remaining indigenous peoples, who, chiefly because of their isolated locations, have managed to survive the terrible depredations of almost four centuries of European contact. Yet despite this widespread tragedy, a relatively large number of Indians whose languages belong to the important Carib stock have been able to adjust to these pressures, and, at least for the present, have escaped the seemingly inevitable fate of indigenous ethnic extinction (see Map 1.1 and Table 1.1). More than 20 distinct Carib-speaking tribal groups, incorporating a much larger number of autonomous villages, presently survive in six South American countries. Though there have been inevitable changes among all of these groups since contact, most Carib-speaking Indians are still able to pursue many of their traditionally defined goals (the few exceptions are mainly those tribes being subjected to aggressive missionization). For these reasons, contemporary Carib-speaking peoples are a valuable source of information to anthropologists, for the comparative study not only of indigenous South American social, economic, and cultural systems, but also of the processes of adaptation to "internal colonialism" (Bonfil Batalla 1973: 23) in the tropical lowlands.

A detailed comparison of Carib groups would offer anthropologists an informed assessment of the variety of adaptive strategies and cultural systems that have arisen in the vast tropical regions of South America. This goal has not yet been achieved, yet it is worth noting that tribes belonging to the Carib linguistic stock are among the best represented in the ethnographic literature on South America. As of 1974, extensive material on 12 separate groups had been published, with most of these data having been collected during the period between 1950 and 1970. In addition, important information is available in the 19th-century publications of Karl von den Steinen on the Bakairi (1886, 1894), W. Ahlbrinck's Carib encyclopedia (1931), the work of Lisandro Alvarado (1956), and Miguel Acosta Saignes' survey of Venezuelan coastal Caribs (1946).

Using Durbin's classification of Carib linguistic families presented in this volume, we find that representatives of almost all the major units have been studied (see Table 1.1, final column). Of Durbin's *Southern Carib* group of languages, the following families are represented in the ethnographic literature: *Bakairi-Nahukwa* by the Kalapalo and the Kuikuru, and to a lesser extent by the Bakairi; and *Southern Guiana Carib* by the Ye'cuana. The *Northern Carib* group includes *Galibi* (represented by the Maroni River Caribs, the Kariña, and the Barama River Caribs) and *East-West Guiana Carib* (represented by the Trio, Waiwai, Wayana, Akawaio, and Kashuyana). Recently, anthropologists have begun field research among another *Southern Carib* group, the Carijona *(Southeastern Colombia Carib),* and among other *Northern Carib* groups: the Panare *(Western Guiana Carib),* the Txicão *(Northern Brazilian Outliers),* the Yukpa *(Northeastern Columbia–Venezuela Border),* and the Akuriyo (probably *East–West Guiana Carib).* Therefore, all major extant Carib language families should be represented by ethnographies of some detail in the near future.

Naturally, the data presently available in the various published sources are not equally detailed, nor are they always of value for comparative purposes. Anthropologists of varied interest, training, and professional background have rarely written with comparative problems in mind. However, it is possible to specify a number of directions for a future comparative study of Carib peoples.

TABLE 1.1

Extant Carib-Speaking Tribes: Location, Population, and Ethnographic Studies (Numbering is Keyed to Map 1.1)

Tribe	Location	Estimated Population	Sources of Data	Ethnographic Studies
1. Akawaio	"Upper Mazaruni Reservation in Northern Pakaraima Mountains," Guyana; "on the frontier of Bolívar state with Guyana," Venezuela	3,000	Butt 1966a Kloos 1972a	Butt 1953, 1956, 1960, 1961, 1962, 1966b
2. Pemong *Includes:* Arekuna, Makusi or Makushi (Taulipang), Kamaracoto	"In the centre and southwest of Bolívar state, chiefly by the river Paraguá and the Gran Sabana"; "Upper Rio Branco Savannas"; a few Arekuna also in Guyana, near Venezuelan border	2,600–7,000	Mosonyi 1972	
3. Caribs	Coastal areas of Guyana, Surinam (especially on or near lower Barima, Barama, Pomeroon, Wayombo, Coppename, and Maroni rivers)	more than 2,100	Kloos 1972a, 1972b	*Barama River Caribs:* Gillen 1934, 1936 *Maroni River Caribs:* Kloos 1968, 1969, 1970, 1971, 1972a, 1972b
4. Parukoto-Charuma *Includes:* Parukoto, Waiwai, Hishkaryana, Waimira, Saluma, and possibly other village groups or remnants thereof	Serra Acarai, headwaters of Essequibo River; "between Trombetas, Branco River, and the Guyana border"	1,500	Frikel 1957, 1958	*Waiwai:* Fock 1963 Yde 1960, 1965 *Hishkaryana:* Derbyshire 1965
5. Trio *Includes:* Tiriyó, Rangu, Akuriyo, Pianakoto, Triometesen, and possibly other village groups or remnants thereof	Southwestern border between Surinam and Brazil	500	Frikel 1957, 1958 Kloos 1972a	Figueiredo 1963 Frikel 1960, 1971b Frikel and Cortez 1972 Rivière 1969, 1971
6. Wayana (see *Aparai*, no. 12 below)	Southeastern border between Surinam and Brazil (formerly in Jari-East Paru River area in Brazil); French Guiana in southwestern Brazilian border area	400–500	Duchemin 1972 Anonymous 1972a	Ahlbrinck 1956 Hurault 1968, 1972
7. Galibi	Eastern coastal area of French Guiana, border of Brazilian state of Amapá	700	Duchemin 1972 Anonymous 1972a	
8. Patamona (Ingarikó)	"Southern Pakaraima Mountains, in the Potaro River and Ireng River areas," Guyana-Venezuela border	more than 850	Kloos 1972a	
9. Xingu Basin Caribs *Includes:* Kalapalo, Kuikuru, Migiyapei (remnants of "Nahukwa" and "Matipuhy" villages)	Upper Xingu Basin, state of Mato Grosso, Brazil	320	Agostinho da Silva 1972 Anonymous 1972a	*Kalapalo:* Basso 1970, 1973a, 1973b, 1975 *Kuikuru:* Carneiro 1956–57, 1956–58, 1961 Dole 1956–57, 1956–58, 1964, 1966

Group	Location	Population	References	References
10. Bakairi	Pôsto Simões Lopes, Batovi River, state of Mato Grosso, Brazil	230	Agostinho da Silva 1972 / Anonymous 1972a	von den Steinen 1886, 1894
11. Txicão (Ikpeng)	Upper Xingu Basin, state of Mato Grosso, Brazil	60	Patrick Menget 1973: personal communication / Anonymous 1972a	
12. Aparai / *Possibly a subgroup of Wayana (no. 6 above)*	"East upper Paru, Jari, Maecuru, between Paru and Jari [rivers]"; states of Pará and Amapá, Brazil	200–300	Anonymous 1972a	
13. Warikyana (Arikeñá) / *Includes*: Kashuyana, Ewarhoyana, Kahuyana, Ingarune, and possibly other village groups	Mid-Trombetas, state of Pará, Brazil	300	Frikel 1958	*Kashuyana:* Frikel 1953, 1955, 1961, 1970, 1971a / Frikel and Cortez 1972 / Galvão 1970
14. Ye'cuana (Maquiritare, Mayongong) / De'cuana a related group?	"In the east of Amazonas territory, and the south of Bolivar state," Venezuela; "Upper Aurisi River," Brazil	1,500	Mosonyi 1972 / Arvelo-Jimenez 1971	Arvelo-Jimenez 1971, 1973 / de Barandiarán 1962a, 1962b, 1965 / de Civrieux 1960, 1968, 1970 / Fuchs 1962, 1964
15. Kariña (Carina, Karinya, Kalina, Cari'na)	"Small enclaves in the centre and south of Anzoategui state and in the north of Bolivar state," Venezuela	2,776–4,000	Mosonyi 1972	Schwerin 1963, 1966
16. Mapoyo	"In the north Amazon Territory [Venezuela]. No concrete data available on these groups."	(?)	Mosonyi 1972	
17. Panare	"Zone northwest of Bolivar state (Caicara, La Urbana, Túriba)"; "from the northwest by the right bank of the Orinoco, to the south as far as the Río Suapure and to the east as far as the basin of the upper and Middle Cuchivero," Venezuela	2,500	Mosonyi 1972 / Dumont 1974	Dumont 1974
18. Yabarana	"Neighborhood of San Juan de Manapiare, Amazonas Territory," Venezuela	50	Mosonyi 1972	
19. Yukpa / *Includes*: Yupa, Yuko, "tame Motilones"	Sierra de Perijá, Zulia state (frontier between Colombia and Venezuela); "mountains of Perijá, Casacara"; Venezuela, Colombia	1,000–2,060	Wilbert 1974 / Mosonyi 1972	Ruddle 1970, 1971, 1973, 1976 / Wilbert 1974
20. Carijona	"Near Miraflores, Vaupés... Yarí, upper Vaupés," Colombia	50–100	Anonymous 1972b	Schindler 1973, 1974

The style of haircut adopted by this teenage boy is typically Trio, and is used by them to distinguish themselves from neighboring groups of Indians who dress their hair differently.

A Kalapalo man decorated for a dance, exhibiting the characteristic men's haircut, toucan feather earrings, and shell necklace (the latter a trade specialty of this group)

Carijona man, in dress typical of the poorer members of backwoods society in the north-west Amazon area

Trio man planting manioc stocks. This task is performed by both men and women, and consists of putting the cuttings into mounds of loose earth.

Ye'cuana women from an acculturated village on the Paragua River returning from the fields with a carrying basket full of manioc

In 1974, Carib-speaking tribes could be found dispersed throughout much of the Guiana regions of Venezuela, Guyana, Surinam, French Guiana, and Brazil, as well as in certain restricted areas of northern Colombia, central Brazil, and southeastern Colombia; their estimated population falls roughly between 20,240 and 27,100 persons. Because of this distribution, it would be misleading to speak of a "typical" Carib habitat. Carib speakers exploit a variety of tropical environments: the Guiana coast, characterized by sandy alluvium, swamps, and marshy forests (Maroni River Caribs); the climax tropical rain forests of southern Guiana (Waiwai, Akuriyo); the riverine gallery forests of central Guiana (Wayana, Barama River Caribs) and of Brazil (Txicão); the lowland forest-*llanos* (Trio, precontact Carijona, Panare); the hilly forest-*llanos* (Ye'cuana, Akawaio); the Upper Xingu Basin, characterized by both gallery and climax rain forests and *cerrados*[1] (Xingu Caribs); the forested subtropical highlands (Yukpa); and the montaña (Yukpa). What makes these environments significantly different for purposes of human habitation is (a) the relative presence or absence of aquatic resources and (b) altitude (particularly in the case of the Yukpa). Tribes that live close to large rivers or lakes or in the littoral zone naturally depend a great deal upon the exploitation of fish, turtles, cayman, and (where present) aquatic

mammals. In areas where major rivers are absent, the inhabitants depend more upon hunting and collecting in both the forests and more open habitats. All tribes exhibit great eclecticism in the variety of floral and faunal species consumed. Kloos's description of Maroni River Carib subsistence as "diversified and unspecialized" (1971: 11) holds true for all Carib speakers, although the Xingu Caribs, who reject most land animals as unsuitable for their diet, are clearly exceptional. However, the variation in diet among Carib groups lies chiefly in the extent of their dependence on gathered foods, and this in turn seems to be related to both the absolute quantity and the seasonal availability of aquatic resources.

In addition to their unspecialized nonhorticultural subsistence practices, the speakers of Carib share dependence upon bitter manioc as a carbohydrate base (the Yukpa are an exception, since they presently occupy territory unsuitable for the cultivation of this plant; Yukpa subsistence is based on a typical montaña complex of sweet manioc and maize). Although other cultivated plants are used by these tribes, only bitter manioc seems to be of consistent year-round importance. Carib subsistence practices thus include a specialized agricultural economy that contrasts with the nonspecialized, seasonal food-collecting endeavors. Again, the Xingu Caribs are to some extent an exception to this rule, since they alone, among all lowland Carib groups for whom evidence is available, depend a great deal upon corn and piqui (notably during the rainy season, when these plants supplement manioc).

The use of the *tipití* (manioc sleeve press) as a processing tool is ubiquitous among the Guiana Carib tribes, but is replaced by the mat strainer and heavy ceramic tub

1. The term *llanos* is used here to refer to a northern South American habitat characterized by grasslands vegetation growing on periodically inundated, poorly drained soils. *Cerrado* refers to a central Brazilian habitat characterized by scrub forests growing on well-drained soils. Both habitats occur in climate zones marked by seasonal aridity. See Eiten (1972) for a classification and discussion of xeromorphic vegetation provinces in tropical South America.

Ye'cuana women grating manioc on boards set with palm thorns

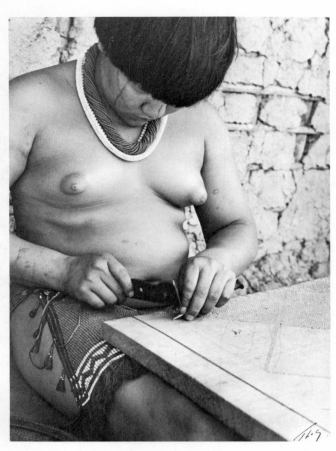

A young Ye'cuana woman making a manioc grater. This article, besides being used by Ye'cuana themselves, is very important in trade with both Carib and non-Carib groups.

Kalapalo girl grating bitter manioc. The ceramic tubs are traded from the neighboring Waura, an Arawakan group.

Kalapalo woman preparing manioc bread on ceramic griddles made by the Waura

Trio woman sieving manioc flour. The baskets are made by men.

The *ättä*, Ye'cuana communal house

among the Xingu Caribs.[2] Furthermore, all Carib groups who process bitter manioc do so in such a way as to obtain both "flour" (actually precipitated starch granules, not a product of grinding) and soup. All groups use the "flour" to prepare large tortilla-like cakes upon a ceramic griddle, but the Xingu Caribs (possibly together with the Txicão) are the only Carib-speaking groups who do not use the soup to prepare a fermented beverage. Where indigenous ceramic vessels are still used for manioc processing, most Carib speakers make their own; once again, the Xingu Caribs are an exception, since they must trade for pottery with the Arawakan-speaking Waura and Mehinaku peoples.

There appear to be four types of Northern Carib villages. Most common is the single communal roundhouse, led by a headman who acts as the faction leader

Traditional beehive-shaped house of the Trio, rarely made today

2. In a survey and discussion of the distribution of manioc processing equipment, Dole suggests that "... the manioc and *tipití* complex appears to have developed in the Orinoco Basin and the lowland region of the middle and lower Amazon.... The *tipití* is seen as a relatively recent invention ..." (1960: 246).

of a group of people who are related through complex (and often cross-cutting or multiple) bilateral kinship and affinal ties. Such villages are small (with no more than 60–70 persons, and averaging about 25–30 persons), flexible in membership, and dependent upon the political strength of the leader for their existence. This type is represented by the villages of the Ye'cuana, Waiwai, and Wayana.

The second type of local group (which has roughly the same population as the first) may be a variant of the communal roundhouse type of village. Here, several communal houses are found in a single settlement; although the membership of each household is small, the relationships of persons within both the households and the village as a whole (and their ties to a headman–faction leader) seem similar to those in the first type. This type is represented by the villages of the Trio and Barama River Caribs.

A third type of settlement, which is poorly understood, may be that of the Carijona, who are described by Schindler (1974) as formerly patrilineal and uxorilocal. The settlement (consisting of a single communal house) thus would include a group of related clanswomen and their husbands, the latter belonging to a number of different clans.

Finally, the Caribs of the littoral (such as the Maroni River Caribs) live uxorilocally in nuclear family houses. Although this is probably a post-contact innovation, it is significant that this type of settlement, unlike the first three, involves little social life at the village level.

The Xingu Caribs live in villages of long-standing duration and relatively high population (more than 100 persons). Each village is composed of a number of communal houses whose adult members are recruited from the bilateral kindred and affinal set of a politically important individual. Thus, each Xingu Carib communal household replicates the structure of a Northern Carib village of either the first or second type. As among the northern tribes, Xingu Carib residence tends to be flexible and shifts several times during the life of any individual. The endurance of a Xingu Carib residence unit also depends upon the success of the household leader in persuading his relatives to form a single group, rather than to live dispersed in the households of other leaders.

Another common characteristic of Carib-speaking tribes is the importance of shamanism as a means for expressing local group solidarity in the face of potential hostility from both human and nonhuman outsiders. The individual shaman is seen as a person with unusual abilities who must act as a mediator between the world of human needs and that of dangerous, ever-threatening nonhuman forces. Carib shamans not only act as curers, but function as diviners, namers of children, and agents of revenge sorcery. They also manipulate the weather and enhance the success of various subsistence activities

Members of a Pomeroon River Carib household cluster. Man seated in foreground is the "house master" of the group; he prepares a "bush rope" for use in basket weaving.

(especially hunting). Shamanistic practices are everywhere intimately associated with a "mirror-image" or "shadow" conceptualization of souls, which is one important means of linking various categories of human and nonhuman beings in fundamental cosmological relationships.

Among all Caribs, the use of tobacco to induce trances, to assist in curing illness, and to establish contact with the world of nonhumans is of central importance. Among several tribes the use of hallucinogens is also found, but their cultural significance is not always clear. The Kashuyana and Makusi, for example, participate in communal rituals during which snuff made from *Anadenanthera peregrina* beans is taken. Ye'cuana shamans are reported by Koch-Grünberg to have made use of *Virola* sp. bark snuff during ritual curing (Schultes and Hoffman 1973: 70–71), and several of the Akawaio bark infusions may also be made from wild hallucinogenic species. Finally, the Carijona traditionally made

Members of a Kalapalo communal household in the work area behind their house. The two seated women are spinning cotton while the young man grooms himself.

use of *Banisteriopsis caapi* during a ceremony in which sacred bark-trumpets were played. The Maroni River Caribs include the consumption of tree latex in certain phases of shamanistic ritual, but it is not known whether this substance possesses hallucinogenic properties. In general, the use of hallucinogens seems to be restricted to those Caribs residing in the northwestern regions of lowland South America, where such use is particularly elaborate and central to many ritual activities. In this respect, then, the northwestern Caribs resemble their non-Carib neighbors more than they do other Carib-speaking groups.

The treatment of pubescent persons is another point of comparison. All Carib tribes for which information is available practice some kind of female puberty seclusion. Male seclusion and subsequent initiation are reported only for the Wayana and Upper Xingu Caribs, but they may be more widespread. Female puberty seclusion is usually associated with a more general concept of menstrual pollution. However, the elaborated symbolic separation of men and women in both household and ceremonial contexts that occurs among the Upper Xingu Caribs does not seem to be shared by other Carib peoples, with the exception of the Carijona, who, in common with their Northwest Amazon neighbors, held certain trumpet and mask rituals that women were forbidden to see.

Finally, in the area of ceremonial activity, we can say that most communal ritual performances are of an essentially secular and commemorative nature. Such ceremonies function to mark social relationships between individual dyads or between groups of persons who are in the process of creating or reinforcing an alliance (for example, those participating in a marriage exchange or assisting a faction leader to build a new residence). In the north, the production and consumption of manioc beer (or chicha, among the Yukpa) seems to be the most critical communal element of such ceremonies, which are not usually initiated for the purpose of influencing non-human forces or of effecting certain mystical ends (as is the case with shamanistic performances). However, two clear exceptions to this rule are found among the Carijona, whose bark trumpet and bark mask ceremonies were apparently adopted from neighboring Northwest Amazon groups, and among the Ye'cuana, for whom Arvelo-Jimenez reports limited communal ritual for propitiation purposes (1971: 212).

To summarize, eight specific "traits" seem to constitute a "typical" Carib complex. Of course, taken individually, each trait can be found among other, non-Carib peoples; what is of interest is the fact that, as a whole, they seem to characterize the tribes whose languages belong to this linguistic group. The eight features, with exceptions to each indicated in parentheses, are these:

Panare tobacco is traded for a resin with the neighboring Salivan-speaking Piaroa.

1. bitter manioc cultivation (exception: Yukpa, living in an area unsuited to its cultivation) and use of manioc products in social prestation;

2. bilateral reckoning of kinship relationships, no descent units (exception: Carijona, with formerly patrilineal descent units);

3. social categorization in terms of kindreds composed of bilaterally related kinsmen and (sometimes) affines (no sodalities or associations such as moieties, age grades, or age sets);

4. shamanistic rituals (especially curing);

5. pan-village communal ceremonies that are secular and commemorative in nature (exceptions: Carijona and to a certain extent Ye'cuana);

6. use of tobacco as the principal means of inducing nonordinary experiences (exceptions: Carijona, Kashuyana, Makusi, Ye'cuana);

7. mirror-image or shadow conceptualization of soul;

8. female puberty seclusion and associated belief in menstrual pollution.

Kalapalo men entering a house to dance during a spear-throwing ceremony. Each house in the village circle is visited by them in turn, after which they finish the dance in the plaza. Spears and spear-throwers are seen only in this ceremony (*ifagaka*).

Trio hosts assembled in a village plaza as a party of visitors arrives.

It is interesting to compare these (tentatively) "typical" Carib attributes with the classic Carib traits reported by the explorers of the 16th and 17th centuries. At least two of these attributes were used by later classifiers of Indian societies to distinguish Carib peoples from persons belonging to other (especially Arawakan) groups. Most significant of these is the offensive, expansionist warfare (coupled with cannibalism) that was thought to differentiate Caribs from Arawakan peoples they overran in the Caribbean (cf. Rouse 1948). During the post-contact period, Arawakan dialects superseded the use of Carib, so that the violent warfare observed by Europeans during the 17th and 18th centuries was probably carried out by Arawakan (rather than Carib) speakers. More recently, such "Carib" bellicosity seems to have been limited to the Bràzilian outlier groups (especially the Txicão, Arara, and Jaguma), to the Carijona in southeastern Colombia, and to the northern Colombian tribes, which were until recently characterized by both intra- and intertribal warfare. Except for the latter case, however, territorial conquest does not seem to have been an objective in most of the warfare and raiding. Yet despite this conspicuous lack of aggression among the majority of ethnographically known Carib tribes, the stereotype persists.[3]

A second trait that has been used to distinguish Caribs from other South American peoples is the couvade, the custom of placing severe dietary and oc-cupational restrictions upon parents (especially the father) during the postpartum period. Father Wilhelm Schmidt considered the Guianas the classic couvade area, and he "emphasizes . . . the Caribs as the actual bearers of couvade in South America with the most characteristic examples, and the most numerous cases of severe couvade" (Fock 1963: 147, in reference to Schmidt 1954: 298). Yet the couvade is also characteristic of both Tupi-Guarani and Gê-speaking tribes, and is found distributed in other groups as well. Furthermore, anthropologists now recognize that the term "couvade" encompasses too great a variety of practices and beliefs about the effects of parental actions upon the newborn to be useful for comparative purposes (Maybury-Lewis 1967: 65–6).

Speaking generally, and upon the basis of admittedly incomplete evidence, it is presently possible to distinguish three Carib "types." The first is represented by

3. For example, the author of a recent work on South American archae-ology states: "The Carib groups placed an unusually high value on interpersonal aggression, warfare as the route to prestige, and being a 'real man,' all of which traits are found in surviving Carib social groups" (Lathrap 1970: 164). Ethnographic sources suggest, how-ever, that the shaman, rather than the warrior, is the person of great-est prestige and influence in these societies.

Men of a Carijona household preparing a bark trumpet

the Carijona, who seem to have shared a number of significant ethnographic features with their neighbors, the Witoto and Bora on the one hand, and the Eastern Tukanoan peoples on the other (Schindler 1974). These features include a distinct system of social classification (named, exogamous patrilineal descent units), aggressive warfare, the use of *Banisteriopsis caapi,* and the personification of various "spirits" during ceremonies incorporating the use of bark masks. Bark trumpets are also shared by the Carijona and other Northwest Amazon groups. Although these appear to be a miscellaneous set of attributes, they are in fact integrated elements of a distinctive cultural system. Their common presence among most tribes of the Northwest Amazon area suggests that a much more intense system of tribal interaction existed in the past than is seen today.

The second Carib "type" is more clearly distinguished, and consists of the majority of Guiana Caribs. We would probably have to include the Arawakan and intrusive Tupian tribes in the "Guiana culture area" as well, however. This region is characterized by: flexible social organization based on bilateral reckoning of kin;

communal family households that constitute a political faction as well as a group of kin and affinally related persons; dependence upon bitter manioc (as opposed to maize, sweet manioc, or palm species); reliance upon shamanism for control and manipulation of nonhuman forces, but without the use of hallucinogenic drugs taken for that purpose; and the importance of girls' puberty rituals.

The third "type" is found in the Upper Xingu Basin. Here a large complex of unique traits—including a dietary system, ceremonial structure, trade specialization, mythology, and social organization—is shared by speakers of mutually unintelligible languages. The villages of Carib speakers cannot be distinguished from those of Tupi, Arawak, or Trumai speakers in the area on the basis of any of these features.

This tripartite division should be taken as provisional and incomplete, recognizing that several Carib groups do not seem to fall into any one of the "types." Forthcoming publications and new research on the Yukpa, Txicão, Panare, and Carijona should help considerably to refine and expand the typology. Each "type" is not uniquely Carib, and in fact each could include non-Carib-speaking tribes sharing many of the features that make the type distinctive for Carib speakers. This suggests that many, if not most, lowland South American tribes should be considered as falling into general social and cultural units that often encompass local groups of different language affiliation and history. These units represent different responses to ecological pressures. More specifically, historically discrete groups, through a process of ecological adaptation, including the establishment of trade, marriage, ritual, and political alliances, appear to have developed a set of shared cultural systems, which in some regions (such as the Northwest Amazon and the Upper Xingu) have resulted in truly "multi-ethnic" societies.

REFERENCES

Acosta Saignes, Miguel
   1946   *Los Caribes de la costa venezolana.* Mexico City: Acta Anthropologica.

Agostinho da Silva, Pedro
   1972   Information Concerning the Territorial and Demographic Situation in the Alto Xingu. In *The Situation of the Indian in South America,* ed. W. Dostal, pp. 252–83. Geneva: World Council of Churches.

Ahlbrinck, W.
   1931   *Encyclopaedie der Karaïben.* Amsterdam: *Verhandelingen der Koninklijke Akademie van Wetenschappen, Afdeeling letterkunde,* n.r. 27 (1).

   1956   *Op zoek naar de Indianen.* Amsterdam: Koninklijk Instituut voor de Tropen.

Alvarado, Lisandro
   1956   Noticia sobre los Caribes des los llanos de Barcelona. In his *Datos etnográficos de Venezuela,* pp. 395–423. Caracas: Ministerio de Educación. (Originally published 1945, Caracas.)

Anonymous
    1972a   Indigenous Groups of Brazil. In *The Situation of the Indian in South America,* ed. W. Dostal, pp. 434–42. Geneva: World Council of Churches.

    1972b   Ethno-Linguistic Groups of Colombia. In *The Situation of the Indian in South America,* ed. W. Dostal, pp. 393–96. Geneva: World Council of Churches.

Arvelo-Jimenez, Nelly
    1971   Political Relations in a Tribal Society: A Study of the Ye'cuana Indians of Venezuela. Ithaca, New York: *Cornell University Latin American Studies Program Dissertation Series* 31.

    1973   The Dynamics of the Ye'cuana ("Maquiritare") Political System: Stability and Crises. Copenhagen: *International Work Group for Indigenous Affairs Document Series* 12.

Barandiarán, Daniel de
    1962a   Actividades vitales de subsistencia de los indios Yekuana o Makiritare. *Antropológica* 11: 1–29.

    1962b   Shamanismo Yekuana o Makiritare. *Antropológica* 11: 61–90.

    1965   El habitado entre los indios Yekuana. *Antropológica* 16: 3–95.

Basso, Ellen B.
    1970   Xingu Carib Kinship Terminology and Marriage: Another View. *Southwestern Journal of Anthropology* 26: 402–16.

    1973a   The Use of Portuguese in Kalapalo (Xingu Carib) Encounters: Changes in a Central Brazilian Communications Network. *Language in Society* 2: 1–19.

    1973b   *The Kalapalo Indians of Central Brazil.* New York: Holt, Rinehart and Winston.

    1975   Kalapalo Affinity: Its Cultural and Social Contexts. *American Ethnologist* 2: 1–25.

Bonfil Batalla, Guillermo
    1973   The Indian and the Colonial Situation: The Context of Indigenist Policy in Latin America. In *The Situation of the Indian in South America,* ed. W. Dostal, pp. 21–28. Geneva: World Council of Churches.

Butt, Audrey J.
    1953   The Burning Fountain Whence it Came: A Study of the System of Beliefs of the Carib-Speaking Akawaio of British Guiana. *Social and Economic Studies* 2: 1–15.

    1956   Ritual Blowing: *Taling*—A Causation and Cure of Illness Among the Akawaio. *Man,* o.s. 48: 49–55.

    1960   The Birth of a Religion. *Journal of the Royal Anthropological Institute* 90 (I): 66–106.

    1961   Symbolism and Ritual among the Akawaio of British Guiana. *Nieuwe West-Indische Gids* 2 (December).

    1962   Réalité et idéal dans la pratique chamanique. *L'Homme* II (3): 5–52.

    1966a   The Present State of Ethnology in Latin America: The Guianas. In *XXXVI Congreso Internacional de Americanistas* (Spain, 1964), *Actas y Memorias,* vol. 3: 19–37.

    1966b   The Shaman's Legal Role. *Revista do Museu Paulista,* n.s. XVI: 151–86.

Carneiro, Robert L.
    1956–57 La cultura de los indios Kuikurus del Brasil Central. I: La economia de subsistencia. *Runa* 8 (2): 169–85.

    1956–58 Extramarital Sex Freedom among the Kuikuru Indians of Mato Grosso. *Revista do Museu Paulista,* n.s. X: 135–42.

    1961   Slash and Burn Cultivation among the Kuikuru and its Implications for Cultural Development in the Amazon Basin. In *The Evolution of Horticultural Systems in Native South America: Causes and Consequences,* ed. Johannes Wilbert, pp. 47–67. *Antropológica,* Supplement 2.

Civrieux, Marc de
    1960   Leyendas Maquiritares. *Memorias de la Sociedad de Ciencias Naturales La Salle* XX: 105–25; 175–88.

    1968   Mitología Maquiritare. *Revista de Cultura de la Universidad de Oriente* 3: 30–33.

    1970   *Watunna: Mitología Makiritare.* Caracas: Monte Avila Editores.

Derbyshire, Desmond
    1965   Textos Hixkaryâna. *Publicações Avulsas* 3, Museu Paraense Emílio Goeldi.

Dole, Gertrude E.
    1956–57 La cultura de los indios Kuikurus del Brasil Central: II. La organizacion social. *Runa* 8 (2): 185–202.

    1956–58 Ownership and Exchange among the Kuikuru Indians of Mato Grosso. *Revista do Museu Paulista,* n.s. X: 125–33.

    1960   Techniques of Preparing Manioc Flour as a Key to Culture History in Tropical America. In *Man and Cultures: Selected Papers of the 5th International Congress of Anthropological and Ethnological Sciences,* ed. A. F. C. Wallace, pp. 243–48. Philadelphia: Univ. of Pennsylvania Press.

1964 Shamanism and Political Control among the Kuikuru. In *Beiträge zur Völkerkunde Südamerikas,* ed. Hans Becher, pp. 53–62. *Völkerkundliche Abhandlung* 1. Hanover: Niedersächsisches Landesmuseum.

1966 Anarchy Without Chaos: Alternatives to Political Authority among the Kuikuru. In *Political Anthropology,* ed. Marc Swartz et al., pp. 73–88. Chicago: Univ. of Chicago Press.

Duchemin, Philippe
1972 The Situation of the Indian Groups in French Guiana in 1971. In *The Situation of the Indian in South America,* ed. W. Dostal, pp. 370–75. Geneva: World Council of Churches.

Dumont, Jean-Paul
1974 L'alliance substituée. *L'Homme* XIV: 43–56.

Eiten, George
1972 The Cerrado Vegetation of Brazil. *The Botanical Review* 38: 201–341.

Figueiredo, Napoleão
1963 Os Aramagóto do Parú de Oeste. *América Indígena* XXIII: 309–17.

Fock, Niels
1963 Waiwai. Copenhagen: *Nationalmuseets Skrifter, Etnografisk Raekke* VIII.

Frikel, Protásio
1953 Kamáni. *Revista do Museu Paulista,* n.s. VII: 257–74.

1955 Tradições histórico-lendárias dos Kachúyana e Kahyána. *Revista do Museu Paulista,* n.s. IX: 203–33.

1957 Zur linguistich-ethnologischen Gliederung der Indianerstämme von Nord-Pará (Brasilien) und den anliegenden Gebieten. *Anthropos* 52: 509–63.

1958 Classificação lingüístico-etnológica das tribos indígenas do Pará Setentrional e zonas adjacentes. *Revista de Antropologia* 6: 113–87.

1960 Os Tiriyó (notas preliminares). *Boletim do Museu Paraense Emílio Goeldi,* n.s. Antropologia 9.

1961 Morí—a festa do rapé. *Boletim do Museu Paraense Emílio Goeldi,* n.s. Antropologia 12.

1970 Os Kaxúyana: Notas etno-históricas. *Publicações Avulsas* 14, Museu Paraense Emílio Goeldi.

1971a A mitologia solar e a filosofia de vida dos índios Kaxúyana. In *Estudos Sôbre Línguas e Culturas Indígenas.* Brasilia: Summer Institute of Linguistics.

1971b Dez anos de aculturação Tiriyó: 1960–70. *Publicações Avulsas* 16, Museu Paraense Emílio Goeldi.

Frikel, Protásio, and Roberto Cortez
1972 Elementos demográficos do alto Paru de Oeste, Tumucumaque Brasileiro: Índios Ewarhoyána, Kaxúyana e Tiriyó. *Publicações Avulsas* 19, Museu Paraense Emílio Goeldi.

Fuchs, Helmut
1962 La estructura residencial de los Maquiritare de "El Corobal" y "Las Ceibas," Territorio Federal Amazonas, Venezuela. *América Indígena* XXII: 169–90.

1964 El sistema de cultivo de los Deukwhuana (Maquiritare) del Alto Rio Ventuari, Territorio Federal Amazonas, Venezuela. *América Indígena* XXIV: 171–95.

Gillin, John
1934 Crime and Punishment among the Barama River Carib of British Guiana. *American Anthropologist* 36: 331–44.

1936 The Barama River Caribs of British Guiana. *Peabody Museum Papers in Archaeology and Ethnology* 14 (2): 1–274.

Hurault, Jean-Marcel
1968 Les Indiens Wayana de la Guyane française: Structure sociale et coutume familiale. Paris: Office de la Recherche Scientifique et Technique Outre-Mer, *Mémoires ORSTOM* 3.

1972 *Français et Indiens en Guyane.* Paris: Union Générale d'Éditions.

Kloos, Peter
1968 Becoming a Pïyei: Variability and Similarity in Carib Shamanism. *Antropológica* 24: 3–25.

1969 Female Initiation among the Maroni River Caribs. *American Anthropologist* 71: 898–905.

1970 In Search of Health among the Maroni River Caribs. *Bijdragen tot de Taal-, Land-, en Volkenkunde* 126: 115–41.

1971 *The Maroni River Caribs of Surinam.* Assen, The Netherlands: Van Gorcum.

1972a Amerindians of Guyana. In *The Situation of the Indian in South America,* ed. W. Dostal, pp. 343–47. Geneva: World Council of Churches.

1972b Amerindians of Surinam. In *The Situation of the Indian in South America,* ed. W. Dostal, pp. 348–57. Geneva: World Council of Churches.

Lathrap, Donald W.
1970   *The Upper Amazon.* New York and Washington: Praeger.

Maybury-Lewis, David
1967   *Akwĕ-Shavante Society.* Oxford: Clarendon Press.

Mosonyi, Esteban Emilio
1972   Indian Groups in Venezuela. In *The Situation of the Indian in South America,* ed. W. Dostal, pp. 389–91. Geneva: World Council of Churches.

Rivière, Peter
1969   *Marriage Among the Trio.* Oxford: Clarendon Press.

1971   The Political Structure of the Trio Indians as Manifested in a System of Ceremonial Dialogue. In *The Translation of Culture,* ed. T. O. Beidelman, pp. 293–311. London: Tavistock.

Rouse, Irving
1948   The Carib. In *Handbook of South American Indians,* ed. Julian H. Steward, vol. 4: 547–65. *U.S. Bureau of American Ethnology, Bulletin* 143. Washington: Government Printing Office.

Ruddle, Kenneth
1970   The Hunting Technology of the Maracá Indians. *Antropológica* 25: 21–63.

1971   Notes on the Nomenclature and the Distribution of the Yukpa-Yuko Tribe. *Antropológica* 30: 18–27.

1973   The Human Use of Insects: Examples from the Yukpa. *Biotropica* 5: 94–101.

1976   *The Yukpa Cultivation System.* Berkeley: Univ. of California Press.

Schindler, Helmut
1973   Warum kann man den Itutari mit dem Gwaruma erschlagen? *Zeitschrift für Ethnologie* 98 (2): 246–76.

1974   Die Stellung der Carijona im Kulturareal Nordwestamazonien. In *Atti del XL Congresso Internazionale degli Americanisti* (Rome–Genoa, 1972), vol. 2: 457–67.

Schmidt, Wilhelm
1954   Gebräuche des Ehemannes bei Schwangerschaft und Geburt: Mit Richtigstellung des Begriffes der Couvade. *Wiener Beiträge zur Kulturgeschichte und Linguistik* 10.

Schultes, Richard Evans, and Albert Hofmann
1973   *The Botany and Chemistry of Hallucinogens.* Springfield, Ill.: Thomas.

Schwerin, Karl H.
1963   Family among the Karinya of Eastern Venezuela. *América Indígena* XXIII: 201–9.

1966   Oil and Steel: Processes of Karinya Culture Change in Response to Industrial Development. *Latin American Studies* 4. Los Angeles: Latin American Center, UCLA.

Steinen, Karl von den
1886   *Durch Central Brasilien.* Leipzig: F. A. Brockaus.

1894   *Unter den Naturvölkern Zentral-Brasiliens.* Berlin: Geographische Verlagsbuchhandlung von Dietrich Reimer.

Wilbert, Johannes
1962   Zur Kenntnis der Parirí. *Archiv für Völkerkunde* 15: 80–153.

1974   Yupa Folktales. *Latin American Studies* 24. Los Angeles: Latin American Center, UCLA.

Yde, Jens
1960   Agriculture and Division of Work among the Waiwái. *Folk* 2: 83–97.

1965   Material Culture of the Waiwái. Copenhagen: *Nationalmuseets Skrifter, Etnografisk Raekke* X.

2. A SURVEY OF THE CARIB LANGUAGE FAMILY

Marshall Durbin
Department of Anthropology, Washington University

The study of Carib languages spans three centuries and has produced commentary by observers of diverse linguistic, national, and occupational backgrounds. In addition to formally trained linguists, there have been hundreds of others who have gathered Carib data —including priests, missionaries, soldiers, colonists, doctors, teachers, explorers, anthropologists, oil men, geographers, geologists, wayfarers, farmers, and a princess. It is often stated that on one·of Columbus's three trips, a sailor gathered a Carib vocabulary, though if this is so the language was probably Island Carib—an Arawakan language that will not concern us here.

As far as we know, the first word resembling *Carib* to appear in the historic literature was *Caraiba,* used by the historian Petrus Martyr in his work published in 1516, ten years after the death of Columbus (von den Steinen 1938: 217). The first reference to the concept of Caribs (that is, Indians of the Caribbean area) is found in the notes of Columbus himself, edited by de las Casas, wherein are references to *Canibales, Caniba,* and *Canima* (Morison 1963: 100, 103). Subsequently, the term *Carib* was used to refer to this geographic grouping.

At present, we are faced with a very difficult and confusing situation concerning the Carib languages. In the first place, a highly varied nomenclature for dialects of the same language, and for tribal and subtribal groups, has resulted from the fact that linguistic observations have been made from a variety of geographical vantage points—including the Caribbean Sea, the Atlantic Ocean, the Pacific coast of South America, Rio Negro, the Amazon, Xingu, Orinoco, and Magdalena rivers, and Lake Maracaibo, among other more local points. In some cases, approaches to a given tribe have been made from different geographic directions, giving rise to commentaries on different dialects of the same language. These different geographical approaches to the same group have also resulted in varying sets of names for the same population or language, since neighboring tribes have different names for a particular group.

Other problems arise from the fact that students of Carib have used at least 11 glossing languages (including Dutch, English, German, Norwegian, Swedish, French, Spanish, Italian, Portuguese, Czech, and Latin). In many cases these observers gathered their data through an intermediary language—English, Portuguese, Dutch, French, or a Pidgin—which neither they nor the Indians understood very well. Often manuscripts that were written in the authors' own languages, or those in which they were fluent, were cast into still a third tongue by an editor, translator, or publisher who failed to observe the original orthographic conventions. Original manuscripts have disappeared after being badly copied (sometimes many times over), and many works available to us today represent third- or fourth-hand attempts.

In addition, we must take into account the history of Carib tribes since contact. Many have become extinct, while others have been dislocated. As a result, surviving Carib languages have been influenced by other Indian tongues, including Arawakan, Tupi-Guaranian, and Chibchan dialects (among other isolated groups), to say nothing of the European, East Indian, African, Pidgin, and Creole languages with which they have been in contact.

The problems I shall confront in this paper are: (1) the location of the original homeland of the Caribs; (2) the directions of their various dispersions; (3) the location at contact time of groups that are presently extinct or dislocated, and for which we have linguistic data; (4) the number of Carib languages and dialects that have ever existed (as witnessed by linguistic material); (5) the subgroupings of these languages and other internal relations; and (6) routes of recent migrations. Although

NOTE: I wish to thank Richard Meier and Ellen B. Basso for their comments on this paper, and Diane Fischer for preparing a preliminary version of the maps. This work was carried out through the generous assistance of the Department of Anthropology, Instituto Venezolano de Investigaciones Científicas, Caracas, while I was a Visiting Researcher there in 1971–72. The results reported here are as much due to Dr. Haydée Seijas of IVIC as they are to me, since we jointly carried on the fieldwork and library research. The only portion of this paper that I have done alone is the writing.

there can be no absolute solutions to these problems, they have served as the focus for the research that Haydée Seijas and I have undertaken.

ANALYSES PRIOR TO THE 19TH CENTURY

The earliest extant linguistic material is that of the missionary priest Pierre Pelleprat (1606–1667), who participated in the Jesuit intrusion into the Guianas that lasted from 1646 to 1681. His linguistic works, considered by del Rey (1971, 1: 210–11) to be a bibliographic rarity, are (1) *Introduction à la langue des Galibis, sauvages de la Tarre [sic] ferme de l'Amérique méridionale*, à Paris Chez Sevastian Gramiosy, and (2) *Introduction à la langue des Galibis*. The first work appeared as part of *Relation des Missions des Pp. de la Compagnie de Iesus dans les isles, dans la terre ferme de l'Amérique méridionale*, Paris. Sometimes it appears as a separate document. Pelleprat left a copy of the work in Guarapiche, Venezuela, when he left there in 1653. The work undoubtedly did not originate with him, since he notes that Fr. Dionisio Mesland's researches had helped him considerably (del Rey 1971, 1: 298–99). Dionisio Mesland (1615–1672) was the great Jesuit intellectual who introduced Cartesianism to America. He apparently studied Galibi and made notes for a grammar, together with a vocabulary of the Indians of Guiana (Carib?) with some conversations and pious sayings (del Rey 1971, 1: 196). However, none of these data, except indirectly those probably used by Pelleprat, have survived today. Pelleprat's grammar and vocabulary are reprinted in del Rey (1971, 2: 9–23). The grammar is inadequate since it appears to be based upon a pidgin Carib used by the French at that time. The vocabulary corresponds to what is variously known today as Carib, Galibi, Kariña, Carina, or Cari'na, which was spoken from French Guiana (near the mouth of the Amazon) to central eastern Venezuela.

The first major attempt to solve some of the problems of classification of Carib languages was made by Fr. Salvatore Filippo Gilij (1721–1789; see del Rey 1971, 1: 118). Gilij spent most of his time at Cabruta, a central Venezuelan town on the Orinoco, though he also traveled widely up and down the river (Gilij 1965, vols. 1–3). He had more than a passing acquaintance with several Carib languages, and apparently spoke Tamanaco (now extinct) with great fluency. He was the first to recognize the Carib (as well as the Arawak) family as a unity, though this classification was based only upon a portion of Venezuelan Carib; Gilij was unaware of most Carib tribes elsewhere in South America.

The most interesting aspect of Gilij's perception of the Carib family was that he recognized what are presently called sound correspondences and cognates. He stated (1965, 3: 137):

Letters together form syllables. The syllables *sa, se, si,* etc., occurring very frequently in Carib *[prob. Kariña]*, are never found in its daughter language Tamanaco, and everything that is expressed in Carib as *sa*, etc., the Tamanacos say with *ča*. Thus, for example, the little shield that the Caribs call *saréra* the Tamanacos call *čaréra*. Pareca is also a dialect of the Carib language. But these Indians, unlike the Tamanacos and Caribs, say softly in the way Frenchmen do, *šarera*.

Further, Gilij took great care to point out that these languages could not be related to or derived from those of Europe, or from Arabic or Hebrew, as was frequently asserted at the time. Nor did he consider these languages primitive in terms of expression, complexity, vocabulary, or grammar. He stated that they merely differed.

It should be pointed out that Gilij came to these conclusions regarding language relationships during his 19 years of residence in Venezuela (1749–1767), long before Sir William Jones's famous 1786 discourse on Sanskrit, Greek, Latin, Gothic, Celtic, and Persian. However, in spite of Gilij's recognition of systematic sound correspondences and cognates as a basis for positing genetic relationships in languages, he consistently viewed Carib (Kariña) as the mother *(matriz)* language of all other Carib languages with which he was acquainted. He never recognized the possibility of a prior parent language giving rise to all the existent daughter tongues.[1]

RESEARCH IN THE 19TH AND 20TH CENTURIES

After the publication of Gilij's work, almost 125 years passed before Lucien Adam published the next great treatise on Carib, *Materiaux pour servir à l'établissement*

---

1. Gilij's classification gave rise to that of Hervás y Panduro (1800–1805). Specifically, the latter noted the following Carib languages: Carib(e) (Kaliña), Maquiritare (Ye'cuana), Pareca, Avaricoto, Tamanaco, Yabarana, Quaqua, Akerecoto, Mapoyo, Achirigotos, Cariabes Mansos, Caribes Huraños, Macuchis, Ocomesianas, Paudacotos, Purugotos, Uarinagoto, Pariacotos, Uokéari, Uaracá-pachilí, Uara-Múcuru, Mujeres Solas, Cumanacoto, Guanero, Areveriana, Guaikíri, Palenco, and Oye. He also noted that Carib languages were spoken on the Peninsula of Paria, near Caracas, and perhaps in other parts of Venezuela. He further noted the similarity of Island Carib to Carib languages. However, Gilij's classification was actually based upon Tamanaco, Pareca, Uokéari, Mapoyo, Oye, Akerecoto, Avaricoto, Pariacoto, Cumanacoto, Guanero, Guaikíri, Palenco, Maquiritare (Ye'cuana), Areveriana,Uaracá-Pachilí, Uara-Múcuru, Mujeres Solas, Payuro, Kikirípa, and Carib (Gilij 1965, 3: 174). Of all the languages mentioned by Gilij, only Carib, Maquiritare (Ye'cuana), Yabarana, Mapoyo (all in Venezuela), Macuchis (Guyana), and Okomesianas (Brazil) still survive.

d'une grammaire comparée des dialectes de la famille caribe (1893). This study includes a comparative list of 329 words, plus some comparative grammar for Akawaio, Aparai, Arekuna, Bakairi, Bonari, Island Carib, Caraibe, Chayma, Crichana, Cumanagoto, Galibi, Guaque, Ipurucoto, Karibis, Karinaco and Makusi, Ye'cuana (Maquiritare), Motilon, Wayana, Palmella, Paravilhana, Pianakoto, Pimenteira, Piritu, Roucouyene, Tamanaco, Tiverigoto, Trio, Waiwai, Wayumara, and Yao. The value of the work lies in its bibliography and the listing of languages, though there were many languages with published sources that Adam did not include. No attempts are made at internal subdivision, except for purely geographical ones. The comparative work uses mainly inspection rather than the comparative method (which was well established by this time in Europe). Nevertheless, Adam's work set the stage for later language classifiers.

Karl von den Steinen was a contemporary of Adam's. He tended to work more with a particular Carib language (Bakairi) than with classifying. Nevertheless, it was he who first made the proposal that the homeland of the Caribs was in the lower Xingu Basin (1892)—a proposal that persists to this day in many researchers' minds. Von den Steinen had studied the comparative method with Dr. Georg Wenker (the author of a German dialect atlas), but it is doubtful that von den Steinen ever grasped the concepts of the comparative method, if indeed Wenker understood them himself. Specifically, von den Steinen established a protophonology *(Grundsprache),* but only by inspection and not by establishing true correspondence sets. For example, he established *p in Proto-Carib and showed how this became /w,f,x/ in Bakairi and /h/ in Ye'cuana under certain conditions, but he actually confused correspondence sets that derive from Proto-Carib *p and *w. Von den Steinen in fact believed (for an unknown reason) that the language that had undergone the greatest amount of change represented homeland Carib, though he took great efforts to demonstrate that Bakairi and Nahukwa are not at all the same as Proto-Carib. As will be seen below, our beliefs are to the contrary.

Von den Steinen made many useful observations, despite his obviously poor training in the comparative method. To Adam's list of languages, he added data for Apiaka, Aracaju, Central American Carib, Carijona, and Carinaca, which indicates that he did not rely solely upon Adam for his comparative materials.

De Goeje was the next great classifier. His first *Etudes linguistiques Caraïbes* appeared in 1910 and contained a comparative grammar and a much larger vocabulary (559 words) than Adam's. Many more published sources had since appeared for the languages Adam had compiled. The bibliography is much more complete and de Goeje was able to add Arara, Mapoyo, Pauxi (Pauxiana), Yabarana, Avaricoto, Opone-Carare, Core, Guanero, Hianacoto-Umaua, Kariña, Caribi, Akuku, Nahukwa, Upurui, Pajure, Palenque, Paria, Piritu, Saluma, Tiverigoto, Trio, Yabarana, and Yauapery. De Goeje, unlike Adam, was an accomplished fieldworker and included vocabularies and short grammars of Kariña, Trio, and Wayana in his work; however, his classificatory work surpasses Adam's in quantity only and is based upon comparison by inspection, though his synchronic studies, like those of von den Steinen, are quite valuable.

Working during the same period as de Goeje was Theodor Koch-Grünberg, who compiled vocabularies of no less than 10 Carib languages: Hianacoto-Umaua, Makusi, Mapoyo, Arekuna, Wayumara, Purucoto, Taulipang, Yabarana, Ingariko, and Sapara (1928). Although Koch-Grünberg attempted little classification, his phonetic details are so excellent that they have contributed a great deal toward our understanding of the groupings of Carib languages.

A second work of de Goeje's with the same title as his first volume appeared in 1944. It gives information on some additional languages: Akuria, Pariri, Yaruma, Azumara, Chikena, Guayana, Ihuruana (Ye'cuana), Kamarakoto, Kumayena (Okomayana), Mocoa (Motilon), Wayarikure (Triometesen), Parechi, Parukoto (Barokoto), Patagona (Guague), Patamona (Ingariko), Quaca (Chayma), Sapara, Sikiyana, Urukuyana, Varrique (Chayma), and Wama (Akuriyo). As can be readily seen, many of these represent dialect names while others represent genuinely new-found languages. The work also includes a short comparative grammar (morphology) and a vocabulary consisting only of a list of reconstructed Proto-Carib words. The dictionary is awkward to use because one must constantly refer to Adam's (1893) and de Goeje's (1910) works through a set of code numbers. It is not clear how de Goeje arrived at the Proto-Carib reconstruction without correspondence sets.[2] Of great value, however, are appendices containing a grammar and vocabulary of Wayana, and vocabularies of Triometesen and Akuriyo.

The next landmark in Carib linguistic studies appeared in 1968, when B. J. Hoff published the most comprehensive phonology and morphology that has yet appeared for any Carib language, one that will serve for a long time to come as a guide to comparativists of Carib languages. His method is that of the structuralist school. The value of the work lies in the fact that Hoff presents us with a complete morphological analysis of a Carib language. Consequently, we now have a complete view of the verbal affix system.

––––––––––––––––

2. See Lounsbury's review (1947) of this work.

During much of the first half of the 20th century, one man had been assiduously collecting bibliographies and vocabularies (from his own fieldwork, from that of others, and from published sources) for all South American Indian languages. By the time of his retirement from South American studies in the 1950s, Paul Rivet had an incredibly large bibliography and a vast collection of vocabularies in his possession. In his publications his principal endeavor was to show that Pance, Pijao, Colima, Muzo, Pantagora (all in Colombia) and Patagon in Peru were Carib languages (Rivet 1943a), and that the Chocó family in Colombia was a part of Carib (Rivet 1943b). However, in retrospect, these conclusions almost certainly seem not to be valid, since Rivet's work was characterized by the crudest sort of inspection.

Rivet cannot, however, be held totally responsible for the type of methodology he employed, since he built upon a number of early Americanists such as Adelung and Vater (1806–17), Balbi (1826), D'Orbigny (1839), Ludewig (1858), and von Martius (1867), in addition to the scholars mentioned above. With the exception of Gilij, they had shown very little originality. The manner of comparison of these early Americanists was to establish relationships by utilizing sources from many different languages. That is, there were no controls or constraints placed upon the comparing process as there are in formal linguistic comparison. Rivet also used history, ethnohistory, racial characteristics, geographical distributions, folk accounts, and folk etymologies to establish relationships (as in his well-known classifications of South American languages published in 1924 and 1952); these techniques were also much in vogue in his time, especially among Americanists.[3]

Wilbert (1968) has pointed out that only Brinton (who attempted to establish a critical evaluation of source materials) was able to confine himself to linguistic material, working principally with a lexicon. Furthermore, as Wilbert suggests, neither Rivet (1924), Rivet and Loukotka (1952), nor Chamberlain (1903; 1913) followed the criteria set forth by Brinton (1891).

The last major classification of Carib has been done by Čestmír Loukotka, a student of Rivet's. His first study appeared in 1935, and it was followed by others published in 1941, 1944, 1948, 1952 (with Rivet), and finally, 1968. It was the work of Loukotka and Rivet that perhaps most influenced Mason in his classification of Carib published in the *Handbook of South American Indians* (1950).

Loukotka's style is similar to Rivet's, though considerably more sophisticated. First, he includes a large number of languages for which no data exist—that is, he depends upon historical sources for part of his classification; for the other part of his classification he depends upon published and unpublished sources. Loukotka enlarged Brinton's basic vocabulary to a diagnostic word list of 45 lexical items, which he tried to compile as fully as possible for each language (Wilbert 1968: 11). Because of different methods of collection he never presents more than 14 words for any given Carib language (head, tooth, eye, water, fire, sun, moon, arrow, man, jaguar, maize, one, two, three). Some languages have as few as two entries for comparative purposes. Since Loukotka was obviously comparing by inspection, he was never able to solve the problems of what he called "mixed languages," languages that are of one structure but have borrowed lexically from another. Thus, he usually was indecisive about Island Carib (Arawakan) and finally classified it incorrectly as Carib. The great value of Loukotka's work lies in the enormous bibliography he provides (both published and unpublished) and in his internal linguistic subdivisions (which are basically correct, though he gives no evidence concerning internal relationships of subdivisions). Most of his work is based upon geographical subdivisions, which in some cases coincide with the linguistic subdivisions and in other cases do not. For example, Loukotka places Carib within his Tropical Forest Division, which is also a geographical and cultural category. Johannes Wilbert, who edited Loukotka's posthumous publication (1968), has correctly recognized the nature of Loukotka's method and has entitled the map accompanying the author's classification of Carib "Ethno-Linguistic Distribution of South American Indians." To our knowledge, no ethnohistorian, historian, or archaeologist has utilized Loukotka's materials, even though they represent a rich source.

Specifically, Loukotka gives us a number of divisions of languages for which linguistic data exist. These are shown in Table 2.1, which excludes all languages for which there are no linguistic data, as well as all subdivisions and languages that our analyses have demonstrated to be non-Carib. What starts out as a confusing plethora in Loukotka can be reduced to 21 major subdivisions by critical evaluation and analysis of the source materials. As Table 2.1 shows, we are dealing with linguistic material from 52 languages rather than the hundreds sometimes thought to be the constituents of the Carib family.

Finally, the works of Greenberg (1959), McQuown (1955), Ortiz (1965), and Swadesh (1955; 1959) should be mentioned in reference to classification of Carib languages. Steward and Faron (1959), Tax (1960), and Voe-

---

3. See Rowe (1951: 15) for an evaluation of Rivet's work with which we wholeheartedly agree.

TABLE 2.1
Major Subdivisions of Carib Languages for which Linguistic Material is Available

Western Languages	Eastern Languages	Trio	Chikena	Waiwai	Yauapery	Pauxiana	Makusi
Galibi Caribisi Kariña Cariniaco †	Wayana Upuri Aparai Roucouyene † Aracaju †	Trio Wama (Akuriyo) Urukuyana Triometesen Kumayena Pianakoto	Chikena Saluma Pauxi † Cachuena	Waiwai Parukoto Wabui Hishkaryana Bonari †	Yauapery Waimiri Crichana †	Pauxiana	Makusi Keseruma Purucoto Wayumara Paravilhana † Sapara

Pemong	Maquiritare	Mapoyo	Panare	Tamanaco †	Yao †	Motilon	Opone †
Taulipang Arekuna Ingarico Patamona Kamarakoto Uaica Akawaio	Maquiritare Ye'cuana Ihuruana Cunuana	Mapoyo Yabarana	Panare	Tamanaco † Chayma † Cumanagoto † Tiverigoto † Palenque † Caraca † Quirequire † Guayqueri †	Yao †	Yupe Chaque Iroca Macoa Manastara Maraca Pariri Shaparru Wasama Japreria Coyaima †	Opone † Carare †

Carijona	Arara †	Palmella †	Pimenteira †	Xingu
Guaque † Carijona Umaua †	Arara † Apingui † Pariri †	Palmella †	Pimenteira †	Yaruma † Bakairi Nahukwa Naravute †

† extinct
{ includes dialects of one language

SOURCE: Adapted from Loukotka 1968: 198, 224.

gelin (1965) have relied upon Greenberg's classification. Greenberg, McQuown, and Ortiz relied upon earlier sources based principally upon inspection, while Swadesh's work is based upon his lexicostatistical method.

I would also like to mention the research of contemporary descriptive linguists (chiefly missionaries) who are working in the area. Notable are Fray Cesareo de Armellada (1972); Fr. Adolfo Villamañan (1970–1974); George and Emilio Esteban Mosonyi (whose work on Carib is largely unpublished but is long, reasoned, and thorough); and those members of the Summer Institute of Linguistics who are working on Carib in Guyana, Surinam, Brazil, and Colombia—especially Grimes (1972), Derbyshire (1961), and Hawkins (1952).

EXTERNAL RELATIONSHIPS

The Carib family is a well-known and easily recognized entity. Up to now there have been only three other linguistic groups that have been proposed as being related to Carib. Chocó (northwestern Colombia) was proposed by Rivet (1943a), but there is no recent or strong evidence that Carib and Chocó are in fact related; consequently, this relationship is generally not accepted. Gê (also spelled Jê or Žê) and Pano (Brazil, Peru, and Bolivia) were proposed as related to Carib by Greenberg (1959); while this hypothesis may eventually prove true, no data or analyses have yet substantiated it. Island, Black, and Central American Carib (related languages found in the Caribbean area) were thought to be Carib ever since Adam proposed them as such in 1893; however, Walter Taylor's extensive work (e.g., 1969) has clearly shown that this group belongs to the Arawak family.

In addition, Shebayo (Arawakan from Trinidad), Mutuan and Pimenteira (probably Tupi-Guarani from Brazil), Hacaritama (Arawak from Colombia), Patagon (isolated language from Peru), and Pijao, Colima, Muzo, Pantagora, and Pančě (language isolates from Colombia) have been proposed as related to Carib, but they definitely are not. Most of these proposals are simply cases of misidentification, though there will probably never be enough evidence to properly identify Pantagora, Pančě, Colima, Muzo, and Patagon.

RESEARCH PLAN

Seijas and I have now collected approximately 1,000 separate references on the Carib languages, some original and some not. The proliferation is such that it is not feasible to list all the sources or to include the evaluations and comments in the references to this paper; in fact, the proliferation is so great that it is not feasible to list here all the different names for each separate language and dialect—all this will have to be included in a later work. Nor can we state with certainty at this point how many separate Carib languages there are, since our survey is not yet complete; however, we do feel there are considerably fewer languages than the names that have appeared in the literature would indicate.

Our own work on Carib has consisted, first, in trying to make a complete bibliography of all references containing Carib language data (either vocabulary, grammar, or texts) that can be used for comparative purposes. By this process we have been able to eliminate many references traditionally given in Carib bibliographies (those containing ethnohistorical information but no linguistic data). Second, we have attempted to obtain copies of each reference. These two processes have consumed a great deal of time, since it can be truly said that there is no best library in the world for Carib materials or for South American Indian language materials in general. We have found the following libraries to have large collections of Carib source materials, each collection differing somewhat from the others: Arcaya Library, Caracas; Bibliotéca Nacional, Caracas; Middle American Research Institute Library, Tulane University, New Orleans; Olin Library and George Meisner Rare Book Room, Washington University, St. Louis; Newberry Library, Chicago; New York Public Library, New York; Fundación La Salle Library, Caracas; Anthropology Library of the Smithsonian Institution, Washington, D.C.; Bibliothèque Nationale, Paris; Bibliotéca Nacional, Madrid; and Bibliotéca del Museo de Antropología e Historia, Bogota. Other libraries we would like to consult are: University of Texas Library, Austin; University of Florida Library, Gainesville; Library of Congress, Washington, D.C.; Peabody Museum Library, Cambridge; Library of the Museu Paraense Emílio Goeldi, Belem, Brazil; and the national libraries of Brazil, Surinam, Guyana, and French Guiana. All of these, we suspect, may have sources not yet noted. Since the publication of some of our work, we have also received notice from several persons about word lists in their possession. Thus, the bibliography will inevitably be expanded.

After obtaining copies of all the accessible Carib language materials from the above-mentioned libraries, we noted for each item (whether a grammar, vocabulary, or text) its linguistic value for comparative purposes, the number of words included, whether a phonetic transcription was used or not, the native language of the observer, the place and date when the material was gathered, and information about the origin of informants, where available; in addition, we recorded bibliographic information regarding publications and later reprintings. We have noted very few unpublished manuscripts for the Carib languages. This annotated bibliography is nearing completion and should be ready for publication soon. It is our hope that this will save future workers a great deal of time.

Our next step was to make source cards for each language, (1) noting all alternate language and dialect names, (2) briefly listing all the sources for that language, and (3) noting those to which we had access. We then proceeded to examine separate geographical areas for related languages. The mass of Carib languages are in the Guiana region, but we began by examining those geographical areas distant from that region where isolated Carib-speaking peoples are found.

Our procedure was to gather as many original and secondary sources as we possessed (using as many original sources as possible). We then attempted to recast data from these earlier works into a set of contrastive phonological statements that are meaningful in light of today's knowledge of Carib. By comparing various transcriptions of related languages and dialects, by using our knowledge of the set of phonological contrasts found in the transcriber's native language, and by referring to present-day Carib languages, we were able to make statements about the phonological systems. After these interpretative statements were made for each separate publication concerning a given geographical area, we proceeded to apply the comparative method to these restated data to arrive at a reconstruction of the Carib languages in that area. The work has been slow and tedious, since we have had to acquire a great deal of knowledge of colonial history, archaeology, geography, botany, and zoology. However, we have been greatly aided by doing fieldwork ourselves on several Carib languages in Venezuela. As of 1974 we have nearly completed the analysis of all groups outside the Guiana mass of Carib languages.

It is our eventual goal to arrive at a large list of reconstructed Proto-Carib lexemes that will shed some light upon the general problems mentioned earlier. In the following sections I shall discuss our findings to date.

GEOGRAPHICAL DISTRIBUTIONS

There are at present three geographical areas of Carib speakers, smaller than they once were, but still substantial: (1) Colombia, which can be divided into two geographic units, (a) southeastern Colombia and (b) northeastern Colombia–Venezuela border; (2) an area south of the Amazon, which can be divided into (a) outlying areas of eastern and northern Brazil and (b) the Xingu River Basin; and (3) the Guiana land mass, which can be considered a single homogeneous unit.

It is well known that Carib speakers once made great incursions into the Caribbean islands as far north as Cuba—onto Hispaniola, Puerto Rico, and the Lesser Antilles (including Trinidad, Tobago, Margarita, and Cubagua off the coast of Venezuela). While the native Arawak speakers on these islands borrowed heavily from the invading Caribs, it is our contention that there was no Carib language in the islands outside of that spoken by invading Carib males for a generation or so after the invasions. As noted earlier, what are called Island, Black, and Central American Carib are certainly Arawak languages. One language identified as Carib has also been reported from northern Peru (near southern Ecuador), but we do not believe it to be Carib (Durbin and Seijas 1973b). Suggestions have been made that

Carib intruded as far north as Florida and Texas, but there is no positive evidence for this. In short, we can say that the vast majority of Carib languages have always been (as they are today) in the Guianas.

INTERNAL SUBDIVISIONS

The following is a discussion of internal subgroupings found in the geographical divisions mentioned above; as will be shown, these do not always correspond with linguistic subdivisions.

Colombia

SOUTHEASTERN COLOMBIA

In southern Colombia between the Vaupés and the Caquetá rivers we find three Carib languages that are closely related: Hianacoto-Umaua, Carijona, and Guaque (see Map 2.1). There are satisfactory published data

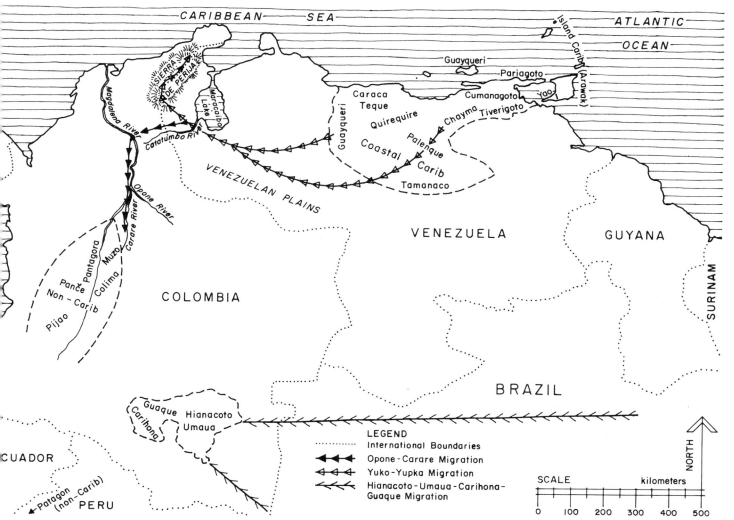

Map 2.1. Some Carib tribes of Colombia and northern Venezuela and their possible migration routes (adapted from Loukotka 1967)

for Hianacoto-Umaua only (Durbin and Seijas 1973c). A few speakers of Carijona still survive (Arthur Sorenson 1973: personal communication; Schindler: this volume). These languages have in common the innovation whereby Proto-Carib *p has become Proto-Hianacoto-Umaua-Carijona-Guaque *p, *b, *h (Durbin and Seijas 1973c: 30). They are not closely related to their northern Colombian neighbors but rather to languages in the southern Guianas, northern Brazil, and Brazil south of the Amazon.

NORTHEASTERN COLOMBIA–VENEZUELA BORDER

In northeastern Colombia, extending down the Sierra de Perijá over into Venezuela (almost up to Lake Maracaibo—perhaps around the lake aboriginally), are the Yukpa (also known as Yuko or Motilon). There appear to be two languages: (1) Japreria (mostly located in Venezuela, with occasional incursions into Colombia); and (2) a series of dialects of Colombian Yukpa or Yuko (Iroka, Las Candelas, Manaure, Maraca, San Genaro, Sokomba, Susa, and Yowa) and Venezuelan Yukpa (Irapa, Macoita, Pariri, Shaparru, Viakshi, Wasama, and Rionegriño), which together constitute another language. All these languages appear to be closely related to a group of Venezuelan Coastal Carib languages that are now extinct: Chayma, Cumanagoto, Piritu, Pariagoto, Palenque, Tamanaco, Tiverigoto, Caraca, and Yao (see Map 2.1).

While the Yukpa dialects are most closely related to the above-mentioned Venezuelan coastal languages, another group, Opone and Carare in northeastern Colombia, appear to be more closely related to Yukpa than they are to any other languages (Durbin and Seijas 1973a). Opone and Carare are found spoken along rivers of the same names, which are tributaries of the Magdalena River in the Department of Santander. They appear to be dialects of the same language, with not more than three surviving speakers, if any.

This distribution suggests to us a movement from the Venezuela coastal area through the plains into the southern part of the Sierra de Perijá. Our own analyses (Durbin and Seijas 1973d; 1975) suggest that Yukpa migration into the Sierra de Perijá came from the south (see Map 2.1), and therefore that the area between Lake Maracaibo and the Sierra may have been occupied by ancestors of these speakers at one time. We surmise that they were pushed into the Sierra, first by Barí speakers (also called Motilones; their language is as yet unclassified), and later by Spanish colonists. In support of this hypothesis we may cite Jahn (1927: 39–73), who mentions a group residing around Lake Maracaibo in early times that he believes to have been Carib. Furthermore, Layrisse and Wilbert's blood studies indicate that

Yukpa mixed intensively during the last 700 years with a large Diego-negative Indian population in the area, who could have been the Barí (Layrisse and Wilbert 1966: 65). Finally, our sound-correspondence studies indicate that Spanish has influenced some of the Venezuelan groups toward change (Durbin and Seijas 1975: 71). Along with or perhaps after the movement into the Sierra de Perijá by the Yukpa (Yuko) groups, the Opone-Carare may have been pushed through the southern foothills of the Sierra onto the Magdalena River in Colombia by the expanding Barí (the Magdalena flows fairly near the foothills of the Sierra de Perijá in the north Colombian Department of Magdalena). The Opone-Carare may then have proceeded down the Magdalena to the tributaries where they were found historically. Alternatively, the Opone-Carare may have been pushed into Barí territory up the Catatumbo River to its source in the present state of Norte de Santander, which again is very close to the Magdalena. There were probably other closely related Carib groups in the general area who accompanied the Opone-Carare. Loukotka (1968: 220) lists several tribes in the same area whose names are drawn from ethnohistorical sources for which there are no linguistic data: Yariqui, Xinguan, Carate, Corbato, Chinato, Zorca, Cariquera, Capacho. He also lists Hacaritama (once spoken around the modern city of the same name in the Department of Santander) and Guane (once spoken in the Department of Santander at the sources of the Carare River). Our examination of the Hacaritama data reveals that it is probably a dialect of Guajiro; Guane is listed as having two recorded words, but we have never been able to locate them.

Nevertheless, Carib tribes must have been widespread at one time throughout northeastern Colombia and northwestern Venezuela, since we find some incontrovertible Carib influences upon Muzo, Colima, Pantagora, Panče, and Pijao, all languages of an unknown affiliation that extend downward through the present central Colombian departments of Santander, Cundinamarca, and Tolima. It had long been supposed that these unclassified languages were Carib, but we were able to demonstrate that the linguistic material included in prior discussion had not been sufficient to properly place them within this language family (Durbin and Seijas 1973b). Certainly the Pijao word list collected by Gerardo Reichel-Dolmatoff in 1943 (Ramirez-Sendoya 1952) substantiates our hypothesis that it is not Carib; thus all of these remain unclassified at the present time, though there seem to be Carib influences. It is quite possible that Opone-Carare and other now-extinct Carib groups displaced the above-mentioned groups. In summary, we believe that we can posit a close unity among the Venezuelan coastal groups, the groups in Sierra de Perijá, and the Opone-Carare. This would seem to represent a western migration across the plains into the Lake Maracaibo area, then north into the Sierra de Perijá, and also south through the foothills of the Sierra and down the Magdalena (see Map 2.1). An important point to keep in mind is that the Carib languages of southeastern Colombia do not fall into this same group.

Areas South of the Amazon

NORTHERN BRAZILIAN OUTLIERS

In northern Brazil the following Carib languages are found: Palmella, Arara, Apiaka, Pariri, Aracaju, Aramayana, Yaruma, and Txicão (see Map 2.2). It is genuinely doubtful that Pimenteira (an eastern language in this general area, now extinct) is Carib, since the only extant material contains more Tupi-Guarani than Carib. Aracaju and Aramayana have counterparts north of the Amazon in Brazilian Guiana and appear to have strayed into their present positions south of the Amazon. It appears that Arara, Apiaka (not to be confused with Tupi Apiaca), Pariri, Yaruma, Palmella, and Txicão have also strayed across the Amazon, because they closely resemble languages from the eastern Guiana areas, including eastern Brazilian Guiana, French Guiana, and Surinam. The movement must have been a concerted one, for Apiaka, Arara, Pariri, Yaruma, and Txicão closely resemble each other more than any one resembles any other group or language. They share the common trait of lacking a fricative series, which is unusual in Carib languages. As far as we know, the only other Carib language without a fricative series is Tamanaco, though we do not postulate a close relation between Tamanaco and these languages.

Palmella, on the other hand, closely resembles a group we call the East-West Guiana Carib languages (see below). There are reports that Palmella society once had European whites as well as blacks in its midst. Although very little is known about Palmella, it is conceivable that it might have been one of several Pidgin or Creole languages frequently found in Guiana, and that its speakers might have been a band of racially mixed refugees who wandered as far south as the border between Brazil and Bolivia. Very small amounts of data have been available to us from Txicão and Yaruma, formerly located on the margins of the Upper Xingu Basin; for this reason the position of these languages is only tentative. Finally, a language called Yuma, for which no data exist, is posited by Loukotka (1968: 222) as being in this group and is so marked on Map 2.2.

Because Aramayana and Aracaju are found south of the Amazon and seem to have definitely emigrated from Brazilian Guiana (north of the Amazon), we have also placed the point of origin for Arara, Apiaka, Pariri, Yaruma, and Txicão approximately in this area (see Map 2.2). It can be seen on the map that the majority of Arara, Apiaka, and Pariri speakers are reasonably close to this point of origin and that most of them could have traveled from the point of origin to the nearby Amazon and down the Amazon to various tributaries. We would like to account for this migration by population pressures exerted in Brazilian Guiana (north of the Amazon) by Tupi-speaking groups. These Tupi groups seem to have appeared in the area just before European contact and to have continued living there throughout much of the colonial period. If this was indeed the case, then all of Brazilian Guiana could at one time have been Carib (except for a few old residue pockets of Arawak).

XINGU RIVER BASIN

Bakairi and Nahukwa form a group of languages in the Xingu Basin area (see Map 2.2). Bakairi appears to have two main dialects, as does Nahukwa. Hermann Meyer gave the names Yanamakapë and Akuku to the Nahukwa subdivisions, and he credited each with a large number of dialects (Krause 1936); however, the latter are mainly names for village groups (Ellen B. Basso 1973: personal communication). The Bakairi were made famous by von den Steinen (1892) when he first demonstrated that Proto-Carib *p developed into an intervocalic manifested in the language of that Xingu Carib tribe. This change has also occurred in Nahukwa.

Von den Steinen also posited that the Lower Xingu Basin was the homeland of the Caribs and that Apiaka represented an intermediate group ("missing link") left behind in the migration of the Guianan Caribs to the north (1940: 226). If this were true, Proto-Carib would have had to change a great deal before migrating very far. We have chosen to explain Apiaka (along with Yaruma, Txicão, Arara, Pariri, Palmella, and possibly Pimenteira) as extensions of Brazilian Guiana Carib languages that crossed the Amazon sometime within the past 500 years. We have done this because they most closely resemble these Brazilian Guiana languages, and because Bakairi and Nahukwa on the other hand more closely resemble Hianacoto-Umaua-Carijona-Guaque and languages in the southwestern and southern Guianas such as Ye'cuana, Ocomesiana, Wayumara, and Hishkaryana, among others. In all these languages Proto-Carib *p has undergone considerable changes, whereas in the rest of the Guianan languages it has remained intact.

The Guiana Land Mass

The next area we turn to is the land mass of Guiana, where the largest geographical and numerical concentration of Carib languages is found. As can be seen in Map 2.3, Carib speakers form one unbroken group, with only

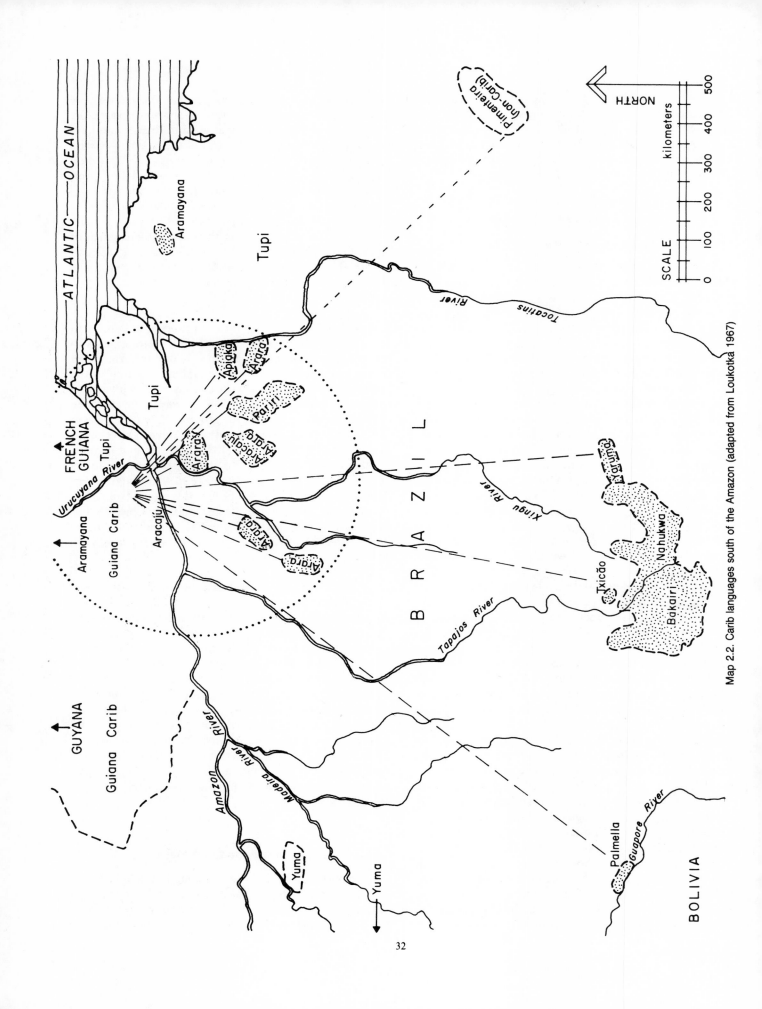

Map 2.2. Carib languages south of the Amazon (adapted from Loukotka 1967)

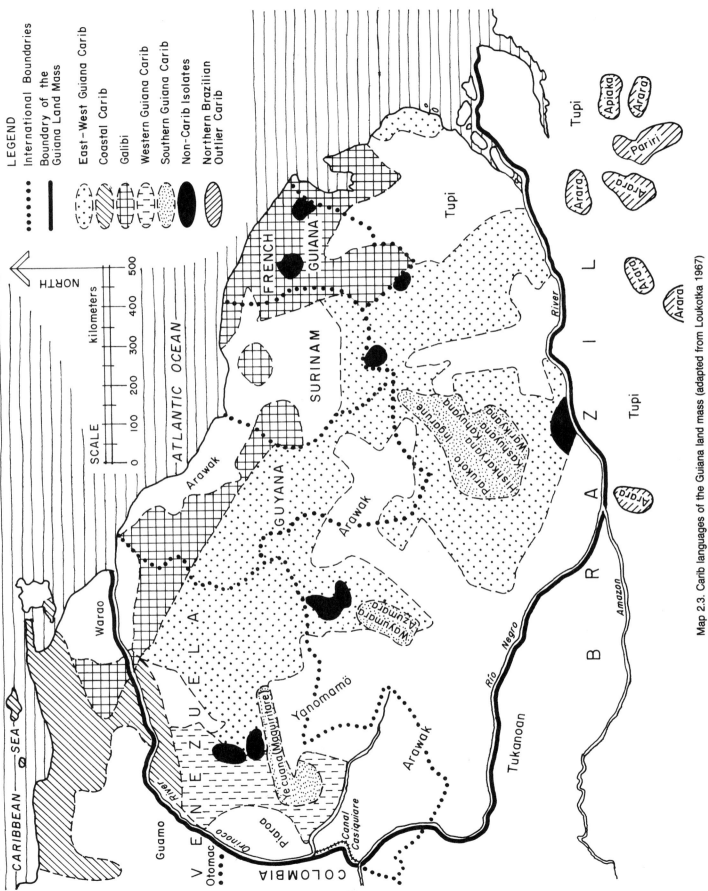

Map 2.3. Carib languages of the Guiana land mass (adapted from Loukotka 1967)

two small islands separated from the rest (one in northern Surinam and one on the Atlantic coast of Brazil).

The region also contains what appear to be recent incursions into the area—Tupi from the south (represented by Mutuan, which has been classified as Carib but definitely is not, and Emerillon), Coastal Carib in the form of Tamanaco, and Yanomamö (an unclassified language, coming from the south).

There are other islands in the area that represent what we believe to be remnants of languages that survived the original Carib expansion. In French Guiana are Tocoyene (no data) and Palikur (Arawakan); in Brazil are the language isolates Taripio and Maracano, for which no data are available; in Venezuela we find Joti (Chikano and Yuana). It can thus be seen that except for recent incursions into the area, the integrity of Carib in the Guianas has been complete since contact time and probably since much earlier.

We suspect that Carib occupied most of the Guiana area until recent incursions of Tupi and Yanomamö speakers from the south (in Brazil). It would seem almost certain that the Caribs replaced Arawaks, since we see the Guiana Carib languages boxed in among Arawaks on all sides—north and south, east and west. Just as recent Tupi and Yanomamö expansions began to dislodge Caribs from various areas, we would hypothesize that the Caribs pushed Arawaks north into the Antilles, to the west, and deep into southern Brazil. In line with this hypothesis, isolated northern language groups such as the Warao, Sape, Arutani, Joti, Auake, Kaliana, Guahibo, Yaruro, Otomac, Taparita, and possibly Yanomamö (among others) would have been the original inhabitants of the Guianas before the Arawaks replaced them.

While we have not yet finished our analysis of the data from the Guiana area, we can nevertheless discern four main linguistic subdivisions. The first is that of *Galibi,* which starts in extreme northern Brazil, covers the entire area of French Guiana, small portions of Surinam, northern Guyana, and northeastern Venezuela, and extends out of the Guiana area into the coastal region of Venezuela. Galibi is commonly called Carib or Carabisce in English, Kribisi in English Creole of Surinam, Caribe in Spanish, Caraiben in Dutch, and Galibi in French and Portuguese (Hoff 1968: 1); it has also been called Cariniaco, as well as Carina and Kaliña, in Venezuela. Of all the Carib languages it has the largest geographical spread and probably had the largest number of speakers (see Map 2.3).

The second linguistic subdivision, which we have called *Western Guiana Carib,* occurs in the extreme western part of the Guiana Carib area in western Venezuela, immediately below the Orinoco River. The languages

are Quaca, Pareca, Panare, Yabarana, and Mapoyo. Quaca and Pareca are now extinct, with very little data available; they are very aberrant from most Carib languages and appear to have been heavily influenced by outside languages.

The third linguistic subdivision we have chosen to call *Southern Guiana Carib.* It consists, on the one hand, of Kashuyana, Warikyana, Kahuyana, and Ingarune (all dialects of the same language), and, on the other, of Hishkaryana, Wayumara-Azumara, Parukoto, and Ye'cuana. In these languages several sound shifts have taken place, the most prominent of which is the change of Proto-Carib *p to Proto-Southern Carib *h. In this respect the group is more closely related to the Southeastern Colombian group and to the Xingu River Basin groups (discussed above) than it is to any of the other Carib languages in the Guiana area.

The fourth subdivision of the Guiana area contains the largest number of languages. These languages range from east to west, hence our term for them, *East-West Guiana Carib.* Starting with Brazil, we have Aracaju, Pianakoto, Urukuyana, Wayana-Aparai, Trio-Rangu, Cachuena, Sapara, Yauapery, Pauxi, Wabui, Bonari, Crichana, Waimiri, Chikena, Saluma, Paravilhana, and Pauxiana. Roucouyene is the name for Urukuyana in French Guiana. In Surinam are Kumayena, Akuriyo, and Triometesen. In Guyana we find Makusi, Akawaio, and Patamona (Ingariko). In eastern Venezuela we find Pemong (Taulipang, Kamarakoto), Arinagoto, and Purucoto.

CONCLUSIONS

I wish to repeat that our work is not complete enough to lead us to a reconstruction of a basic Proto-Carib lexicon. We are at the state of reconstructing various internal subdivisions. Nevertheless, we can state several conclusions with some confidence.

1. Among the Carib there appears to be a basic north-south dichotomy that runs on an east-west axis. We refer to these major divisions as *Northern Carib* and *Southern Carib.* Each can be subdivided further, as outlined in Table 2.2. *Northern Carib* comprises what we have called *(IA)* Coastal Carib (with its Sierra de Perijá and Opone-Carare outliers), *(IB)* Western Guiana Carib, *(IC)* Galibi, *(ID)* the central East-West Guiana Carib languages running through the Guiana area, and *(IE)* their northern Brazilian outliers south of the Amazon. *Southern Carib* consists of *(IIA)* Southeastern Colombia Carib, *(IIB)* Xingu Basin Carib in central Brazil, and *(IIC)* what we have called Southern Guiana Carib, a group of Carib languages in the

TABLE 2.2
**Internal Relations Among the Carib Languages
(Dialects Excluded)**

I. *Northern Carib*

  A. Coastal Carib (mostly outside Guiana land mass)

    1. Venezuelan Coastal Carib

      a. Chayma †
      b. Cumanagoto †
      c. Yao †
      d. Tamanaco (in Guiana land mass) †

    2. Sierra de Perijá (border of northeastern Colombia and Venezuela)

      a. Japreria
      b. Yukpa
      c. Yuko (Colombian Yukpa)

    3. Opone–Carare (Central Colombia) †

  B. Western Guiana Carib (Western Venezuela)

    1. Mapoyo
    2. Yabarana
    3. Panare
    4. Quaca †
    5. Pareca †

  C. Galibi (mostly along the Atlantic Coast from mouth of Amazon to Orinoco)

  D. East-West Guiana Carib (mostly in Brazilian Guiana with outliers in Surinam, Guyana, Venezuela, and French Guiana)

    1. Wayana-Aparai
    2. Roucouyene (French Guiana) †
    3. Aracaju †
    4. Trio-Rangu

    5. Wama (Akuriyo) (Surinam)
    6. Urukuyana
    7. Triometesen (Surinam)
    8. Kumayena (Surinam)

    9. Pianakoto
    10. Saluma
    11. Pauxi †
    12. Cachuena
    13. Chikena
    14. Waiwai

    15. Paravilhana †
    16. Wabui
    17. Sapara
    18. Yauapery
    19. Waimiri
    20. Crichana †
    21. Pauxiana
    22. Bonari †

    23. Makusi (Guyana)
    24. Purucoto (Venezuela)
    25. Pemong (Taulipang) (Venezuela)
    26. Patamona (Guyana)
    27. Akawaio (Guyana)
    28. Arinagoto (Venezuela) †

  E. Northern Brazilian Outliers (south of the Amazon)

    1. Palmella †
    2. Pimenteira? †

    3. Yaruma †
    4. Txicão

    5. Pariri †
    6. Apiaka †
    7. Arara †
    8. Yuma †

II. *Southern Carib*

  A. Southeastern Colombia Carib

    1. Hianacoto-Umaua †
    2. Guaque †
    3. Carijona

  B. Xingu Basin Carib (Brazil)

    1. Bakairi
    2. Nahukwa

  C. Southern Guiana Carib (mostly in southern Venezuela and Brazil)

    1. Ye'cuana (Venezuela)
    2. Wayumara-Azumara (Venezuela)
    3. Parukoto
    4. Hishkaryana
    5. Warikyana (Kashuyana-Kahuyana-Ingarune)

† extinct
{ possible subgroupings

southern part of the Guiana Carib area north of the Amazon.

2. There appear to be approximately 50 to 55 Carib languages, though further research should reduce this number.

3. Although we are not sure how the division has come about, we do feel relatively sure that Coastal Carib, Western Guiana Carib, Galibi, and East-West Guiana Carib (four of the five *Northern Carib* subdivisions) are closer to Proto-Carib than any of the *Southern Carib* languages are.

Throughout our work we have used the hypothesis that the more changed a language is from the protoform, the farther it is likely to have traveled from its origi-

nal homeland. For this reason we have excluded any Southern Carib languages or locations as being possibly close to the homeland of the original Caribs. We would tend to place the homeland of the Caribs in the Guiana area of Venezuela, Guyana, Surinam, or French Guiana, but probably not in Brazilian Guiana. When we have been able to reconstruct more Proto-Carib forms, we may be able to substantiate this hypothesis and perhaps even make the location more precise.

According to Layrisse and Wilbert's preliminary rough glottochronological counts, Proto-Carib began to break up about 4,500 years ago, when 30 percent of the separation occurred. About 3,400 to 2,400 years ago approximately 56 percent of the separation of Carib tribes occurred in a second phase, and finally, about 2,300 to

1,000 years ago some 14 percent of the present diversity of the Carib groups originated. Of course, since colonial contact a great deal of movement has occurred. Layrisse and Wilbert (1966: 105) correlate these glottochronological dates with an archaeological period established by Cruxent and Rouse (1958–1959, 1: 238). From 4,500 to 3,000 years ago (Layrisse and Wilbert's first stage), the Proto-Caribs are believed to have been agricultural hunters and gatherers, which would have accounted for approximately 30 percent of the total linguistic diversity we see today. Stated in another way, the present-day diversity of approximately 50 languages would have been roughly 15 languages about 3,000 years ago. In the second stage (3,000–1,600 years ago) the first traces of manioc cultivation are noted. Presumably this new subsistence technique would have been successful enough to have brought about population increases, the possibility of greater density of population, and movements and migrations out of the central homeland area. By the end of the second stage there could have been approximately 45 languages. The third stage would have been characterized by stability, with only a few divergences being added until the time of contact. Layrisse and Wilbert (1966: 106) further suggest that Bakairi represents the earliest split from Proto-Carib; our data also suggest this, but we would add to Bakairi the other Southern Carib languages, including Hianakoto-Umaua-Carijona-Guaque, Nahukwa, Ye'cuana, Wayumara, Azumara, Hishkaryana, and Warikyana.

REFERENCES

Adam, Lucien
   1893   *Matériaux pour servir a l'établissement d'une grammaire comparée des dialectes de la famille Caribe.* Paris: *Bibliothéque Linguistique Américaine* 17.

Adelung, Johann Christoph, and Johann Severin Vater
   1806–17 *Mithridates, oder allgemeine Sprachenkunde, mit dem Vater Unser als Sprachprobe en beynahe funf hundert Sprachen und Mundarten,* vol. 3 (of 4 vols.). Berlin.

Armellada, Cesareo de
   1972   *Pemonton Taremuru (Invocaciones mágicas de los indios Pemon).* Caracas: Universidad Católica Andres Bello, Instituto de Investigaciones Históricas, Centro de Lenguas Indígenas.

Balbi, Adriano
   1826   *Atlas ethnographique du globe, ou Classification des peuples anciens et modernes d'après leurs langues, précédé d'un discours sur l'utilité et l'importance de l'étude des langues appliquée à plusieurs branches des connaissances humaines . . . avec environ de sept cents vocabulaires des principaux idiomes connus. . . .* Paris.

Brinton, Daniel G.
   1891   *The American Race: A Linguistic Classification and Ethnographic Description of the Native Tribes of North and South America.* New York: N. D. C. Hodges.

Chamberlain, Alexander F.
   1903   Indians, America. In *The [Encyclopedia] Americana,* vol. 9. Revised in *Encyclopedia Americana,* 1941, vol. 15: 43–58.

   1913   Linguistic Stocks of South American Indians, with distribution map. *American Anthropologist* 15: 236–47.

Cruxent, José M., and Irving Rouse
   1958–59 An Archeological Chronology of Venezuela. 2 vols. Washington, D.C.: *Pan American Union Social Science Monographs* 6.

Derbyshire, Desmond
   1961   Hishkaryana (Carib) Syntax Structure. *International Journal of American Linguistics* 27: 125–42.

D'Orbigny, Alcide D.
   1839   *L'homme américain de l'Amérique méridionale considéré sous ses rapports physiologiques et moraux.* Paris.

Durbin, Marshall, and Haydée Seijas
  1973a   A Note on Opon-Carare. *Zeitschrift für Ethnologie* 98 (2): 242–45.

  1973b   A Note on Panche, Pijao, Pantagora (Palenque), Colima and Muzo. *International Journal of American Linguistics* 39: 47–51.

  1973c   Proto Hianacoto: Guaque-Carijona-Hianacoto Umaua. *International Journal of American Linguistics* 39: 22–31.

  1973d   Linguistic Interrelations Among the Yukpa. Paper read at the 1973 annual meeting of the American Anthropological Association, New Orleans.

  1975   The Phonological Structure of the Western Carib Languages of the Sierra de Perijá, Venezuela. In *Atti del XL Congresso Internazionale degli Americanisti* (Rome–Genoa, 1972), vol. 3: 69–77.

Gilij, Filippo Salvatore
  1965   *Ensayo de historia americana,* trans. Antonio Tovar. 3 vols. Caracas: *Biblioteca de la Academia Nacional de Historia* 71–73. (Originally published 1782, Rome.)

Goeje, Claudius H. de
  1910   Études linguistiques Caraïbes. Amsterdam: *Verhandelingen van de Koninklijke Akademie van Wetenschappen, Afdeeling letterkunde,* n.r. 10 (3).

  1944   Études linguistiques Caraïbes. Amsterdam: *Verhandelingen van de Koninklijke Akademie van Wetenschappen, Afdeeling letterkunde,* n.r. 49 (2).

Greenberg, Joseph H.
  1959   The General Classification of Central and South American Languages. In *Men and Cultures: Selected Papers of the 5th International Congress of Anthropological and Ethnological Sciences,* ed. A. F. C. Wallace, pp. 793–94. Philadelphia: Univ. of Pennsylvania Press.

Grimes, Joseph, ed.
  1972   *Languages of the Guianas.* Tlalpan, Mexico: Summer Institute of Linguistics.

Hawkins, Neil W.
  1972   A fonologia da lingua Uaiuai. *Faculdade de Filosofia, Ciências e Letras, Universidade de São Paulo, Boletim* 157, *Etnografia e Lingua Tupí-Guaraní* 25.

Hervás y Panduro, Lorenzo
  1800   *Catálogo de las lenguas de las naciones conocidas, y numeración, división, y clases de estas según la diversidad de sus idiomas y dialectos.* Vol. 1: *Lenguas y naciones americanos.* Madrid.

Hoff, B. J.
  1968   *The Carib Language.* The Hague: Martinus Nijhoff. *Verhandelingen van het Koninklijk Instituut voor Taal-, Land- en Volkenkunde* 55.

Jahn, Alfredo
  1927   *Los aborígenes del occidente de Venezuela: Su historia, etnografía y afinidades lingüísticas,* vols. 1 and 2. Caracas: Lit. y Tip. Comercio.

Koch-Grünberg, Theodor
  1928   *Vom Roroima zum Orinoco.* Vol. 4: *Sprachen.* Stuttgart: Strecher und Schröder.

Krause, Fritz
  1936   Die Yarumá- und Arawine-Indianer Zentralbrasiliens. *Baessler-Archiv Beiträge zur Völkerkunde* 19: 32–44.

Layrisse, Miguel, and Johannes Wilbert
  1966   *Indian Societies of Venezuela: Their Blood Group Types.* Caracas: Editorial Sucre. *Instituto Caribe de Antropología y Sociología, Fundación La Salle de Ciencias Naturales, Monograph* 13.

Loukotka, Čestmír
  1935   Clasificación de las lenguas sudamericanas. *Lingüística Sudamericana* 1 (Prague).

  1941   Roztřídění jihoamerických jazyků. *Lingüística Sudamericana* 3 (Prague).

  1944   Klassifikation der südamerikanischen Sprachen. *Zeitschrift für Ethnologie* 74 (1–6): 1–69.

  1948   Sur la classification des langues indigènes de l'Amérique du Sud. In *Actes du XXVIIIe Congrès International des Américanistes* (Paris, 1947), pp. 193–99.

  1968   *Classification of South American Indian Languages.* Los Angeles: Latin American Center, UCLA, *Reference Series* 7.

Lounsbury, Floyd
  1947   Review of *Études linguistiques Caribes [sic],* vol. 2, by C. H. de Goeje. *Language* 23: 308–11.

Ludewig, H. E.
  1858   *The Literature of American Aboriginal Languages.* London: Trubner.

Martius, Karl Friedrich Philipp von
    1867   *Beiträge zur Ethnographie und Sprachenkunde Amerikas, zumal Brasiliens.* 2 vols. Leipzig.

Mason, John A.
    1950   The Languages of South American Indians. In *Handbook of South American Indians,* ed. Julian Steward, vol. 6: 157–317. *U.S. Bureau of American Ethnology, Bulletin* 143. Washington: Government Printing Office.

McQuown, Norman A.
    1955   The Indigenous Languages of Latin America. *American Anthropologist* 57(3): 501–70.

Morison, Samuel Eliot
    1963   *Journals and Other Documents on the Life and Voyages of Christopher Columbus.* New York: Heritage Press.

Ortiz, Sergio Elias
    1965   *Lenguas y dialectos indígenas de Colombia: Historia extense de Colombia,* vol. 1, book 3. Bogota: Academia Colombiana de Historia.

Ramirez-Sendoya, Pedro J.
    1952   *Diccionario indio del Gran Tolima.* Publicaciones del Ministerio de Educación Nacional. Bogota: Editorial Minerva.

Rey, Jose del
    1971   *Aportes Jesuíticos a la filología colonial Venezolano.* Caracas: Universidad Católica Andres Bello, Instituto de Investigaciones Históricas, Seminario de Lenguas Indígenas.

Rivet, Paul
    1924   Langues américaines. II: Langues de l'Amérique du Sud et des Antilles. In *Les langues du monde,* ed. A. Meillet and Marcel Cohen, pp. 639–712. Paris: La Société de Linguistique de Paris, *Collection Linguistique* XVI.

    1943a   La influencia karib en Colombia. *Revista del Instituto Etnológico Nacional* 1: 55–93, 283–95 (Bogota).

    1943b   La lengua Chocó. *Revista del Instituto Etnológico Nacional* 1: 131-96 (Bogota).

Rivet, Paul, and Čestmír Loukotka
    1952   Langues de l'Amérique du Sud et des Antilles. In *Les langues du monde* (new ed.), ed. A. Meillet and Marcel Cohen, pp. 1099–1160. Paris: Centre·National de la Recherche Scientifique.

Rowe, John H.
    1951   Linguistic Classification Problems in South America. *University of California Publications in Linguistics* 10: 13–26.

Steinen, Karl von den
    1892   *Die Bakaïri-Sprache.* Leipzig: K. F. Koehler's Antiquarium.

    1940   *Entre os aborígenes do Brasil Central.* São Paulo: Departamento de Cultura. (Originally published in *Revista do Arquivo Municipal* [São Paulo] XXXIV–LVIII.)

Steward, Julian, and Louis Faron
    1959   *Native Peoples of South America.* New York: McGraw-Hill.

Swadesh, Morris
    1955   Towards a Satisfactory Genetic Classification of Amerindian Languages. In *Anais do XXXI Congresso International de Americanistas* (São Paulo, 1954), pp. 1001–12.

    1959   Mapas de clasificación lingüística de México y las Américas. Mexico City: *Cuadernos del Instituto de Historia, Serie Antropológica* 8.

Tax, Sol
    1960   Aboriginal Languages of Latin America. *Current Anthropology* 1: 431–36.

Taylor, Douglas R.
    1969   Consonantal Correspondence and Loss in Northern Arawakan with Special Reference to Guajiro. *Word* 25: 275–88.

Villamañan, Adolfo, ed.
    1971–74 Lingüística, antropologia, misionologia Bari-Yukpa-Xapreria. *Hoja Semanal,* pp. 1–140. (Sirapta, Venezuela; mimeographed bulletin.)

Voegelin, Charles F., and Florence M. Voegelin
    1965   Languages of the World: Native America Fascicle Two. *Anthropological Linguistics* 7 (7), pt. I.

Wilbert, Johannes
    1968   Loukotka's Classification of South American Indian Languages. Preface to *Classification of South American Indian Languages,* by Cestmír Loukotka, pp. 7–23. Los Angeles: Latin American Center, UCLA, *Reference Series* 7.

3. SOME PROBLEMS IN THE COMPARATIVE STUDY OF CARIB SOCIETIES

Peter G. Rivière
Institute of Social Anthropology, Oxford University

The publication in 1971 of Peter Kloos's *The Maroni River Caribs of Surinam* was a particularly important event in Carib studies. Among the many virtues of this work, the aspect I would take to be the most important is the demonstration that this Carib society, despite centuries of contact, change, and near extinction, has maintained intact fundamental structural principles or features—features that the Maroni River Caribs share with all known Carib societies. The retention of these features in the face of the vicissitudes suffered by the Maroni River Caribs clearly indicates their vital importance in the ordering of Carib society. It seems probable that these persistent elements are central to all Carib societies.

The first and most important of these elements is the principle of direct or symmetric exchange, which is revealed through a two-section or two-line relationship terminology and is often associated with a prescriptive marriage rule. There is no Carib society from which this feature has not been reported. This does not mean that all Carib relationship terminologies are identical in the sense that they all have the same number of terms covering the same genealogical specifications. They do not, and the published terminologies exhibit considerable variation in this respect; the merging or distinguishing of genealogical levels is the most obvious and frequent difference.

A further word on what is meant by a two-line terminology is in order here. All known Carib societies have relationship terminologies whose categories may be ordered logically into two sets between which a direct exchange relationship exists. How these sets are defined varies, but apt terms for them are *lineal* and *affinal*. It must be stressed that these lines are a feature of the terminology and that they are not necessarily represented by groups of people on the ground. On this score there is a useful lesson to be learned from Carib societies for the study of prescriptive alliance. A feature of these societies, or at least of those north of the Amazon, is the absence of any formal social groupings that have any

permanency—there are no corporate bodies of any sort. Therefore, it is useless in the Carib case to try to see a prescriptive system operating between any forms of social grouping, such as families or villages. Further, the relationship categories themselves are not represented by any definable groups. The prescriptive system operates as a consequence of a certain systematic interrelationship of the categories. When two individuals marry, they do so as members of certain categories in relationship to one another and not as members of certain groups. It has been the tendency to confuse groups and categories that has proved such a hindrance to understanding this type of society.

This is not to say that groups and other practical considerations do not enter into the choice of spouse, for of course they do. There are, however, two levels of investigation to be distinguished. At one level there is the rule, which is part and parcel of the categorical system and by means of which marital exchanges are manifested as an aspect of the structure. At the other level it is a matter of *which* individual is chosen from the prescribed category, and here all sorts of other considerations come into play: residence, age, and so on. It is essential to keep these two levels distinct, for while one, the direct exchange rule, is universally reported for Carib societies and should be considered as one of their fundamental articulating principles, the other, the actual marriage preferences and patterns, shows considerable variation from one society to the next. For example, the Trio and the Maroni River Caribs have very similar relationship terminologies, but there is a strongly expressed preference for close marriages among the former and for more distant unions among the latter. It is often argued that if marriages do not fall in line with the prescription, the prescription will change: demographic decline, for example, will prevent the marriage pattern from following the prescription because of a lack of people in the prescribed category. While I regard this argument to be badly founded through a misunderstanding of the nature of prescriptive systems, the Maroni River Caribs can be cited as a case in which the argument is wrong even in its own terms. Indeed, that these people have maintained an ongoing system of direct exchange despite near extinction is a clear indication of the central importance of this system to the structure of Carib societies.

Ethnographically speaking, there is no doubt about the presence of the principle of direct exchange in Carib societies, and there is considerable evidence to support the view that it is one of the most important organizing principles in these societies. The second principle with which I want to deal is more problematic—it concerns the notion of asymmetric relationships. Asymmetric might not be the right term in this context, because I am not referring to the indirect form of prescriptive alliance, but rather to hierarchical relationships of the superior-inferior order. One difficulty is that in its most acute form, that of domination-subordination, this sort of relationship is extremely rare among Carib peoples. Most Carib societies lack any political organization or institutions, and where these do occur they do not often involve the notion of domination. The exception to this state of affairs appears to arise under certain abnormal conditions, such as during times of hostilities, when the Carib Indian seems willing to bow to some temporary authority. Kloos shows that village leaders among the Maroni River Caribs are able to assume greater authority during periods of political tension. I would argue, therefore, that even if the actual occurrence of dominant-subordinate relationships is rare, the fact that they are able to emerge at all indicates their latent existence in Carib society. What other relationship, then, is there in Carib society whose conceptualization possesses the right connotation, the right idiom for expressing an asymmetrical relationship? The answer would appear to be the affinal one, and I wish to discuss this with reference to one particular Carib word—*pito.*

The term *pito,* which appears in the literature in various orthographic forms, is found among many different Carib peoples. It has variously been translated as slave, servant, client, brother-in-law, son-in-law, and sister's son. This range of meanings covers a continuum from the potentially equal (brother-in-law) to the totally inferior (slave); however, slave and servant are concepts that are out of keeping with the nature of Carib societies as we know them today. There seem to be two ways in which the existence of these concepts might be explained: (1) they reflect an earlier, more complex, and more hierarchical form of society that has now disappeared, or (2) they are postcontact adaptations of indigenous ideas modified by European influence. Although I do not think that the two explanations exclude each other, I would favor the second position on the following grounds. There is little doubt that the translation of *pito* as client, which is given by Henri Coudreau for the

Roucouyenne (Wayana?) (1893: 238–40), is a distortion, and that the so-called patron-client relationship is an affinal one. Williams (1932: 157, 160) gives, in addition to the meanings "dependent" and "servant," the meaning "daughter's husband, used also of any young man in reference to his subordinate position." The terminological identification of daughter's husband with servant is important for the argument, but the identification can be taken a step further: Farabee, writing of the same people, translates the term as both "daughter's husband" and "sister's son" (1924: 81)—an identification that is to be found in a large number of Carib relationship terminologies.

So far, and with only a few examples, it is possible to show a close link between affinal relationships and those of superiority-inferiority. The problematic case is that in which the term *pito* seems to imply equality, and here the Trio afford an excellent example. I have already discussed this term at some length (Rivière 1969b: 81), but I have to some extent changed my views on the subject since the writing of that work. Among the Trio the term *pito* is a reciprocal one, and one of only two reciprocal terms of address; the other is *yako,* which also has a wide distribution among Carib speakers. Both these terms imply equality, although of different sorts. *Yako* lacks any connotation of mutual obligation, which is the central feature of the *pito* relationship. The *pito* relationship is one of exchange; it is closely associated with trading and political alliances—that is to say, alliances between relative equals rather than between unequals. The affinal content of the term is not pronounced, although a *pito*'s sister belongs to the prescribed spouse category.

The range of meanings covered by this term, from slave to equal, is not in my opinion as important as the fact that in almost every case the term also has an affinal content. The variation in the degree of domination and subordination expressed in the term is a matter of cultural variation, and will reflect other features of the particular society. Thus, among the Trio, the relationship between affines is fairly equal, and it would be wrong to describe the son-in-law as living in a state of submission to his father-in-law. The relationship is two-way, with obligations and duties on both sides, and the content of the *pito* relationship is consistent with this. In societies where the son-in-law's behavior is expected to be more submissive, I would postulate that the term *pito* takes on the potential connotations of servant or client; the Wayana would seem to be a suitable ethnographic example of such a case.

I have concentrated on the term *pito* because its meanings, while wide-ranging, always connote affinal relations. However, I would like to suggest that in all Carib societies the relationship between affines—and specifically between parents-in-law and their children-in-law—is always asymmetrical in nature, and this being the case, affinal relationships offer the best idiom for expressing political relationships that involve domination and subordination. We are here dealing with ideal and conventional attitudes, and it is at this conceptual level that we find the picture of the Carib village composed of a leader and his sons-in-law, who are the subordinate in-marrying husbands of his daughters, the leader's sons having married out in accordance with the typical Carib uxorilocal tendency. This is, however, an ideal situation, and it can readily be modified by other factors, such as lack of age difference between son-in-law and father-in-law or the stronger character of one of the individuals concerned. Nor does the ideal situation wherein brothers-in-law live in different villages always hold true (and I might add that I think the whole question of the patrilocal residence of the sons of strong chiefs needs further investigation). However, none of this denies that Carib affinal relationships carry some notion of asymmetry, the degree to which it emerges in any given case varying with other features of the society concerned.

I would now like to turn to the question of whether there exists any uniquely Carib culture. If we were to examine the distribution of such features as subsistence practices and related technology, the division of labor, or dietary systems, it would immediately become apparent that there is little uniformity and that the minute variations existing between one people and the next are well worth close attention. The distribution of certain material objects seems just as variable; I have attempted to show elsewhere that in one small area, two forms of hollow tube, blowguns and hair tubes, are mutually exclusive in distribution, and that their use or nonuse is consistent with other features of the culture of the peoples concerned (Rivière 1969a). Within the Guiana region other features that would seem amenable to the same sort of treatment include house types, forms of disposal of the dead, and the use of drugs, alcohol, and tobacco separately or in combination (these last three show a very uneven distribution). Such studies could undoubtedly reveal numerous minutely varied but internally consistent subcultures, each subculture forming a pattern of selections from the total inventory of available culture elements. However, this is not meant to imply that each subculture is a statistical aggregate of the available traits. If such a view were adopted it would be possible to determine that any two subcultures shared no traits in common, and this situation would raise the question as to whether the two societies concerned were representatives of the same culture.

I wish to claim that it is possible to talk about individual Carib societies as subcultures of a general Carib culture, and that this is so because all Carib societies exhibit certain fundamental principles as an invariant core. This view permits each subculture to be seen and understood as a transformation of the others, in what might be called the variation-on-a-theme approach to comparative studies. The "theme" is not defined by the principle of direct exchange (which Caribs share in common with most other "tropical forest peoples") but by the fact that for the Carib, "wife givers" are superior to "wife takers." This fact, together with certain other features of Carib culture—such as a tendency towards matrilocal residence, the lack of unilineal descent rules, and the absence of any corporate groups—seems to produce a pattern of culture that may be peculiarly Carib.

It is true that tropical forest societies of other language groups exhibit similar, even identical, patterns, and that these principles are by no means confined to Carib societies. However, all other language groups are also represented by societies that have more formal social institutions, and the presence of these institutions changes the pattern of relationships. One or two examples will make this obvious. A particularly good contrast is afforded by the peoples of the northwest Amazon area, who have virilocal residence, a rule of patrilineal descent, and corporate groups. In these societies there is no way for affinity to express asymmetry, because marital exchanges between different corporate groups tend to be balanced and to represent political alliances. Among the Yanomamö, for another example, in some cases affinity is an expression of political friendship, while in other cases "wife takers" could appear to be superior to "wife givers." In still another variation, the Shavante "wife giver" is superior to the "wife taker," but the relationship is one of political hostility.

These few examples should be enough to indicate the nature of my argument, although I should make it clear that I am not suggesting that variations in language and in culture go hand in hand in the tropical forest region; they quite clearly do not. I am simply suggesting that Carib culture contains one feature that it shares with most other "tropical forest cultures," and another feature, closely associated with the first, that by its particular form may set Carib culture off from the others.

REFERENCES

Coudreau, Henri A.
  1893   *Chez nos Indiens.* Paris: Hachette.

Farabee, William C.
  1924   The Central Caribs. *Anthropological Publications* 10. Philadelphia: The University Museum, Univ. of Pennsylvania.

Kloos, Peter
  1971   *The Maroni River Caribs of Surinam.* Assen, The Netherlands: Van Gorcum.

Rivière, Peter G.
  1969a   Myth and Material Culture: Some Symbolic Interrelations. In *Forms of Symbolic Action,* ed. Robert F. Spencer, pp. 151–66. Proceedings, 1969 Annual Spring Meeting, American Ethnological Society. Seattle: Univ. of Washington Press.

  1969b   *Marriage Among the Trio.* Oxford: Clarendon Press.

Williams, James
  1932   Grammar, Notes, and Vocabulary of the Language of the Makuchi Indians of Guiana. *Bibliothèque Linguistique Anthropos* 8: 389–408.

4. THE AKAWAIO SHAMAN

Audrey Butt Colson
Department of Ethnology and Prehistory, Oxford University

The first references to shamanism among the Indians of Guyana, while interesting, are mostly superficial and misleading, and frequently inaccurate. Reading them during the period between two field research visits, in 1951–52 and in 1957, I could scarcely recognize what I had already begun to study. However, first-hand research in the sphere of shaman practice has its difficulties, mainly because of the discrepancies between the reality observed and the ideal to which informants refer. The process of learning to become a shaman offers good examples of such discrepancies. I try in this paper to correct some of the erroneous conceptions that have persisted in works devoted to this subject and to clarify certain points that have a real importance in a study of Akawaio shamanism. I also present as precisely as possible the ideal that is implied in the practices of the shaman pupil, in all its complex symbolism, and I contrast it with the reality on which these practices are based.

The material presented here frequently recalls what we know of shamanism in other parts of America and even in Asia. However, for reasons of space and clarity, I have deliberately avoided making a wider comparison and have also limited the references mainly to the literature on the shamans of the Guiana region of South America.

THE TERMINOLOGY

The general Guyanese term for the shaman is *piaiman,* a corruption of an original Amerindian form, which is spelled various ways in the literature. Charles Waterton first recorded this hybrid word as "Pee-ay-man" and inferred that the "Warow, Arowack, Accoway, Carib, and Macoushi" tribes all had the pee-ay-man (1903: 136, 138). Roth (1915: 328) discussed the various forms of the word in the different tribes and its derivations, which he considered ultimately to be early Carib and probably related to the Carib word *piače.*

Among other Carib-speaking peoples the word is very similar. The Barama River Caribs refer to the shaman as *piaiyen* (Gillin 1936: 169); the Makusi call him *piazoŋ,* the Taulipang, *piatzaŋ;* the Akawaio speak of the *piai'čaŋ.* The Akawaio also, on occasions, identify the shaman so closely with the order of spirits that he most frequently consults—*imawali,* the forest spirits—that he may be referred to in terms of *imawali.* People speak of "consulting *imawali"* or "getting *imawali* help," meaning that they go to the shaman in order to do this. The word *eneoge* (pl. *enewïdoŋ)* is invariably used to refer to the shaman in the Akawaio spirit songs sung during the seance. *Eneoge* is said to be the *piai'čaŋ,* the "real *piai'čaŋ,"* the "true *piai'čaŋ."* It was also asserted in the early literature that *"Imawali* calls the *piai'čaŋ, 'eneoge.'"* Several spirits have this duplicate reference, one name being used chiefly in the spirit songs and the other in daily conversation. *Eneoge* means "one who sees" (*ene* = see); since this refers to the seeing of spirits and of those aspects of life normally hidden from others, *eneoge* may perhaps be more appropriately translated as "one who perceives," that is, a clairvoyant.

THE SHAMAN PRACTITIONER

The qualifications necessary for a shaman's career among the Guyana Indians have been considered by many authors. One of the commonest fallacies is that the profession is inherited. Referring to the Arawak, Bolingbroke (1947: 103–4) wrote: "The office of peii is hereditary, being conferred only on the eldest son." He also said: "Each family has a priest, or peii, who performs the twofold office of priest and physician. . . ." Richard Schomburgk, writing in the 1840s, remarked that the Makusi *piai* who had no son of his own picked the craftiest from amongst the village boys (1922, vol. 1: 331). Nevertheless, Farabee, three quarters of a century later, asserted that among the Makusi the office of sha-

NOTE: I wish to express my gratitude to the Colonial Development and Welfare Corporation, the American Association of University Women, the London Central Research Fund, and Oxford University for financial aid that made possible my two periods of field research among the Akawaio, in 1951–1952 and in 1957.

An earlier version of this paper was published in 1962 under the title, "Réalité et idéal dans la pratique chamanique" (*L'Homme* II (3): 5–52); I wish to thank the Editor of *L'Homme,* Dr. Jean Pouillon, and also Mouton publishers, for giving permission to use much of the material contained in that paper.

man was formerly hereditary, ". . . but apparently it is not so to-day. A boy is selected by the piazong and put through a certain amount of practical training" (1924: 72).

A second fallacy, also relating to Makusi shamanism, was introduced by im Thurn:

If there was no son to succeed the father, the latter chose and trained some boy from the tribe—one with an epileptic tendency being preferred. . . . It has been said that epileptic subjects are by preference chosen as peaimen, and are trained to throw themselves at will into convulsions; and it is at least certain that the peaiman, when in the midst of his frantic performance, seems as though overcome by some fearful fit, or in the extreme of raving madness. [1883: 334–5]

It is to the credit of W. F. Roth that he disputed both contentions. Of the one, he wrote: "It is likely that the secrets and mysteries of the profession may also have been imparted to outsiders for a consideration. I happen to have known one of the fraternity who taught another his profession for the sum down of eleven dollars together with the gift of his daughter" (1915: 333). An Akawaio shaman may learn his profession from his father or from some other relative, but there is no strict inheritance of the skill. Specific cases show this clearly (see Appendix for a list of shamans working in the 1950s). Francis of Tagaikapai intended, he said, to teach his son how to practice, but he died before the boy was old enough. Francis himself had learned not from his father, but from his brother-in-law (his father's brother's daughter's husband), who was an Arekuna from the Gran Sabana in Venezuela. (Parallel cousins are classified as brothers and sisters in the Akawaio kinship system; using the classificatory terms, a shaman pupil can always manage to establish some relationship with his shaman teacher, for ultimately kinship terms embrace the entire membership of the tribe.) Francis also stated that when a man wants to be a shaman he goes to one who is fully established and asks to be taught. George of Sagaraimadai and his deceased brothers (except for one who died young) were taught by their father. George is not teaching his sons "because people do not like to *piai* now—they have to drink too much tobacco juice." He had wished to teach his son Ronald, but the latter said that he did not like tobacco juice and so the matter was dropped. Joe of Chinawieng learned from his elder brother William. Ernest and Edwin, the Ataro brothers, learned from their father. In turn, Ernest taught Elias, his mother's brother's son. Bengie and Albert were learning from Freddy, who was not a close relation. Donald of Amokokupai taught himself, it was said.

In sum, anyone can become a shaman if he wishes to do so. If a father is unable to teach the necessary skill and knowledge, then a father's brother, a brother, or any relation will do so if requested. If by chance there is no close relative (either by blood or marriage) who is a shaman, then the candidate may apply to any friendly shaman and ask to be taught. Whenever possible a shaman wishes to teach at least one of his sons.

As for im Thurn's second contention, Roth pointed out that victims of epilepsy would be unconscious during the convulsions and hence unable to carry on the customary shaman activities. Akawaio practice, differing little from that of other Guyana tribes, both Carib- and non-Carib-speaking, similarly contradicts the opinions expressed in much of the literature. During my research I encountered two, possibly three, Akawaio who were subject to fits. None of them were shamans, and Akawaio do not consider that epileptics have any part to play in shaman activity. One woman, definitely an epileptic, was the daughter of the Sagaraimadai shaman, George. He had never taught her his skill, although he had attempted to cure her by his own spirit consultations. A person who is subject to fits is regarded as ill, and those who are ill do not engage in any activity whatsoever; they merely rest. Deafness, as in George's case, was considered a definite disability in contacting the spirits—for how could a deaf shaman hear the spirits? If deafness is a disadvantage, then unconsciousness would be even more so.

Among present-day Akawaio, the shaman is usually a man. Women may undertake to practice if they wish, but there were no female shamans at the time of my fieldwork. Several shamans offered to teach me when I displayed great interest in the profession, and they did not consider it odd that a woman should think of joining their ranks. When I was collecting genealogies, informants occasionally mentioned the fact that certain individuals had been well-known shamans; among these were a few women. One such female shaman was Chiwai, the long-deceased sister of a very old woman living at Kataima village in 1952. Chiwai had been a spinster, which is most unusual among the Akawaio. Another, Christina, the shaman grandmother of Dolphus, had had a husband. Several other female shamans were recalled as having had husbands, which indicates that female celibacy when holding that office is by no means usual. Various inquiries led me to the conclusion that in all essentials the practice of the female shaman is like that of the male shaman. Several Akawaio confirmed this.

Age is of little significance to the candidate for shaman skill. A number of present-day shamans are young men. Joe, Ernest, Edwin, Elias, and Henry are young men who began learning shortly after marriage, at a time when they were between 18 and 25 years of age. Older men with adult children may also start learning, as did King George of Chinawieng. As a shaman grows older, his reputation increases until he becomes elderly. As an old man he may be recognized as wise and highly skilled; old age alone implies this, according to Akawaio concepts. However, bodily infirmities may interfere with the practice of his skill. When this occurs the aged shaman retires, performing at fewer and fewer seances and then finally giving up altogether. George had reached this stage in 1952, and on one occasion when his relatives were sick he invited Francis of Tagaikapai to conduct the seance for him. By 1957 old age and deafness had, for all practical purposes, ended George's career as a shaman. There were several old men at Uwi village in the Ataro who were pointed out to me as former reputable shamans who had ceased to practice on account of advanced age.

The evidence amounts to this: while young, a person has the energy and strength for shaman practice, but he has to spend some years practicing in order to attain the degree of skill that makes him a really good shaman of widespread reputation. In old age, he has the skill and experience but not the necessary energy, for shaman activities are both physically and mentally exacting. Estimation of a shaman's ability by other Akawaio takes all these factors into account. The best shamans, therefore, are those in middle age, who are both strong and skillful. Such a skilled, mature person was Francis of Tagaikapai, who in 1952 was recognized as the best shaman in the tribe and was most frequently consulted by people outside his own settlement and circle of relations. By 1957, after Francis's untimely death, Ernest and Joe were on the way to acquiring something of the same reputation, although they were still considered to be rather young and lacking the maturity and genuine achievement that comes with longer practice.

Contrary to some assertions, the shaman is not necessarily the "Leader" (ebulu) of his village settlement. Francis was both Leader and shaman, but none of the other Akawaio shamans combined the two offices. It is unlikely that the situation differed greatly in the past, when there appear to have been more shamans, according to the genealogies, and frequently several in the same family and the same settlement. Nowadays leadership and shamanism are neither mutually exclusive nor necessarily connected, nor could they have been so in the past, by reason of the number of practitioners.

During the 1950s a new factor entered into Akawaio life—Hallelujah, a semi-Christian, prophet-inspired religion that developed in the latter half of the 19th century (see Butt 1960). All present shamans are believers, and many are enthusiastic adherents, taking part in church activities and feasts. Ernest, for example, sometimes leads the Hallelujah dancing in the Kwatin area when he is visiting relatives there, and he preaches and prays publicly on these occasions. Like all other aspects of their culture, Hallelujah occasionally enters in a minor way into the shaman's seances. A spirit may come and devoutly sing an Hallelujah-type chant, or it may make a speech and zealously condemn alcohol, dancing, and shaman practice! In so doing the spirit conspicuously apes the admonitions of the more extremist missions, Seventh-Day Adventist and Pilgrim Holiness. When recording one of Ernest's seances I was subjected to one of these sermons, delivered by the hawk (kukui) spirit. Said the hawk, who was obviously an adherent of Hallelujah:

You must not take a song from *Imawali* [the forest spirit] for that isn't good, but only if you want to get Hallelujah I will give you one. I like Hallelujah too. I don't want to give you *imawali* song. Hallelujah is good and you may get God through it, but *malik* [spirit songs] may be sinful because of the *paiwadi* drink taken when we sing *malik* and dance *tugoik* and *palična* [the old spree dances]. If you enjoy *imawali* you cannot reach heaven.

In spite of such pronouncements, the Hallelujah faith does not itself exclude shaman activity, as formal Christianity has often done through the opposition of missionaries. The Hallelujah Indians can, without any hypocrisy, believe in and practice shamanism because the two systems of belief exist side by side, without mutually contradicting each other or being in any way incompatible.

The average Akawaio shaman is noted for being attractive to women, and is likely to have more than one wife or to have had a succession of wives. By 1957 Edwin and Ernest had three wives each. In 1952 Joe had two wives and was angling for a third. The father of the latter was opposing the union on the grounds that Joe already had two wives and was a lazy fellow anyway. Joe did obtain his third wife for a short time, but by 1957 his first wife had died and the last one deserted him. At that same time, Elias was busy switching from a second to a third wife, in spite of the scandal caused by divorce in the Anglican Mission village of Jawalla where he resided. Francis, on the other hand, was firmly established as a family man, monogamous over a long period and showing no inclination to change. My Akawaio cook apparently summed up the situation correctly when she remarked that "women always like *piai'čaŋ* husbands." The Akawaio explain any great interest shown in a shaman by saying that the charms (*muraŋ*, which means "attraction"), used in attaining skill and gaining control over the spirits also attract women and control their affections. If a shaman (especially one who is a pupil) allows these affections to go too far, he will ruin his practice. Edwin of the Ataro was considered to have spoiled his practice in this way.

There is no secret about the attractions of present-day shamans. They are, in several instances, good-looking young men; even more important, they have a ready understanding, a good sense of humor, and a personality that enables them to outshine many of their non-shaman contemporaries, who are perhaps steadier, but also duller, companions. This more flamboyant temperament is often difficult to cope with, and a young shaman— or any Akawaio of equivalent temperament—can be a great nuisance if he is offended or annoyed. The Ataro brothers, Ernest and Edwin, proved this to a series of employers, being an exceptionally lively and obstreperous pair. There is little doubt that the more successful shamans are those who are lively, intelligent, and responsive to others, quick to see the implications of every social situation. Moreover, the shaman's profession appears to attract just this type of personality. This may be because a shaman's practice provides an outlet for energies and ambitions that otherwise would have little opportunity for expression; this egalitarian society traditionally did not make use of public display for personal advancement, nor did it applaud individual enterprise.

The average Akawaio shaman, then, has a great deal of personal appeal, much common sense, and considerable perception, as well as an ability to· apply himself to the task in hand. Apart from being almost invariably "a personality," the successful Akawaio practitioner in other respects is just an ordinary individual in his community. He is not necessarily a Leader, and frequently there are others equally intelligent in the same settlement. No psychopathic symptoms are manifest in candidates for the profession: any abnormality of this kind would be regarded as inappropriate and more likely to scare away patients than to encourage them to apply for aid. Akawaio shamans themselves say that no special aptitude is required for their profession—"anyone can learn."

THE DECISION TO BECOME A SHAMAN

The decision to become a shaman may be reached in one of several ways. The father or a near relative of a youth may persuade him to undergo training, or he may desire to follow the expected and natural course of events. Young Henry is an example of this category of learners. His father had been a shaman, and "people expected him to *piai*—it had been passed on to him by old time people." Some may feel the desire to become a shaman even though they have no close relatives who practice. Friends may persuade them, or the motive may be no more than an individual interest or inclination to acquire this useful form of self-expression. In this category was King George of Chinawieng, who wished to have shaman training and had actually started on it but was dissuaded by the Leader of his village. Joe was inspired to learn when he heard a Patamona Indian sing-

ing shaman songs at a seance. "He liked it and kept singing it. Then his wife, Ellenjola, told him he must become a *piai'čaŋ.*" He sought instruction from his brother William.

Excessive grief for a deceased relative and the desire to be in touch with the departed one may also be a motive (comparable in Britain to becoming attached to the Spiritualist Church in the hope of receiving messages from one who has "passed over"). Ernest of Uwi related how he came to learn shaman practice: "My father," Ernest said, "was a *piai'čaŋ* but I was too young to learn from him when he was living. I grew to manhood and went out to Kurupung. When I was coming back I heard that my father had died. I could not eat and I cried and cried and mourned, and when I was crying by the grave one day my father's ghost spirit came to me and told me to learn to be a *piai'čaŋ*. My father's ghost spirit taught me *piai.*" (Going to Kurupung, to work in the mining areas of the Lower Mazaruni below the Pakaraima escarpment, is a regular practice and is now often regarded as part of the education of a young man; as soon as he reaches maturity, frequently before he takes a wife, he spends three or four months there. The depth of affection and feelings expressed in Ernest's statement is also to be noted; in the literature these Amerindians are often described as being totally unemotional and lacking in sentiment.) Later, Ernest said that when he slept he dreamt that someone told him not to be too sad—if he took *piai'čaŋ* leaves he would see his father's ghost spirit (*akwalupï*).

A dream is frequently the inspiration for beginning a shaman's career. However, even though a person may dream and may be told to start drinking tobacco juice and use the leaf bundles, he need not do so if he does not wish to become a shaman. The spirits are not considered to be angry at a refusal.

Another factor that sometimes sparks an interest in shamanism is a genuine desire to help one's family and the people of the settlement when they fall ill. The shaman's chief function is to cure illness and to prevent death caused by nefarious spirit activity. Pity for those who are ill and a wish to help overcome sickness are sentiments frequently expressed by individuals who are contemplating a shaman's career. One Akawaio remarked, when considering such a career for himself, "A good *piai'čaŋ* keeps sickness away from a place. The spirits cure people."

THE SHAMAN TEACHER (ladoi)

That shamanism is a serious profession is indicated by the months, even years, of training that learners pass through before they become fully recognized practitioners. The average period of time for initial apprenticeship is about one year. However, there is no set course of training, and exact periods of time have no special value in themselves. Akawaio allow the timing of events to be determined within very broad limits by what they themselves feel to be necessary in their own individual circumstances.

Once a learner has conducted a public seance, he is recognized as a fully fledged but not very good shaman. Several years must pass before he is generally considered to be a skilled practitioner. Not everyone attains this status, even after years of practice, for it is recognized that, as with other skills, some people never become proficient. Donald of Amokokupai, even after seven or more years, was invariably labeled as "knowing only a little of *piai'čaŋ*," and it appeared as if he would be going on learning indefinitely.

During the initial months of learning, and also during the entire period of his professional and public performances, the shaman is aided by his teacher, who is referred to as *uladoi*. The literal meaning of this word is "my side." It might be translated most accurately as "partner," but in the beginning the essential role of the *ladoi* is that of teacher and guide. When the shaman is fully initiated and increases in skill and practice, his *ladoi* becomes less and less a teacher and more and more a helper and partner in his spirit experiences. As we shall see, the shaman has many helpers in the spirit world; each of them may be referred to as *ladoi*, but the shaman teacher is particularly known by this term and he alone is addressed by this one word, without any additional modifier, when his spirit or ghost spirit comes to the seance.

Kenswil's description of the part played by the shaman teacher is misleading. He wrote:

Every Aboriginal Indian with whom I have come in contact, and they have been many, believes that every human being has a being from the spirit world who is his predestined servant, and who can assist him to secure many other spirits as his servants. This spirit being is called in their language "Wi-Iladwi" meaning my other self. The Medicine-man professes to have found his spirit servant, hence he is much feared by his fellow-men. [1946: 8–9]

The description of shaman training that follows suggests that Kenswil, who had been taught something of shaman arts by a living practitioner, never realized that the *ladoi* could be either a living shaman or the ghost spirit of a deceased one. This "spirit servant" is not predestined but is chosen, often on the basis of kinship relations. Kenswil's use of the word "servant" is an unhappy one. There is no implication of dominant status of master and lower status of servant in the word *ladoi*. Those Indians who can speak a little English translate *ladoi* as "teacher" or "helper." "Other self" is not an accurate inter-

pretation even of the literal meaning "side." Finally, the "medicine-man" is not necessarily feared by his fellows. This is a common fallacy.

It was several months before I realized the significant fact that some of the present Akawaio shamans had learned their profession from ghost teachers—that is, from shamans who were already dead. I was also surprised to learn that it did not make much difference whether a teacher was dead or alive. No form of payment is proffered to a dead shaman, whereas gifts are presented to a living teacher in payment for his services and assistance to his pupil. As in other instances of Akawaio indebtedness, the nature, extent, and occasion of payment vary according to individual circumstances and demands. A pupil visits his living shaman teacher during the course of learning. The living teacher should be present in person at his pupil's first public seance, when the pupil is publicly recognized as a newly qualified shaman. The shaman teacher is not necessarily present in person at any succeeding seance and has no special part to play in his pupil's future career. That is to say, the teacher no longer assists by his bodily presence, but his spirit *(akwalu)* may come to the seances to talk, give advice, and help in the control of other spirits. For example, Elias was visited in this way by his teacher, Ernest of the Ataro, who came down in spirit during two seances that I attended. A dead teacher is also present, but necessarily as a ghost spirit, at his pupil's first seance, and he readily attends subsequent performances throughout the shaman's career. For example, Francis's dead teacher's ghost spirit always came to Francis's seances, and there would almost always be long conversations between him and Francis at the very beginning. The teacher's ghost spirit would say which spirits were coming down; he would give news of the spirit world and would hear in turn any special news concerning the settlement and its inhabitants. At the end of the seance he would say goodbye and go.

Although a man who learns from a living shaman has the advantage of direct instruction from his teacher under seance conditions, the one who learns from a ghost teacher is not very much at a disadvantage. All Akawaio know the mechanics of the seance, for they frequently attend seances with their families from the time of birth onwards. Moreover, they hear people talking about the shaman's activities and they learn to take part in the seance themselves, as part of the audience, by making inquiries of the spirits and listening to them. At some of the less solemn seances, when no one is seriously ill, boys in the audience often heckle the spirits and engage in a great deal of backchat. Even small boys know some of the most frequently sung spirit songs, and the day after a seance one or two of them may be heard singing the bush spirit's song or the mountain spirit's song while paddling in the river, playing about the village, or lying idly in their hammocks. A spirit that has caused much amusement is imitated by them with malicious enjoyment. I have recorded on tape several spirit songs of two other Carib groups, the Arekuna and Kamarakoto, as well as of the Akawaio, sung by a young man of the Kamarang River who was not a shaman pupil, although he was thinking about becoming one. Anyone who has a father or close relative who is a shaman inevitably knows about shaman practice at a very early age, since he would hear the seances conducted at night in his own home and would be able to ask questions the next day if he felt any curiosity about what had been happening.

The Akawaio shaman pupil, therefore, has most likely been brought up with shaman activity going on around him, and his learning consists chiefly in making the effort of transferring his role from that of relatively passive listener to that of active practitioner of a familiar art. This accounts for the fact that direct instruction from a shaman is not always a necessity. Ernest said that his father used to tell him of many things used by a shaman, but he was too young to learn from him while he was alive. However, he inherited his father's shaman equipment, spirit stones, and special types of tobacco. He learned not only from his father's ghost spirit, but from other spirits as well. "While sleeping," Ernest said, "I used to dream and walk all about on the mountains with many people [spirits]. *Imawali* used to tell me to get *malik* [the spirit songs], and learn *piai*. *Imawali* knew I was thinking about *piai*." From all this it is legitimate to conclude that much of Ernest's learning was the process of recalling his father's words and early instruction. Presumably, those who have had no close contact with shamans at any time would not be able to recall shamanist activities or to dream of them satisfactorily. It would be these candidates for the profession who would feel the necessity for a living teacher and would apply to one.

Having decided to become a shaman, the pupil begins his training. He either approaches a living shaman and asks him to be his teacher, or he starts getting instruction from a ghost teacher, through dreams and retrospective contemplation. At this time he begins a period of special observances and restrictions that all shaman pupils must follow in order to gain entry into the spirit world—"to see *imawali*," as they say.

SECLUSION

The numerous descriptions I obtained from present-day Akawaio shamans show a consistent pattern of conduct that is followed by the shaman pupil in his efforts to achieve spirit contact.

The shaman pupil must spend a great deal of time alone. He must avoid women and, if already married,

Sammy, shaman pupil at Kataima village, Mazaruni River (1952). He is decorated for a drinking and dancing feast.

should live apart from his wife. A female shaman pupil must have no lovers and, if married, must not cohabit with her husband while learning. The shaman pupil must spend long days in the forest. In the literature are various reports of periods of complete seclusion lasting one, two, or more years. Kenswil reported some six months among the mountains or along the rivers, away from human contact.

Most of the present Akawaio shamans solved the problem of their period of seclusion in similar ways. They went among strangers, spending much of the period of training either outside the tribal territory, visiting foreign tribes or working in the mining areas, or within it, working at a mission or at the government station. Some traveled around in the employ of officials visiting the area. This habit of spending the training period abroad makes it difficult for the anthropologist to check up on the actual activities of the shaman pupil during this time. If he spends the entire learning period away, then inquiry even among his relatives or fellow villagers is of little use because they themselves have not been witnesses.

The shaman pupil gains several advantages by working abroad. He enlarges his experience and sees some of the strange things and different peoples that exist outside his tribal area. Akawaio have an immense curiosity about this outside world, and shamans in particular are always on the lookout for fresh material to incorporate into their seances. Spirits of non-Indians who belong to the mixed population of Guyana come within the shaman's sphere. They are called down to the seance and a bastard English phraseology and intonation is used to denote their speech. Shamans considerably enliven their seances in this way. One of Joe's seances, for example, was attended by a Ye'cuana spirit from Venezuela, who, said one informant in explaining some curious phraseology, "speaks like Spanish." *Piait'ma,* the mountain spirit who had been patiently listening to the strange mode of speech but who was evidently not a Spanish speaker, then complained bitterly that Joe was conducting seances for English people (namely, the anthropologist) while he, *Piait'ma,* could not understand what the Ye'cuana spirit was saying. Commenting on the tape recording I had made of this conversation between spirits, Joe said that he himself did not understand exactly what the spirit was singing, though as usual it was something to do with a cassava grater (the Ye'cuana are famous as makers of this item). One of my most vivid memories of research is that of Ernest listening intently to the strange dialect of some Taulipang Indians, shortly after our arrival at one of their villages near Mount Roraima. His eyes held a gleam of excitement and his expression was a mixture of amusement and contempt. He kept casting significant glances at his traveling companions and was clearly savoring accents and phraseology and storing them up for dramatic presentation at future seances. In utilizing their linguistic gleanings from abroad, the shamans are usually able to reproduce the intonation and characteristic sounds of the language and also the general mode of delivery; some phrases and sentences might even be discernible, although the English and Spanish I heard during seances was mainly gibberish. Nevertheless, it all sounded most convincingly like the language it was supposed to represent. The seance audiences were satisfied that the spirits were speaking a foreign language, since they could not understand what was being said and it sounded authentic.

A shaman pupil abroad probably finds it easier to train for his profession because his departure automatically breaks off his everyday relationships and removes him from his family and ordinary settlement life. He can observe what restrictions he thinks fit and more easily remain secluded and remote over a long period. Before the mining operations on the Lower Mazaruni, which began in the latter half of the 19th century, and before missionary and administrative penetration into the Upper Mazaruni, there were fewer opportunities for this type of seclusion. The accounts given in the literature suggest that the only way of obtaining it was to withdraw into the forest or climb a mountain and camp there for a period, either alone or with a living shaman teacher or other learners. There are various waterfalls and mountains in Akawaio country with names that recall shaman observances and commemorate the fact that a succession of shaman pupils went and established themselves there. These landmarks are still visited for a few hours, possibly a few days, by shaman pupils.

One conclusion is inescapable: today the period of seclusion is not nearly so long or arduous as it was made out to be in the graphic 19th-century descriptions of the trials of shaman pupils. Years ago a learner might have gone off and existed as best he could for certain periods of time, away from his settlement, alone in the forest or on the mountains. Today he can fulfill the seclusion requirement in greater comfort by working abroad for at least part of the time. Nevertheless, the requirement of being cut off from one's natal group, in order to concentrate and to contemplate, is considered a necessary preliminary to spirit experience. It should also be understood that any form of isolation tends to be an ordeal for Akawaio, who use the same words for "being alone" and "being sad" *(bogoibe).*

FOOD RESTRICTIONS *(jeruma)*

The period of learning is also one of privation. Antony, who was working at Paruima village while a shaman pupil, maintained that he could not eat anything for a year. There were wide grins and amused laughter from his fellow workers on hearing this, for his strength and health belied any possibility of malnutrition. His meals at that particular time of his training were obviously more than "nothing" and indeed seemed to have been perfectly adequate.

Exaggerated statements of this kind are commonly made about shaman food restrictions. Joe of China-wieng said that during his year of training he ate no food and was able to drink nothing but water. Elias of Jawalla maintained, "You go into the Bush and you eat nothing. It takes two years to learn, and *kaširi* and *paiawalu* are the only things taken during that time." (*Kaširi,* the main fermented drink, is made from boiled cassava pulp, usually with a little purple sweet potato added; fermentation may be assisted by adding sugar cane juice. *Paiawalu* is made from thin, burnt cassava bread, soaked and left in water to ferment.)

Such extreme assertions are greatly modified when further inquiry is made. According to one informant, "in order to learn, people have to go a long time without food. They must eat nothing—or very little." Another recalled that her grandfather, who had been a well-known shaman, had said that "being a *piai'čaŋ* is a hard thing, for when learning they eat little." Ernest related that he endured many food restrictions during his four-month period of learning. He ate mainly thin cassava bread and drank a little *kaširi* and *paiawalu.* He ate a little fish and a few bananas, some sugar cane, plantains, and a little pepper pot. He did not go hunting, for he was eating no meat. Had he gone hunting, he said, he would not have been able to shoot any meat. He also stated that he got little to eat when working for the Medical Officer on one of his periodic tours of the Sierra Pakaraima, so he considered this a good opportunity for learning. Even such a modified statement of the restrictions, which amounted to no more than avoiding meat and consuming other foods in moderation, scarcely describes the real circumstances of the tour that Ernest's brother Edwin made while learning. On his tour with the Medical Officer, Edwin did not noticeably eat much less than the other Akawaio carriers; he ate heartily on some occasions and joined in several village festivals, being particularly free with the drinks offered at Kataima village.

For the major part of the learning period, the restrictions relating to food are not nearly so intensive as Akawaio make out. At the most, the pupil's meals are smaller and perhaps less frequent; some items, such as meat, are cut out completely. No doubt the pupils do get hungry on a curtailed diet, but for most of the time they are certainly nowhere near the starvation that their own descriptions of dieting suggest. Moreover, even the exaggerated claims relating to shaman training would apply only to very short periods of time—a few days or a few weeks at the most. Although an Akawaio may take a year or two to train, normally only a very small portion of that time is devoted to intensive learning; the descriptions of shaman training in the literature concern these short, intensive periods. The rest of the time the pupil may be leading a life which, although quiet, is not noticeably different from usual.

Information from Francis of Tagaikapai is particularly interesting because in many respects his first, intensive period of training is a typical account of the sequence of events. Francis was learning from his parallel cousin's deceased husband, his "brother-in-law" Jenness. He first started by going two whole days without food, continually drinking small quantities of tobacco juice instead. Everything began revolving and he started to faint; he could not see properly and he was sick. Then he became very hungry but soon he had to retire to his hammock, where he was looked after by an old woman. On the third day he drank plenty of water; he went to the river for this purpose and he drank and drank, all day long. The following day he allowed himself one pepper and one small fish in his pepper pot, and one small, thin piece of cassava bread to eat; on the second day following this he had two small peppers, two small fish, and two small pieces of cassava bread; on the third day his allowance

Francis of Tagaikapai, Mazaruni River, with leaf bundles and a cup of tobacco juice prepared for seance at Kataima (1952)

was increased to three of each item. There was a gradual extension of his diet in this way over the whole of his initial training, which took one month. A year then elapsed before Francis's first public seance, when he qualified as a fully fledged shaman.

The older practice of retiring into the forest or up a mountain for the period of seclusion must in itself have involved severe food restrictions. The shaman pupil, prohibited from hunting and finding little to eat by collecting, could have had no garden produce beyond what he himself brought in his carrying basket. Even fish would have been in very short supply in mountain country. Hence observations like that of Schomburgk, who wrote that the Makusi novice returned "more like a skeleton than a human being" (1922, Vol. 1: 331).

Many of the earlier ethnologists understood such hard practice to be the means of building moral fiber. Roth stated, for example: "During his course of training, in addition to his other instruction, the apprentice was taught to suffer the pangs of hunger and thirst, and to experience the martyrdom of pain without complaint or murmur" (1915: 339). Perhaps such training has the function of creating the disciplined and devoted practitioner, but certainly the Akawaio, who have the ideal of a starvation diet in mind, are concerned with quite different effects. The shaman pupil eats little because he wants to become thin *(etotsali)*; he wishes to become thin because then, he believes, the spirits will come and possess him and he will be "as a support" *(yaboŋ)* for the spirits.

THE TREE-BARK CHARMS *(yei bipa muraŋ)*

The shaman pupil, whether at home or working abroad, is supposed to spend part of his time of seclusion in the forest, staying by a waterfall or along the banks of a river, alternately drinking and vomiting quantities of water and tree-bark infusions. Tobacco juice in water is also sometimes drunk and tobacco pellets may be sucked. Tobacco pellets consist of a piece of damp tobacco leaf rolled into a ball with charred water weed *(uliŋ)* to add a salty flavor. Sucking these pellets is an everyday practice of Akawaio men, not a special practice of shamans.

At first, any type of tree bark is mixed with water and the infusion drunk; later on, special tree barks are sought. There are three particularly important ones, known because "old time people tried out all the trees and barks and found out which were the best ones." These three tree barks have been tentatively identified[1] as follows:

1. *Miligawa (Virola* sp.?): A common tree found all about Akawaio country.

2. *Maibaima (Lauraceae* sp.?): Difficult to find, as it grows mainly to the west in the savanna area of Brazil and Venezuela.

3. *Taiugu (Pagamea* sp.): *Taiugu* is said to be the *"Imawali* name for the tree." In everyday speech it is often called *aiyuk* or *aibiak.* This is also a savanna tree, occasionally found in Akawaio country, especially on the Gran Sabana in Taulipang country. It is said to be like the *miligawa* tree but to have a smaller leaf.

Sometimes these barks are more carefully prepared than the ordinary ones. For example, Ernest used to boil his infusion of *taiugu* bark before drinking it. During seances the shaman, or a spirit using the medium of the shaman, sings of these barks that are his "helpers" or "partners." Thus one of Elias's songs has the line:

Taiugu wana uladoiyu,   eneoge   ladoiyu.
Taiugu is   my partner, clairvoyant partner.

Informant's Comment: "This tree bark helps the *piai'-čaŋ.*"

Note that the bark is referred to here as *ladoi,* the same word as for shaman teacher (see the discussion of meanings of *ladoi* in the earlier section, *The Shaman Teacher*).

---

1. For these tentative identifications I wish to thank Mr. Rufus Boyan, Botanist of the Forestry Department, Georgetown, who spent several weeks with me in 1957. His knowledge and companionship were invaluable.

Akawaio shamans regard tree-bark infusions as special charms for obtaining spirit contact. As noted earlier, the shaman charms, if not used carefully, may serve to attract other objects than those intended. In particular, any charm can easily become a love charm, attracting women. It is for this reason that the shaman pupil—and also the fully fledged shaman, who continues to take the charms from time to time—must, like the hunter, avoid women while directly under the influence of a charm. Akawaio are fully explicit about this. As one of my informants said, "Any *muraŋ* can make a girl love you, but in fact you must keep apart from women or the *muraŋ* will be spoiled. The reason why the *piai'čaŋ* usually has two or more wives is because he is drinking barks and having *muraŋ.*"

Concomitantly, one of the reasons a shaman pupil should not go hunting or eat meat is that he might spoil his spirit charms by using them, inadvertently, to attract the animals. *Miligawa,* for example, is said to be a good charm for hunting deer and birds. To take it and then go hunting would mean a successful catch of meat—but no spirits. It is also said that the spirits of the animals killed might become angry, and this would be unfortunate at a time when the shaman pupil is aiming to get in touch with all the nature spirits, including animal spirits, to obtain their help in his future seances. The attraction that *miligawa* is supposed to exert on spirits is illustrated by the use to which it is sometimes put as a medicine *(debik),* frequently by non-shamans. A smoking branch of *miligawa* may be taken all round a settlement and the spirit of a sick person called upon to return to the body. *Miligawa* is a strong spirit; it is released in the smoke and is believed to rescue the wandering human spirit from its captor.

In Akawaio beliefs relating to the spirit world the tree barks are given a collective name: *kasamarawa.* The spirit *kasamarawa* frequently comes down during the seances, and its function is said to be as follows: "*Kasamarawa* is a tree bark—any tree bark—that enables the *piai'čaŋ* to rise into the sky easily. The *piai'čaŋ* drinks bark and vomits in order to get *kasamarawa. Kasamarawa* cares for the *piai'čaŋ* when he drinks bark." Ernest on one occasion said that *kasamarawa* was a reed charm (a *kumi muraŋ);* by this he meant that a special reed charm could be used by the shaman to obtain contact with *kasamarawa,* the tree-bark spirit, which gives the shaman power enabling him to rise easily into the sky (that is, to enter the spirit world).

A closely associated spirit is *kalawali,* the "ladder" or "steps" spirit, also attracted by using a charm, though one of a different sort. The *kalawali* charm is the one that has frequently been described in the literature as the "string nose bena" (im Thurn 1883: 229; *beena, bena,* or *bina* is the general Guyanese word for "charm" and is sometimes used by Akawaio when speaking to foreigners). The Akawaio call it *kalawali muraŋ*, and it is either a hunting or a shaman charm, according to the circumstances in which it is used. It usually consists of a plaited cotton string with *sala* grass or tufts of *waiabi* and an ant tied to the end. *Sala* grass (*Scleria* sp.) is known as "razor grass" in Guyana, because the edges of this reed cut and scratch the flesh of anyone pushing through it. *Waiabi* (probably *Desmoncus* sp.) is a cane used for binding the edges of baskets; it is very stiff and hard and has sharp edges when shredded. The charm is made by an old woman and would be spoiled if a young one were to plait it—another instance of the necessary dissociation between the shaman and female attraction. The charm is taken by inserting one end in a nostril and drawing the whole out through the mouth, inch by inch, an extremely painful process causing much bleeding. Joe of Chinawieng took this charm. He used a very long piece of cotton that was attached loosely to the roof. He inserted one end into his nose and drew it out through his mouth. A girl then pulled on the end until the entire length of the cotton went up to the roof and down again, then through his nostril and out through his mouth. The girl in this instance helped the shaman get the *kalawali* spirit by attracting the spirit to the shaman and so temporarily becoming a charm herself. When the shaman pupil has taken this ladder charm his spirit will be able, it is believed, to climb up into the sky during seances.

Kalawali and *kasamarawa* are both "ladder spirits," but they are not exactly the same and should not be confused. The difference was carefully explained to me. *Kasamarawa* is the spirit of tree barks and it functions as a ladder type of spirit in that it causes the shaman's spirit to leave the body and fly off. At the same time, it enables *imawali*, the various nature spirits of the forest, to come down and occupy the shaman's body, which is emptied of its usual spirit occupant. *Kalawali*, on the other hand, is the spirit of ladders and as such is conceived of as the spirit link between the sky and the earth, which the other spirits use in passing up and down. One of the shaman's spirit songs tells of how, when water is poured over the tobacco leaves, the ladder *(kalawali)* comes from the sky down to the stool where the shaman is sitting, and *imawali*, the forest spirit, comes down the ladder. The shaman's own spirit, departing from the seance, climbs up to the roof of his house by means of the ladder spirit, and at the end of the seance it returns by the same route.

The symbolism in the process of taking the *kalawali* charm and in the results it is believed to achieve is clear. Although strings and tree vines may be used to symbolize contact between earth and sky, the ladder connection is thought of primarily as a tree. With its roots embedded in the earth, its long trunk towering more than 100 feet overhead, and its crown of foliage reaching into the sky to bask in the life-giving sunlight, the forest tree is a most appropriate symbol of the link between the

people of the earth and the spirit world. A house ladder is a tree trunk with notches or steps cut into it. A wooden pole, with a pointer to the east, is driven into the head of graves, and the spirit *(akwalu)* of the deceased can climb up it in order to go into the sky (Butt 1953: 11–12).

Kalawali is of primary importance to the shaman pupil. One of the criticisms of Edwin's practice was that he "went with girls when learning and spoilt his *kalawali*, and that is why he not such a first class *piai'čaŋ*." Ernest, on the other hand, made a virtue of not getting the *kalawali* spirit. A skilled shaman can remove the ladder when a shaman rival of his is holding a seance, so that the shaman's spirit is unable to come back down the ladder and return to its body; if this happens, the shaman falls sick and, deprived of his spirit, will eventually die. Ernest was afraid that this might happen to him so he did not get *kalawali;* instead he "flew by leaves" —that is, by using the bundles of leaves that shamans rustle rhythmically throughout their seances. It was said that Francis of Tagaikapai died because Antonio of Paruima "cut his *kalawali*"—that is, broke the connection between the spirit realms and the material world, keeping Francis's spirit permanently away from his body and so causing his body to die.

The shaman pupil may also vomit bark from the *wariŋa* tree, which is a species of bamboo, in order to get this *imawali* inside himself. The shaman who has taken this tree bark has the power to capture an enemy's spirit and shut it up inside the hollow wood of the *wariŋa* tree; this isolation of the spirit away from its body likewise causes the death of the person's body.

The explanation given by Akawaio for the practice of drinking and vomiting bark infusions are several. One informant said rather vaguely, "*Imawali* is pleased when he sees the learner doing this and *imawali bazi [imawali* woman] is especially pleased." (*Bazi* means a sister older than the speaker; it is also sometimes used to mean "woman" and is probably best translated so here.) Another explanation was very similar to that of Kenswil: "They vomit up to make the *ewaŋ* [the central part, trunk, of a person] clear so that *imawali* or the tree-bark spirit or others will stay inside the body. *Imawali* gives everything he has to the *piai'čaŋ*—a drink, something to eat, and so on. This is if the shaman doesn't eat and goes and vomits water and bark; then, he may get *imawali* food and drink and the spirits will stay in him." Ernest's explanation is interesting because of its implied symbolism: "Tree bark vomited turns to be [becomes] *imawali*. *Imawali* is the forest spirit and the trees have this spirit."

Another function of the tree-bark charms is clearly portrayed in a picturesque description of how the *taiugu* bark helps the shaman: "*Taiugu* is a strong spirit helper for the shaman. He helps the shaman by directing him the way to go on his spirit flight. *Taiugu* has the strength to force open the door of *imawali*'s house in the mountains and to get back the captured [human] spirit." In other words, this tree-bark infusion enables the shaman to breach the spirit world and so find out the location of his patient's captured spirit.

In an elaborate system of symbols the Akawaio conceive of the vomiting of barks as being a process whereby the body is cleansed and the ladder provided for the shaman's spirit to climb up into the spirit realms. This connection is also a ladder for the spirits to climb down from the sky into the shaman's body. It is believed that the forest and tree spirits (*imawali*) in particular will come inside by reason of the vomited bark.

At the same time, the practice of vomiting bark, combined with a spare diet, increases the hunger of the shaman pupil. He becomes "straight," or thin—the necessary condition, it is believed, before he can achieve the main object of detaching his spirit and enabling other spirits to come and possess him. The Akawaio consider that the shaman's body can be occupied by several other spirits or ghosts and the shaman's own spirit, all at the same time. Said Basil of the Kamarang River, referring to one of Joe's seances: "Even if Joe's spirit [Joe *akwalu*] is in his body, other spirits can still come down and be inside him. With a real *piai'čaŋ*, an *eneoge* [clairvoyant], the spirits stay down and all go back at the end of the seance, one after another, as with Joe and Antonio. With Elias the spirits go back almost immediately: he is not so good" (Elias was still learning).

The shaman's aim, then, is to attract down a number of sympathetic spirits and ghosts who arrive and "occupy the shaman's stool" (on which he sits). The shaman talks with these spirits, the audience joining in. If the need for assistance is urgent, the shaman's own spirit flies away quickly and more spirits come down to the seance, occupying the shaman's body or hovering around his stool. These spirits talk to each other and to the audience, in a dialogue from which the shaman is absent.

Another group of charms sometimes taken by the shaman and the shaman pupil is known as *kumi*. These are reed or grass charms of different kinds. A *kumi* charm can also be a tapir charm (*maipuli murano*) used by the shaman for hunting (ordinary folk use the hunting charm reed). Sorcerers (*edodo*) may possess a reed charm that will kill people.

Since he is concerned that his voice should be strong the shaman not only practices the spirit songs but also takes the cicada charm (*analawa murano*). The cicada (or "sun bee") is an insect that makes a loud, continuous whirring noise in the forest, morning and evening. The shaman pupil crushes and eats the insect so that his voice, too, will achieve a ringing note. The *wamoŋ* bee (probably another variety of cicada) "has a loud voice," so it also is squashed and drunk and "makes your voice come good." A flying beetle called *sakiliwa* (*Euchroma*

gigantea) is eaten as well. After eating the beetles, the shaman pupil collects their shiny, green-gold iridescent shards and strings them on his ceremonial armbands (*malik*), which he wears during his first public seance. Because these beetles fly quickly, they help the shaman's spirit to fly with similar speed to meet the other spirits.

Even established shamans take these kinds of charms, though with age and experience, only an occasional charm is felt to be necessary to renew the power to summon a certain spirit or to achieve or improve on special shaman skills.

TOBACCO JUICE *(kawai egu)*

When the shaman pupil is learning to drink and vomit tree barks, he also begins to drink tobacco juice and on occasion to vomit it. His success as a fully fledged shaman will depend upon taking tobacco juice. There are several different sorts of tobacco recognized by the Akawaio. Among them are:

1. *Kawai:* A broad-leafed variety; also the name for tobacco in general.
2. *Tamu:* A narrow-leafed variety; the name for cigarette or cigar.
3. *Kumeli:* "Tiger tobacco," because it is named after a species of jaguar ("the large one with spots") and the leaf has tiger-like mottling on it. *Kumeli* tobacco is used when the shaman wants to summon this type of jaguar spirit to eat up and so destroy another, evil spirit.
4. *Abasarawa:* Another type, unidentified by me.

Tobacco is grown in the gardens and around the house, but it may also be picked from plants that grow wild, high up in the mountains. Seeds of these wild plants are frequently obtained and brought back for planting in the shaman's garden. It was generally said that tobacco came from the top of the mountain and that seeds had fallen or blown down the cliff face. At Chinawieng village, during the course of a seance, Joe brought down a minor mountain spirit, *Baidotma*, who said that there was one large tobacco tree on Karowrieng Mountain and that its seeds drop below the cliffs and make small bushes. It was said that this one large tobacco tree had *kumeli* tobacco growing on one side and *abasarawa* on the other. (The idea of the propagation of fruits and vegetables from one large tree seems to have a fascination for Akawaio, and it is frequently found in their myths of origins of vegetable products. The "food tree" story is widespread in South America.)

Akawaio say that wild tobacco is *piait'ma kawai* —that is, tobacco belonging to *piait'ma*, the order of mountain spirits. All the spirits use this tobacco. "Just as white men buy tobacco from the store, so the spirits come and get *kawai*, tobacco, on the mountains. *Piait'ma* gives tobacco to the *piai'čaŋ*. The *piai'čaŋ* sees the tobacco as his spirit flies round the mountain during a seance." Shamans value wild tobacco more highly than the ordinary garden plants for ritual purposes. Obtaining this tobacco is sometimes an important feature of shaman preparation, and considerable efforts may be expended by the pupil in getting it. He will climb to the top of a high mountain and pick it and then be able to claim that it is given him by *piait'ma*, by virtue of the fact that the mountain spirit is believed to live on the mountaintop.

Only a shaman can use this tobacco, for it has been obtained from a spirit. It is sometimes said that a person cannot conduct seances before he gets his tobacco from *piait'ma*. For this reason, apparently, Francis carried his own tobacco when he went to conduct seances outside his settlement. Joe and some of the other shamans were less discriminating and used any that was provided if they ran short of their own.

A small gourd *(kasakïlï)* that grows on a wild vine is occasionally seen about the settlements and is of a useful size for holding charms and medicines. To obtain one, Francis undertook a long journey (in person) to where the plant grew on top of a cliff at the edge of a mountain. It was said that Francis did not keep the gourd himself, but that *piait'ma* who lived on the mountain kept it and Francis used it occasionally during his seances, drinking his tobacco infusions from it and sniffing the juices up his nose. If *piait'ma* kept the gourd, this merely means that the *piait'ma* spirit brought it with him on coming down to the seance.

As a contrast to all this tremendous activity on Francis's part, Ernest's special *kumeli* tobacco, carefully wrapped up and gingerly brought out of a tin for my inspection, had been inherited from his father; he had gotten it from some Venezuelan Ye'cuana who had come on a trading expedition to Uwi village many years before.

The tobacco obtained by the shaman is converted into tobacco juice for drinking. Every shaman pupil knows how to make it. If others make it while he is learning, then it must be given him by an old woman. Girls who have reached puberty *(mazipïatai)* cannot give it to him, "for such girls would spoil the *piai'čaŋ*," said Ernest. The mode of preparation is simple: tobacco leaves are soaked and squeezed in a little water and sometimes salt is added, either trade salt or a little pulverized water weed. The salt content is not necessary, it is said, but merely imparts a pleasant taste. This is understandable among a people who generally lack salt and salt-containing foods. Very small quantities of tobacco juice are in fact agreeable, being reminiscent of peppery cucumber.

Occasionally, a shaman pupil or a newly established shaman may make more elaborate preparations of tobacco juice. In Chai-chai gorge, where the Mazaruni River flows at the foot of the Ayanganna Plateau, a mountain and waterfall were pointed out to me as a place that shamans often visit. The stream is called Kawaibalu, "Tobacco Creek." There the shamans collect the water from the falls to mix the tobacco juice, and there they can also obtain the salty water weed, which is added to the wild tobacco found on the mountains around.

Tobacco has a two-fold importance in shamanism; it helps to bring down spirits to the seance and it also assists in carrying off the shaman's spirit. Akawaio say that it can do both these things because it possesses an exceptionally powerful spirit. They also maintain that the tobacco obtained from the mountains has more spirit than that planted in the garden, and that it is consequently stronger and more effective. Perhaps wild tobacco is stronger, or perhaps it is believed to be stronger because it comes directly from the mountaintops, which represent the world of the spirits.

At the beginning of a seance, when tobacco juice is drunk, the tobacco spirit *(kawai akwalu)*, thought of as an old man, comes and can be heard making characteristic little whistlings: "pwee, wee, wee." The whistling is shortly followed by the noise of a spirit coming to drink the juice, through the medium of the shaman, who has a cupful of it by him. A succession of spirits comes during the seance, each in turn seeking to drink the tobacco juice. At each arrival there is a loud and elaborate gurgling, sucking, and spitting noise, which indicates that the spirit possessing the shaman is sipping its share of the tobacco. The tobacco spirit has the power to entice other spirits because no spirit can resist the attraction of tobacco—just as, the Akawaio confess, they themselves are unable to resist it either. Once a spirit has drunk tobacco juice it is "glad" and satisfied, and can be induced to help the shaman by allowing itself to be interrogated. Thus in this context, tobacco juice functions as a charm.

The powerful tobacco spirit also carries the shaman's spirit away, out of the house and into the sky, where it roams about the mountains, the forests, and the rivers, seeking other spirits and ghosts. In this connection the Akawaio state their beliefs succinctly: "*Kawai* makes the spirit fly away if the *piai'čaŋ* takes a lot." If the shaman wishes to detach his spirit quickly, then he takes the tobacco juice through the nose, a process that is made known to the seance audience by a great deal of violent sneezing, coughing, choking, and retching coming from the shaman's direction.

According to general belief, one of the essential attributes of the powerful tobacco is that it makes the shaman small. Some of the spirit songs *(malik)* tell of how the shaman's spirit is seeing the mountains because the tobacco has made him small and able to fly away.

The shaman's bird, *kumalak* (swallow-tailed kite, *Elanoides forficatus*)

Photo courtesy Ray O. Green

(The *comment* given after each quoted song records the explanation given to me before detailed translations were worked out. Although occasionally the comments are not very accurate, they are in all cases enlightening.)

Uyewañaigaik   wïbu   yenebïk kawai
Has made me small mountain seeing tobacco

   uyewañaigaik.
   has made me small.

Informant's Comment: "The *piai'čaŋ* says he is getting small for going out through the cracks of the house."

Although it was said that Antonio, having used up all his tobacco, drank *miligawa* bark in water on one occasion, this is a most unusual expedient. Normally, a seance cannot take place without tobacco, tobacco juice being essential to the shaman because of its power of enticement and of detaching the spirit of the one who consumes it. For these same reasons, *kawai algasak*, vomited tobacco juice, has great importance for the shaman pupil. By

drinking and vomiting it he practices the shaman's essential skill—that of enabling his spirit to leave the body behind in order to go traveling about in the spirit realms. As Francis of Tagaikapai remarked, "The special *piai'čaŋ* spirit is, above all, *kawai*."

THE KUMALAK-BIRD SPIRIT
(kumalak akwalu)

Drinking tobacco juice initiates the shaman pupil's spirit experience. Similarly, at the seance, this act marks the point at which the shaman starts to get in touch with the spirit world. While drinking, the shaman begins to tremble all over. What happens afterward is the subject of an intricate web of beliefs relating to the shaman's movements and the assistance he obtains from spirit helpers. These beliefs are marked by imaginative analogies and symbols taken from natural life and applied to the changes that the shaman undergoes.

First, there is the tobacco spirit; this spirit brings down the *kumalak* bird, which is the shaman's chief

Malik, the ceremonial armbands of the Akawaio shaman, worn at the first public seance

spirit helper. *Kumalak* is the swallow-tailed kite, a most beautiful and graceful black and white bird. The bird is so closely associated with shaman practice that Akawaio frequently refer to it as "the *piai'čaŋ* bird" or "*ima-wali* bird," or as "*eneoge bazi*"—that is, "clairvoyant woman."

Kumalak bazi (kumalak woman) is regarded as the spirit wife of the shaman's spirit as it flies about the world of the spirits during the seance. "*Kumalak* can take you for a husband or boy friend if you are a good *piai'čaŋ.* She can give you a baby even if you talk to her or dance with her. There is *kumalak bibi* for woman *piai'čaŋ.*" *Kumalak bibi* literally means *kumalak* elder brother; in a wider frame of reference, as here, it means *kumalak* man. The advantages of fathering a *kumalak* child were explained by Elias: "When you *piai, kumalak bazi* is nice to you and dances with you and you might make a child with her. The spirit child grows and becomes big and helps the father in his *piai* work." Because of his relationship to the spirit child, the shaman is often addressed as *papago,* "father," by the spirits in the spirit songs (this usage contrasts with the everyday evocative *papai,* "father").

The importance of the *kumalak* spirit lies in its raising and carrying powers. First of all, it assists the tobacco spirit in getting the shaman's spirit airborne. There is believed to be a close connection between the spirit of the *kumalak* bird and the tobacco spirit—so much so

that at Chinawieng village some said that the tobacco spirit lives in the *kumalak* bird. Further inquiry established that the two, although closely allied, are nevertheless separate spirits. It is the tobacco that brings the *kumalak* bird, but *kumalak* also has its own tobacco. Both Joe and Ernest stated that when it is necessary for the shaman's spirit to fly away quickly, *kumalak* comes and gives him its own tobacco from the mountains, which is especially strong. *Kumalak* gives it to him through the nose, and this makes the shaman fly away. "But if he is a real *piai'čaŋ,* an *eneoge* [clairvoyant], he can still fly away, without *kumalak,* provided he takes a lot of tobacco." Thus the *kumalak* spirit comes at the beginning of a seance, just after the tobacco spirit, frequently bringing a stronger tobacco spirit to reinforce that deriving from the cupful of tobacco juice made up by the shaman himself.

The shaman's spirit flies up and out of the house, together with the *kumalak*-bird spirit. This occurrence is portrayed in the seance by the rustling of bunches of leaves, the sounds being such as to suggest two spirits going out separately, one after another, and flying off into the distance. It is said that the shaman's flight can take place because the tobacco spirit and the *kumalak* spirit helper have given him wings.

The wings that carry the shaman away are like those of a bird. They are referred to as *malik.* The majority of the songs (also called *malik*) sung by the shaman at the beginning and end of the seance contain references to these wings. The material form of *malik* is the shaman's traditional ceremonial ornament, which consists of arm bands of white cotton, bound above the biceps of the upper arm and connected together across the shoulders and back by cotton strings that sag loosely to the waist or below. White bird down covers most of the length of the strings, which are said to represent the white markings on the upper wing surface of the kite. From each arm band hang loose cotton strings, ending in a small pompon of yet more white bird down. In the spirit songs these feather pom-pons are called *činik,* translated as "flowers" (the usual word for "flower" is *dibulu*). Together with other ornaments, such as ear pendants of white down, they are worn by the shaman only at his first public seance. However, at succeeding seances, the shaman's spirit is supposed to be clad in these ceremonial ornaments. Years ago, it is said, the shaman also had white feathers and bird down stuck with gum across his forehead (the *kumalak* bird has a white head). When the *kumalak* spirit comes to the shaman, or to the practicing shaman pupil, it is believed to give him the "hat" and wings so that he can fly away. Even the shaman pupil's complexion, growing pale from vomiting, is associated with the *kumalak* bird's appearance; when he gets white like the *kumalak* bird he is ready to fly away.

Beliefs concerning the power of flight given by the tobacco juice and the mechanism of flight provided by the swallow-tailed kite are expressed in a large number of songs learned by the shaman and sung during the seance. This is one of Elias's songs, which refers to the power of *taiugu* tree bark as well.

Mialï, wïbu   kusendan Yumawali kawaiyu yabilibe
Go on, mountain see   *imawali*   tobacco wing-like

Taiugu yabililube   mialï, wïbu   sendan
Taiugu wing sort of like go on, mountain see

  Yumawali.
  imawali.

Informant's Comment: "*Kawai* is getting wings for the *piai'čaŋ* to go to the mountains. *Imawali* tells the *piai'čaŋ* to fly with the *kawai* spirit to see the mountains and to see *imawali* who lives there."

Ernest, shaman of Uwi village, Ataro River, wearing the shaman's ear pendants made of cotton strings, white bird down, and white seed beads (1952)

A similar song of Ernest's stated that tobacco makes the shaman fly away and gives him the arm bands and ornaments—that is, the wings (*malik*). After singing this the shaman, supposedly drunk on tobacco juice, flies off around the mountains, followed by the *kumalak* bird. In short, the successful shaman is one who is possessed by the various spirits that can help him to enter the spirit realms.

The *kumalak* bird takes the shaman's spirit with it on its travels. While there is silence in the house and the leaves are held still, poised over the shaman's head, these two spirits are ranging through the various landscapes of Akawaio country, "seeing everything and finding everything," as one song aptly puts it. Seeking out spirits (*akwalu*) and ghosts (*akwalupï*), they travel in the mountains and the forests and along the rivers, just as the *kumalak* bird is seen habitually flying about. The characteristic flight of the scissor-tailed bird, powerful yet effortlessly graceful, explains why it, above all others, has appealed to Akawaio imagination. It is seen hovering around the mountaintops, occasionally swooping down past the forest canopy to glide a few inches above the surface of the rivers, then soaring once more into the sky. The spirit of the bird, which communicates so easily with all the main cosmic regions (of sky, water, forest, and mountains), is the shaman's most appropriate spirit conveyer and guide when he seeks other spirits from all these regions. When the *kumalak* bird is seen skimming the surface of the river like a swallow and then rising above the forest and over the mountaintops again, the Akawaio say that it is taking up water from the river into the sky to put in its tobacco juice.

All birds that have a mountain habitat are closely associated with shamanistic practice, for the mountains are the places where the spirits dance and feast. The shaman's songs refer to these birds time and time again and describe their dancing. In contrast, the birds of the forest have little value as shaman helpers, although their possession of wings and the power of flight occasionally allows them to assist him in his attempts to perform a spirit flight. For this reason, while the *kumalak* bird is the primary helper, the shaman occasionally sings that he is getting wings like the *kukoi*, a species of hawk. He also sings sometimes that *lamolamo*, one of the hummingbirds, is dancing with him, and that the *cadouri* (*waiowra*) is teaching him shaman lore (the *cadouri*, or moriche oriole, is valued for its singing and its power to mimic other birds).

The shaman's spirit rises with the aid of wings and steps (or a ladder) for crossing from one part of the spirit realm to another. It may also have a vehicle to carry it into the spirit realms. Every sky bird is thought to have its own means of conveyance, and this, in accordance with the traditional Akawaio level of technology, is the woodskin canoe (*kanow*, possessive form *guŋwa*), made from the bark of the purple heart tree. (The concept of sky vehicles seems to have been a traditional one for these Amerindians—the Wayana of French Guiana also have a "sky boat" associated with sky birds. The airplane, when it first appeared in Akawaio skies, was called "the king vulture's canoe" [*amwana guŋwa*] because its silhouette reminded people of this bird.) As every sky bird has its own means of conveyance, expressed in terms of navigation, so do the spirits of all sky creatures, including the shaman on his spirit flight. Elias brought down the ghost spirit of Edwin's father, and he sang about this. (*Yanayana*, in the third line of the song, is the fierce "master of the peccary.")

Enewoge   guŋwa yawï utïbïduma
Clairvoyant canoe inside going far away

Weidïdï guŋwa   yawï utïbïduma
Weidïdï bird canoe inside going far away

Yanayana   guŋwaiyow utïbïduma
Peccary spirit canoe in   going far away

Amwana   guŋwaiyow utïbïduma
King Vulture canoe in   going far away

Dwaidanogomasibra zenugomasibra   gïrïduma.
He must not get sick he must not get sad crossing over.

Informant's Comment: "When the *piai'čaŋ* is going inside these birds and in the hog boats he must not get sick. All these spirits have canoes, like people, and he must not get sick or sad when crossing over in these canoes."

Thus the shaman utilizes all the means of conveyance used by the inhabitants of the sky. The shaman's spirit crosses the rivers like the *kumalak* bird and, with the aid of his wings, he even goes under the earth and inside the mountains. In performing these feats he is in danger, since this new world is full of perils for earthbound human spirits. Thus he is admonished not to fall sick or be sad in the course of his flight. Much of the time the shaman sits on the top of one of the mountains he is visiting, and there he dances with the spirits, especially with the bird women. The mountain is the "stool," that is, the place occupied by these bird spirits. Some of the songs, with lilting melodies, describe how the shaman is dancing with all the mountain birds, with one bird woman on one side and a second on the other side.

Enewoge   bazi   siŋwinalï
Clairvoyant woman on this side

Weidïdï   bazi   siŋwinalï
Weidïdï bird woman on this side

Sawrogogo   bazi   siŋwinalï
Sawrogogo bird woman on this side

Yanarigo   bazi   siŋwinalï
Yanarigo bird woman on this side

Jiajia   bazi   siŋwinalï
Jiajia bird woman on this side

Enewoge   kumanumbai
Clairvoyant wants to dance

Weidïdï   bazi   kumanumbai
Weidïdï bird woman wants to dance

Eneoge   bazi   malikï yawï
Clairvoyant woman wings inside

Waigïyiŋbo.
Waigïying Mountain at.

Informant's Comment: "All these birds dance on the mountain while the *piai'čaŋ* sings *malik*, the spirit songs. When dancing Hallelujah you have to get a woman on one side and on the other side of you and link arms and dance—so with the *piai'čaŋ* when he sprees with the birds."

Although I was unable to identify all the birds mentioned in the song, the Akawaio, significantly enough, classified them all as "mountain birds."

When the tobacco juice is finished and many spirits and ghosts have come to the seance, the shaman's spirit is brought back by the *kumalak* bird, or occasionally by some other helper such as the *kukoi*, a hawk. The shaman gives his wings (*malik*) back to his bird assistant and once more re-enters his everyday existence. His return is heralded by a great rustling noise, suggestive of the flight back, and a thump on the floor of the house as he lands.

Although the full role of the *kumalak* bird can be manifested only during a seance, the shaman pupil has to practice beforehand and learn how to implement it. He must try to establish contact with the *kumalak* spirit when drinking tobacco juice and singing. According to Ernest, the pupil may dream of the *kumalak* bird, which tells him to drink tobacco juice and use the leaves.

The elaborate imagery of the beliefs associated with this phase of the pupil's training consists basically of this: his spirit flies by the wings of the *kumalak* bird, which are symbolized by the *malik*, the wing-like arm and shoulder ornaments. It is essentially the tobacco spirit that gives these wings. For this reason the same training applies for obtaining the *kumalak* spirit as for getting the tobacco spirit. It is said that by maintaining food restrictions and vomiting tree bark, and so becoming thin, the shaman becomes a support (*yaboŋ*) for the wings (*malik*) that will carry him on his spirit journey.

THE SPIRIT SONGS (malik)

The *malik*, or spirit songs, sung by the shaman fall into several categories. First there are the songs sung at the beginning of the seance about flying away to contact the spirits with the aid of tobacco, wings, and the feather pom-pons (*činik*). Kenswil (1946: 9) has called these "songs of invitation." Other songs, which may be sung at the end of the seance, tell of how the shaman has been on the mountains and flying about the spirit region. Still another category includes the songs sung by the spirits during the course of the seance, through the medium of the shaman. Each spirit has its own *malik*, it is said, just as the shaman has his own. Each spirit on arrival at the seance should call its name or include it in its song—but it does not invariably do so.

Malik, then, is best translated generally as "spirit song," whether it refers to one sung by the shaman about the spirits, or to one that is supposed to be sung by a spirit itself about spirit activities. Basically, *malik* songs are "flight songs" or "wing songs" of the shaman, and it is probably for this reason that they have the same name as the wing ornaments.

The part played by song and rhythm in helping the spirit to fly away is expressly stated by the shamans. The day after one of Ernest's seances, I was humming an accompaniment to one of the more tuneful spirit songs that I was playing back to him on my tape recorder, when Ernest stopped me with the warning that if I "caught" this song my spirit might fly away. On another occasion, Ernest sang a mountain spirit *(piait'ma)* song for me in broad daylight, imitating at my request this spirit's raucous voice. After two such songs he stopped. He could not go on, he said, or his spirit might fly away. Singing in an ordinary voice was one thing, but reproducing a spirit song exactly was dangerous in such circumstances because he might be carried away by its effects. This elevation of the spirit through music is a concept that enters into Akawaio Hallelujah ritual as well as shaman practice and is a basic attribute of any song and dance that is energetically performed.

The shaman pupil, when drinking tree-bark infusions and learning shaman practice by himself, must also learn to sing the spirit songs. A seance may last anywhere from about 1½ hours to 5 hours; most of them average about 3 hours. During this time as many as 20 to 40 spirits may be summoned and all of these are "made to sing," so it can be appreciated that a shaman has to have an extensive repertoire of songs. According to the various accounts by present-day Akawaio shamans, all have learned these songs in a similar way, partly from other shamans and partly from spirits. Elias, who had Ernest as his teacher *(ladoi)*, said that Ernest had first taught him *malik*. Then *imawali*, forest spirits, taught him others afterwards: "For when he flies away he finds the spirits dancing on the mountains and so he learns the spirit songs."

When a shaman or a shaman pupil states that the spirits have taught him their songs, and that he learned them when drinking bark or tobacco juice, when dreaming, or during a spirit flight, it means that he has already been familiar with the songs. He is merely recalling them or improvising on them as inspiration moves him. The importance of improvisation and personal composition was strikingly demonstrated to me during my second period of research. While staying in Uwi village in 1952 I

had heard several seances conducted there by Ernest. At nightfall he began by singing his first spirit song, a *malik* with the most beautiful and haunting melody; it invited the spirits to come down and drink the tobacco juice that had been prepared for them. I wrote down the words and learned the song myself. In 1957, at Ernest's new settlement of Elema, I asked him to sing this particular song for a tape recording to be made. He could not remember either the tune or the words, although he sang several very similar songs in an effort to comply with my request. I had to sing the song to him before he could recall it. Then Ernest explained that all shamans "get others from time to time and cannot remember them all."

In societies that have written music, changes are often wrought by deliberate arranging and rearranging of old tunes. Among the Akawaio this process is going on, perhaps unconsciously, all the time. The individual interpretations are continually being lost, because there is no method of permanently recording them, but the tunes continue indefinitely. When the shamans or the shaman pupils are obtaining new songs from the spirits, they are merely producing variations on themes that are a tradition of their profession. For this reason, while various shaman performances produce what to the listening foreigner often seem identical sounds, a greater familiarity with them soon reveals considerable differences, as degree of skill, personality, and individual creativity become recognizable within the pattern common to all performances. It is like seeing the characters in the same play or opera being performed by different individuals in different companies. The shaman pupil practices all branches of his shamanistic skill, but particularly his mastery of spirit songs. Thus he gradually becomes an exponent of a new expression of his art. His individual inspiration is fostered by the conditions of his learning, which suggest to him that his relationship with the spirit world is a personal, unstereotyped one. This makes him something of a composer—and this in turn, I am certain, is one of the satisfactions he derives from his profession.

THE SHAMAN'S LEAVES *(piai'čaŋ yale)*

The shaman pupil has to master the art of using the shaman's leaves *(piai'čaŋ yale)*. No seance can be held without them. They are used to provide rhythm and sound effects, accompanying song and portraying movement. The leaves consist of several large sprays of twigs, tied up with forest creeper to form a bundle. Three or four such bundles are used together during a seance, one or two being grasped in either hand. The leaves are collected just before a seance from any kind of forest tree. In the past the Akawaio had the *maraka*, the hollow gourd rattle with pebbles or seeds inside, but they used it only to provide rhythm in dancing.

The mode of giving the leaves to the shaman is important. They should be collected and made into bundles either by the patient on whose behalf the seance is held, or by one of the patient's relatives or associates. The shaman should not get the leaves unless it is his own very close relation who is ill. Telling the shaman "to take the leaves" is the first step in initiating the seance. Its special significance is suggested by the assertion sometimes made that the person who gets the leaves for the shaman should not go to sleep, although anyone else in the seance, including the patient, may do so. At one of Ernest's seances, after the arrival of various helping spirits, his spirit went up into the sky on its customary flight but immediately returned, for "the girl who got the leaf had gone to sleep and was blocking up his path to the spirit world." Ernest asked some of his audience to wake her up "because her spirit was lying in his way." The culprit was duly awakened and Ernest's spirit departed again, this time successfully.

"Giving the leaves" is the act of commissioning the shaman to undertake a cure. It is significant because it indicates that the patient and his family group are prepared to entrust the shaman with the welfare of the spirit of the sick person; they open up the way for his spirit flight, there being no obstruction in his way through reserve, suspicion, or unwillingness on their part.

The leaves provide a continual background of sound in the seance. Every spirit coming to the seance blows on the patient to express good will and to help in achieving a cure. This is indicated by the shaman, who approaches the hammock in which the patient is lying and then shakes and rustles the leaves over it; sometimes loud blowing sounds accompany the flapping: "swoosh-woooosh" or "swaik, swaik, swai-ii-k." Just the flapping of the leaves alone over the occupants of nearby hammocks and over the patient or patients is said to represent the blowing of spirits making a cure.

The leaves are also rustled rhythmically as the accompaniment to the spirit songs. From time to time they are manipulated in such a way as to suggest that something is coming down from the roof or going up through it. Thus, when a spirit is supposed to be going out of the house, through the roof, the shaman starts by rustling one bundle of leaves in one hand, at floor level. These he then jerks upwards in short stages, rustling them loudly at first and then more and more softly as he jerks them higher and higher towards the roof. Eventually, the shaman is standing erect with one hand holding a bundle of leaves aloft over his head, near the roof, and the other hand holding the second bundle down by his knees. There are some moments of complete silence, then the lower bundle is rustled slightly, followed by the one that is held aloft. The latter is then jerked downwards with in-

creasing noise, until both bundles are rustling loudly near the floor. They are given a final smack with the hand, and a thump on the floor is made by the shaman's feet. This final thud, often accompanied by an ear-splitting yell, indicates that a spirit has arrived. The rustling of leaves is thus designed to portray the approach of the spirit from afar and its progress into the midst of the seance. The use of the leaves throughout the process is cleverly suggestive of aerial flight.

Although the house in which the seance occurs is usually too dark for anyone to see these procedures, it is easy to guess what is going on from the sounds of slight movements that the shaman makes when manipulating his leaf bundles. Francis once held a seance in a house that had a gap between the top of the wall and the roof, at the gable end. By strategically placing myself I was able to see his hand holding the leaf bundles aloft, outlined against a starlit sky, every time a spirit left or entered the house. On another occasion, gaps in the bark walls of a tumbledown house enabled me to witness Ernest's movements. In any case, the Akawaio make no secret of what the shaman does, for the mode of shaking the leaves is only the mechanical aspect of the seance, the way in which the spirits and ghosts arrive and depart again and express themselves.

The rhythmic swishing and rustling is important because, together with the spirit songs, it is said to help the shaman's spirit to fly away. According to one spirit song, the leaves give the shaman spirit wings (the *malik* discussed earlier) to enable him to go to the mountains and under the ground. The rhythm and song also cause many of the seance audience to fall into a deep, peaceful, and refreshing slumber, and this in spite of the fact that the noise being produced in the seance is loud enough to be heard all over the considerable area of a village and even beyond.

THE PRACTICE OF SHAMAN TECHNIQUES

During the entire period of training, while secluded, observing various restrictions, and taking charms, the pupil practices the shaman's skills described above. He learns to drink more and more tobacco juice. He practices shaking the leaves in a particular manner, so as to be able to produce, for hours at a time, exactly the sound effects and the rhythm required. He practices singing the spirit songs, learning the words and tunes of a considerable number and improvising on them as inspiration seizes him. He practices very hard, and when he has the techniques correct and has learned to drink considerable quantities of tobacco juice, the spirits begin to come. At first, it is said, one spirit only comes; later, after more practice, another spirit comes; and then, still later, others arrive. With each practice seance and, eventually, with each public seance of the professional shaman, more and more spirits can be summoned, and the spirit world is successfully penetrated.

The shaman pupil has as his model the great *piai'čaŋ* Maijabï, whose story is this:

Maijabï took Amwana Bazi, King Vulture Girl, as his wife. When visiting his in-laws her father gave him a number of impossible tasks to perform, each within the space of a day. One day he had to cut a big garden; another day he had to bail water from a large pool until it was dried up; finally he was told to build an enormous house. Maijabï accomplished each task in the stated time because he was able to obtain spirit help. For example, fishing-bird spirits came and helped him empty the pool and get the fish and water snakes at the bottom. Other bird spirits, the bunia birds who make complex hanging nests, helped him build the house in record time.

Eventually, Maijabï was told to carve a stool from a red rock *(kako)*. He called down the spirits of the wood ants, who are excellent borers, and they made the stool for him. Maijabï was by now furious with his father-in-law for setting him all these tasks so he instructed the stool to destroy him. The stool chopped down Amwana Bazi's father and Maijabï went off.

"Maijabï is a real *piai'čaŋ*, he can bring all the spirits," said the narrator, Basil of the Kamarang River.

Kenswil's account of learning shaman practice is of interest, although it is also misleading. He writes:

If a man or woman, for they have women practicing the profession as well, desires to become a Medicine-man, he or she must get a fully qualified Medicine-man as their teacher. They must implicitly submit themselves to this gentleman's instructions. They are first carried to the top of the highest mountain range in the surrounding country for initiation. Their food, drink, and place of abode are chosen by this instructor. Certain hours of the night they are taken to the different spots, which are considered the homes of the various spirits, and taught to sing the different spirit songs, drinking at intervals small doses of tobacco juice mixed with salt. This course takes three or more moons to be completed. When it has been completed by the student, and only then, he has power over his other self. [1946: 8–9]

Kenswil, when he writes of the journeys at night to the mountaintops and homes of the spirits, does not state whether the pupil is physically taken there or whether his shaman teacher detaches his own and his pupil's spirit and performs the customary spirit flight of the seance. Unless particular care is taken by the investigator it is easy to misinterpret accounts of such journeys. Akawaio shamans who had had living teachers stated that the pupil learns by going into his teacher's house and remaining inside with him for instruction, learning some of the spirit songs, how to use the leaves, and the general technique of shaman practice. On these occasions, the shaman teacher, in seance conditions, takes his pupil stage by stage through the mechanics of a seance, teaching him the appropriate songs and explaining what is happening in the spirit world as each stage is enacted in song and accompanying rhythm.

On the other hand, an energetic shaman teacher, or the shaman pupil on his own, might fulfill the task of learning after the style of Kenswil's description. He might camp at night in the forest, on a mountaintop, or by a waterfall, and there he might practice the songs he already knows from hearing shaman seances. At the same time, he might believe that he is visiting the spirit realms, for in the forest dwell the forest spirits *(imawali)*, on a mountain are the mountain spirits *(piait'ma)*, and by the water are the water spirits *(lato)*. Whether the shaman pupil practices his songs and his spirit flight in the settlement or "in the bush," and whether he does one or the other under instruction of either a living or a ghost teacher, is of little importance. The essential point is that by using one method or another (or both combined) he is certain to obtain spirit experience.

Only once did I hear one of these practice seances. It was at dusk when loud noises, spirit songs, roars, and scraps of conversation came from a darkened house next to mine at Kataima village. The noise lasted only a few minutes, but since it sounded like a shaman at work I made inquiries the next day. Sammy then confessed that he was learning shaman practice and had been engaged in contacting spirits. Some people never go beyond this rudimentary stage. John David, for example, of the same village, admitted to engaging in shaman activities a little, but he never did more than amuse himself and try to aid his family with a few minor demonstrations of the art. He was never a qualified practitioner, for he had never undergone the full training and had never given a public performance. Only when the shaman pupil has practiced hard and acquired all the necessary skill, when he has undergone a period of seclusion and restriction and has used various charms, when in his hungry and tobacco-addicted state he has had a series of dreams relating to his performance—only then will he feel that he is ready to embark on his first public performance.

THE FIRST PUBLIC SEANCE

The first seance that the shaman pupil conducts in public is the climax of all of his months of training; he has been working for this event since he began seriously to take up the profession. During its enactment he becomes recognized as a fully fledged shaman. Afterwards he can return to live a normal life, eat as usual, go back to his wife, live socially, and take only the occasional shaman's charm.

The first seance takes place at the shaman's home settlement and therefore may coincide with his return from the seclusion of working abroad. A great number of relations and friends attend, and the shaman teacher *(ladoi)* must be present, either in the flesh or in spirit. Certain preliminary preparations are made by the shaman pupil. He does not eat anything before the seance. Instead, he may go to a waterfall or stream and drink a lot of water, which he vomits up time after time. Then when the seance is due to start, he drinks tobacco juice in considerable quantities. Years ago, it is said, the shaman pupil used to make a small drink barrel, *korialï,* about three feet long, to hold tobacco juice for his first public seance *(korialï* is the word for a dugout canoe, and also for a tree trunk hollowed out to hold drinks for a feast). The result of drinking so much tobacco juice is drastic. What happens is perhaps best explained in the words of the Akawaio themselves:

After a year or two—one year is enough—the *piai'čaŋ* learner then starts to make a great amount of *kawai* in the *kašili'iŋ* [a large gourd, or a dugout, literally "*kaširi* container," *kaširi* being the main fermented drink among the Akawaio]. He fills it right up with water and tobacco and drinks and drinks; eventually, he falls down in a dead faint. He would die were it not that another *piai'čaŋ* is present to *piai* for him. He is placed in the hammock and looks as if dead. He dies virtually. The other *piai'čaŋ* goes to the mountains and finds the new *piai'čaŋ* spirit there, dancing with *imawali* and all the spirits. Eventually, during the seance, the new *piai'čaŋ* is restored to life and he starts to *piai*—to bring down the spirits—and his teacher is silent. After this first seance the new *piai'čaŋ* can return to his wife and start eating normally.

Apart from this ordeal with the tobacco juice, the first public seance does not appear to be very different from any other seance conducted by an experienced shaman. Nevertheless, a great deal of symbolism is involved that is not immediately obvious. The preparations in several ways suggest that a feast or "spree" *(eborikma)* is made by the new shaman for the spirits who are to be invited down to the seance to witness his change to a new status. There is the use of the small drink barrel, the *korialï,* which is a replica of the large one used for holding the fermented liquor during the ordinary sprees, to which the people of one settlement invite relations and friends from another for drinking and dancing. Then the shaman's arm bands, the *malik,* are in form similar to the arm ornaments, called *abïda,* donned by the men when dressing up for dancing; the major difference is in color, white being used for the down strings and pompons on the shaman's ornaments. A comment to a spirit song suggested that some Akawaio are aware of the similarities between ordinary feasts and spirit feasts: "When *imawali* gives the *piai'čaŋ malik* he has to wear it; he dresses up to go to the mountains as we dress up to go to church" (that is, to dance Hallelujah).

The spirits feast on tobacco juice offered them at the seance, and so does the shaman pupil, who loses consciousness as a result or at least goes into a state of trance akin to drunkenness. The Akawaio say that he gets drunk on the tobacco juice. His spirit leaves the body and flies off to the mountaintops, where it joins the other spirits and ghosts in dancing and spreeing. His body is left behind and, being without its spirit, is said to be dead. This is the crucial time for the shaman pupil on his first formal spirit flight to the spirit world, for there is the possibility that his spirit will not find its way back again and that the temporary death will become permanent. This is where the shaman teacher, who is at the seance, comes to his aid. If the teacher is a ghost teacher *(ladoi akwalupï),* then he is already in the spirit world and leads his pupil's spirit back. If he is a living teacher, then he is at the pupil's side, conducting the seance for him while he is unconscious or temporarily too sick to carry on for himself. With the ease born of many seances of his own, he can himself make a spirit flight to rescue his pupil from a perpetual spirit existence on the mountaintops.

A living shaman teacher's presence must be of inestimable help at this time of physical and mental stress, and Joe of Chinawieng said that he did not believe those who said they were taught shaman practice by a ghost —"because a ghost spirit could not have conducted the seance for him when he died after taking the tobacco juice." Nevertheless, the two most reputable shamans in the tribe, Francis and then Ernest, had both learned from ghost teachers (although it is notable that when Ernest's younger brother Edwin held his first seance, Ernest substituted for the presence of their father). There is, therefore, nothing to prevent the shaman pupil from having both a ghost teacher for the full course of his training and a friendly shaman to assist him on the occasion of the final and most exacting trial of all.

After the first formal penetration of the spirit world, the feat of his first public seance, the shaman pupil is a pupil no longer. He has become a shaman in his own right. Before his first public seance he is learning, and he practices alone or in his immediate family circle only; afterwards, he can conduct seances in public whenever he likes. Before, he is regarded as a learner, not a proper shaman; afterwards, he is known as a *piai'čaŋ,* even though it is generally recognized that he is not yet a very good or skillful one, because of his lack of experience and the necessarily slow acquisition of spiritual powers. Above all, the first public seance allows him to begin his major task of curing illness and averting death. It is the difference between a medical student and a qualified doctor, a theological candidate and an ordained priest. With the shaman the change in status occurs at this first public seance, which is both a test of his capacity and a public ritual of inauguration. As an ordinary individual he "dies" during it, and then is brought back to life. With a new status, having control over his own spirit and those of others and having made contact with the spirit world, he is on the way to becoming a real shaman—an *eneoge,* one who perceives.

CONCLUSION

The actual processes of shaman training are matched at every stage by an ideal, envisaged as the correct procedure but never fully attainable. Each process is also significant as a symbolic expression of an activity which, according to this ideal pattern, is taking place sympathetically in the spirit world.

I have tried to find the heart of shaman practice by stripping off its layers and examining each segment of reality with its accompanying ideal conceptualization or its symbol. Does an essential conceptual core remain after such a process, and what are the fundamentals of the shaman reality and of its ideal? The Akawaio say that only one thing is essential, the drinking of tobacco juice; but they also maintain that a seance can be conducted properly only if the shaman has observed food restrictions *(jeruma)* beforehand. It is significant that, for each seance, a shaman repeats only these two facets of his professional training. He eats little or nothing that day and during the seance, at night, he drinks a cup of tobacco juice. In these two acts reality and the ideal meet in shaman practice. There is no doubt that the basis of the Akawaio shaman's experience lies in this deliberate act of taking nicotine on an empty stomach.

However, these combined acts make no sense in themselves, even if they are real ones, and it is their result that is culturally and socially significant. This result is fascinating to us because presumably it will have a different function and be expressed in different images according to the cultural heritage and social circumstances of the participants. Thus the imagery described by the Akawaio is an expression of the poetical and imaginative side of their culture. This is one sort of result. Yet the shaman's experience in trance is not totally individualistic, nor is it uncontrolled. Thus, another sort of result is the immediately practical one, relating to spheres of social control and group interrelationships. The basic acts of the shaman's technique and the poetical, symbolic images ultimately make sense through the fact that they are translatable into a number of meaningful social and cultural spheres.

APPENDIX: AKAWAIO SHAMANS WORKING IN THE 1950s

AKAWAIO SHAMANS WORKING IN 1951–52

Kamarang River Area

PARUIMA VILLAGE AND SEVENTH-DAY ADVENTIST MISSION AREA

No shamans were working officially, owing to the opposition of the missions at Paruima and Waramadong villages.

Antonio (a shaman pupil). Of mixed Arekuna and Akawaio descent, Antonio was learning to be a shaman. For a part of this time he was engaged in work on Paruima Mission buildings. He was learning from Arekuna relatives in Venezuela, particularly from his brother-in-law.

Mazaruni River Area

TAGAIKAPAI VILLAGE

Francis learned from a ghost teacher, his deceased brother-in-law, Jenness, who was an Arekuna. Francis intended to teach his son as soon as he was old enough. Considered to be the best and most experienced shaman in the tribe, Francis was regularly consulted by Mazaruni and Kako River people.

SAGARAIMADAI SETTLEMENT

George and his brothers had learned from their father. None of George's sons had learned or intended to learn. Elderly and going deaf, George conducted seances for his immediate family only.

KATAIMA VILLAGE

Sammy (a shaman pupil). Sammy came from the Kukui River area and married into Kataima village of the Mazaruni River area. He was learning from his deceased father, who had himself learned from Francis of Tagaikapai. As there were no fully qualified shamans in the village, the people were applying to Francis for necessary assistance.

CHINAWIENG VILLAGE

Joe, a young shaman, learned from his older brother, William, who had married into the Patamona tribe to the south of the Akawaio. William gave the instruction when Joe visited him.

King George (a shaman pupil) was starting to learn but was dissuaded by Austin, the Leader of Chinawieng, on the grounds that shaman practice is bad.

Kukui River Area
AMOKOKUPAI VILLAGE

Donald learned on his own. He was said to know very little and to conduct seances mostly for his immediate relatives.

Ataro River Area
UWI VILLAGE

Ernest and *Edwin* were brothers, Ernest being the elder. Their father had been a shaman but had died before they were old enough to be taught. They learned from his ghost spirit. Ernest learned first, although they went through much of their training together. A young shaman, Ernest was nevertheless rapidly establishing his reputation.

Also at Uwi there were said to be some old men who had given up practicing because of old age.

There may have been other shaman pupils. These are difficult to discover as they tend not to talk about their intentions until they are ready to give a public seance and become fully qualified.

AKAWAIO SHAMANS WORKING IN 1957

Kamarang River Area
PARUIMA VILLAGE AND SEVENTH-DAY ADVENTIST MISSION AREA

Paruima is occasionally visited by Arekuna shamans from Venezuela (for example, Abraham stayed there in September 1957). They do not practice their profession unless asked to do so and in any case not near the Mission itself, owing to the opposition noted earlier.

Antonio. By 1957, Antonio was a fully established shaman to whom many Kamarang River people went for help, even those from the missions. He was considered by some to have used his skill to kill Francis, the Tagaikapai shaman up the Mazaruni.

WALBAIMA AND ERUWANKING SETTLEMENTS

Freddy had been brought up in Uwi village, Ataro River area. On marrying into a Kamarang River family he went to reside with his in-laws. His shaman teacher was Edwin of Uwi, his father's sister's son. He was regarded as young and inexperienced but nevertheless was frequently consulted by the people living in the region of Kamarang Mouth and the Mazaruni settlements below.

Mazaruni River Area
SAGARAIMADAI SETTLEMENT

George held very few seances in 1957, being deaf and also unable to sing in tune.

JAWALLA AND NEIGHBORING SETTLEMENTS

Elias had learned his skills at Kataima village, and when this was abandoned he came to Jawalla to practice. His shaman teacher had been Ernest of the Ataro River; his wife was Ernest's mother's brother's daughter, and she was the sister of Freddy.

Henry. Henry's father had been a shaman but had died before Henry was old enough to learn. His shaman teacher was Ernest of the Ataro. Henry had just become a shaman in 1957.

Bengie (a shaman pupil) had lived in Kataima village before its abandonment. He was learning from Freddy and had traveled the day journey to Walbaima to see him for this purpose.

Albert (a shaman pupil) was a stepson of Bengie and was also learning from Freddy.

CHINAWIENG VILLAGE

Joe. In 1957, Joe was fully established as a shaman and was gaining in reputation even outside his village and river area.

Kukui River Area
AMOKOKUPAI VILLAGE

Donald, who had been learning in 1951–52, was still considered to know only a little of shaman skills.

Dolphus was a young shaman whose teacher was Ernest of the Ataro. His grandmother, Christina, had been a shaman years before. She had died some years previously.

Ataro River Area
ELEMA SETTLEMENT

Ernest (formerly of Uwi, which had been abandoned by 1957). Ernest was considered to be the most proficient shaman in the tribe, and he succeeded Francis when he died. The Kwatin River area people in Brazil frequently applied to Ernest for help. Nearly all the shamans practicing in 1957 had been taught by Ernest, either directly or indirectly (as when his pupils in turn passed on their knowledge); a notable exception was Joe.

Edwin had fallen behind his brother Ernest in reputation. He was said to have spoiled his practice by not carrying out the necessary observances. His practice was in both the Ataro and Kwatin River areas.

REFERENCES

Bolingbroke, Henry
    1947   *A Voyage to Demerary.* Georgetown: Daily Chronicle. (Originally published 1807, London.)

Butt, Audrey J.
    1953   The Burning Fountain Whence it Came: A Study of the System of Beliefs of the Carib-Speaking Akawaio of British Guiana. *Social and Economic Studies* 2: 1–15.

    1960   The Birth of a Religion. *Journal of the Royal Anthropological Institute* 90 (I): 66–106.

Farabee, William C.
    1924   The Central Caribs. *Anthropological Publications* 10. Philadelphia: The University Museum, Univ. of Pennsylvania.

Gillin, John
    1936   The Barama River Caribs of British Guiana. *Peabody Museum Papers in Archaeology and Ethnology* 14 (2): 1–274.

im Thurn, E. F.
    1883   *Among the Indians of Guiana.* London: Kegan Paul, Trench.

Kenswil, F. W.
    1946   *Children of the Silence.* Georgetown: Interior Development Committee.

Roth, W. E.
    1915   An Inquiry into the Animism and Folk-lore of the Guiana Indians. *U.S. Bureau of American Ethnology, 30th Annual Report (1908–1909),* pp. 103–386. Washington: Government Printing Office.

Schomburgk, Richard
    1922   *Travels in British Guiana, 1840–1844,* trans. and ed. W. E. Roth. 2 vols. Georgetown.

Waterton, C.
    1903   *Wanderings in South America.* London.

5. CARIJONA AND MANAKÏNÏ: AN OPPOSITION IN THE MYTHOLOGY OF A CARIB TRIBE

Helmut Schindler
Arbeitsgruppe für Humanethologie, Max-Planck-Institut für
Verhaltensphysiologie, Percha/Starnberg

The Carijona used to occupy the tropical lowlands of southeastern Colombia. Their territory encompassed the area between the tributaries of the Rio Yarí and the headwaters of the Rio Apaporis.[1] Today, descendants of Carijona who were recruited to work as rubber gatherers during the first decades of the 20th century live near La Pedrera on the Rio Caquetá and in Puerto Nare on the Rio Vaupés, close to Miraflores. These groups number approximately 30 persons each, and intermarriage with non-Carijona has taken place within them.

Carijona is the name the members of the tribe gave themselves, but to the Creole population they were known by various other names (see Friede [1948], Koch-Grünberg [1908, 1910]; different spellings of names referring to the Carijona have been compiled by Durbin and Seijas [1973: 22]). The Brazilians named them Umaua, while the inhabitants of the tributary regions of the Rio Caquetá called them Huaque or Mesaya Indians. Population estimates for the Carijona as a whole dating from the middle of the 19th century are as high as 4,000–10,000 persons (Cuervo 1894: 474, 490ff., 500; Pérez 1862: 472).

In the literature one can find several names for the Carijona that can now be identified with certainty as clan names. It is not surprising that these clan names entered ethnological literature as tribal appellations, since the Carijona themselves call these clans nowadays by the Spanish term *tribus*. Table 5.1 lists clan names, together with their English glosses and variant spellings.

Carijona clan affiliation was reckoned patrilineally, and residence was uxorilocal. In the literature it has been occasionally maintained that all male inhabitants of a village belonged to the same clan (Schindler 1974: 459). This cannot be reconciled with the uxorilocal rule, which is referred to so frequently in the myths that it cannot be a recent innovation. On the other hand, it is possible that a village was named after the particular clan that commanded the greatest number of male residents, or after the clan to which its headman belonged.

None of the extensive reports on the Carijona fail to mention that they were cannibals and that for this reason they were continually at war with the neighboring Witoto (Cuervo 1894: 260, 475; Marcoy 1869: 386ff; Marcoy 1875: 379ff; Martius 1867: 545; Pérez 1862: 430, 438, 471ff, 475). Moreover, the Arawakan and Tukanoan tribes to the east of the Carijona still remember the attacks by their once-dreaded neighbors (Jacopin 1970: 155; Reichel-Dolmatoff 1971: personal communication).

At least as early as the 18th century, but most probably even earlier, the Carijona had trade contacts with the Spanish-speaking population of the Piedmont region to the northwest; from at least the 19th century onwards

---

1. The Rio Yarí is one of the tributaries of the Rio Caquetá-Yapurá; its own headwaters wind through savannas that stretch from the Sierra de Magdalena southward to the vicinity of the Rio Caguan. At approximately 1° north latitude, the Rio Yarí then enters the tropical forest. In its lower stretches, it receives the waters of the Rio Mesay, whose northern sources spring from the Mesas del Iguaje, in a region characterized by forest interspersed with stony savannas.

NOTE: My fieldwork with the Carijona as well as part of the elaboration of the material was made possible by grants from the Deutsche Forschungsgemeinschaft. I am also indebted to Mr. Laszlo Vajda for his critical comments on an earlier version of this article.

TABLE 5.1
Carijona Clan Names

Carijona Term	English Gloss	Other Terms Used in Literature
Sahasaha	ant people	Tsahatshaha, Cabacabas
Kaikutshiyana	jaguar people	Caicushana
Mahotoyana	fire people	
Hianakoto	harpy eagle people	Riama, Piana
Yakaoyana	green fly people	
Tshohone	duck people	
Roroyana	loro-parrot people	
Sukahasa	digging-stick people	

they traded with the Brazilians as well, exchanging wax and curare for iron goods, glass beads, mirrors, and other trinkets (Coudreau 1887: 161; Cuervo 1894: 260, 262, 266, 492; Pérez 1862: 430, 464, 468). At the beginning of the 20th century, the Carijona were incorporated into the extraction industry along the middle Rio Apaporis, working as *caucheros* (rubber gatherers) for the Creole Salvador Perera. Until 1970 they worked for Marcos Mora, whose father had also been a *patron* of the Carijona in the rubber industry. As of 1970, the Carijona workers have taken over the rubber processing ports for themselves, and most of the young men are engaged in this industry.

My fieldwork took place in 1970–71 in Puerto Nare on the Rio Vaupés. The older men of this settlement were especially willing to tell me about their former way of life, their religion, and their folktales. These men had extensive knowledge of the traditional culture, which had been almost completely lost among the young people. Marcos Mora put himself at my disposal and acted as translator. He had been living with Carijona for nearly four decades, ever since his father had brought them to the Vaupés around the year 1933. Marcos Mora speaks the language fluently, and young Carijona like to point out that he speaks it better than they themselves.

The body of this paper consists of abstracts of seven

Carijona man preparing a roof covering

folktales of the Carijona,[2] and a discussion of some characteristics of Carijona ideology that are embedded in them. My explanations are based upon the content of all Carijona folktales known to me, a corpus of 38 stories.

I should state here that I use the term "ideology" in the same way that Sebag (1964) used it. It coincides largely with terms like "religion," "belief," and some others that Hahn (1973: 208) has listed. In the following discussion, ideology refers to that level of the belief system which is corroborated by statements in the folktales. Obviously, there are other levels of Carijona ideology that are not expressed in the folktales.

THE TALES

Tale 1

Several brothers went into the jungle to get smoked meat for a dance festival. Their two sisters decided to visit them. On the way, the girls came to a brook where intestines were floating downstream, and they assumed that these came from the animals their brothers had

Carijona men at dance festival

2. The detailed texts of these folktales will be published in German.

killed. As the sisters followed the brook they came to a hut, which they thought was their brothers' hunting camp. Inside the hut there was much smoked meat and a large frog. It was the house of the *itutarï* [a jungle demon], who soon returned with a lot of game. As he caught sight of the girls, he jumped towards them in order to grab them. He caught the older sister, while the younger managed to escape. The older sister was tickled by the *itutarï* until she died of laughter. The younger ran home and told her relatives what had happened. Some men sneaked back to the hut, where they heard the *itutarï* sing his song: "I cannot be killed with the axe, because my shoulder blades are axes. I cannot be killed with a club, because my arms are clubs. I cannot be killed with a bludgeon, because my legs are guns. I can be killed only with the *warumaimï* reed." The people returned home and reported all they had heard. Thereupon the girl's brothers went to the *itutarï*'s hut and cooked a dish of palm larvae, to which they added a lot of pepper. While the *itutarï* was gone they broke all the water containers in his hut and smashed the mouth of the frog. One man then hid in the roof truss. When the *itutarï* came home, the frog wanted to draw his attention to the man above him, but it could not speak distinctly any more, and therefore the *itutarï* could not understand it. He tried the dish of palm larvae and immediately the pepper burned his mouth terribly. Since the *itutarï* could not find any water in the house, he ran to the brook, threw himself on his stomach, and began to drink. The man climbed down from the roof truss and killed him with the *warumaimï*.

Tale 2

A man went to the river to fish. On the bank, the *itutarï* was scooping water into the man's canoe. Surprised, the man thought to himself, "He has big testicles." The *itutarï* turned around and asked the man, "What did you say?" But the latter denied having said anything. "If you want to have your canoe back, bring me *peraman* [an adhesive made from wax and resin] to eat," ordered the *itutarï*. The man promised to fetch this immediately from his house.

He returned home and didn't dare go out for three days. On the third day he said to his wife, who was roasting manioc cakes, "I am going to fetch the fruits of the *mariha* palm" [species unknown], and he went on his way. As he came to the palm tree, the *itutarï* approached him. Because the man hadn't brought any *peraman,* the *itutarï* tried to hit him with his club, but the man succeeded in avoiding the blow with a swift movement. "The fruits of this palm tree are very good to eat, too," said the man, and he climbed up. He cut off one fruit,

Itutarï mask

took the stone out, and threw the pulp down for the *itutarï* to try. The latter found it excellent and wanted more of it. Thereupon the man said to him, "You had better lie down on your back with your arms and legs stretched out and catch the fruits I will cut for you, so none of them will get lost." The *itutarï* followed this suggestion. The man then cut a large cluster of fruits, which fell down and squashed the *itutarï* completely. Three days later the man returned to the spot where this had happened and burned the body. When he returned after some time, many kinds of plants with edible fruit were growing there, except for manioc.

Tale 3

In the river there lived a giant snake that always devoured people when they sat down on a rock on the riverbank. For this reason a man made a basketry framework out of strong lianas and gave it the appearance of a human being by using a certain tree bark [from which masks are made]. He placed this basketry figure on a rock and then sat inside, equipped with a drum and a sharp knife. As soon as the snake had swallowed the figure with the man inside, the man began to drum continuously in the snake's belly. This continual noise coming from its insides made the giant snake madder and madder. Desperately, it swam up and down the river. When it finally came to a shallow spot, the man cut open the snake's belly and jumped out, thereby killing it. But the worms that lived in the belly of the giant snake had attached themselves in the man's ears, nose, and eyes, and he died shortly thereafter.

Tale 4

Two sisters were alone at home. A water demon came to them in the form of their older brother and suggested that they dance with him. The older sister agreed and the three held hands with each other. The demon sang a song that the older brother often used to sing, and they danced to it. The younger sister whispered to the older, "This is not our brother." But the older answered, "Naturally, it's he. This song is the one he always sings." After the dance the demon suggested that they go closer to the riverbank and continue dancing. The younger sister repeatedly warned the older that this was not their older brother, but the older sister disregarded her warnings. After each dance they went closer to the riverbank. All of a sudden the demon jumped into the water and dragged the older sister with him. The younger was able to pull away at the last moment and rescue herself by jumping backwards.

Tale 5

A man had a wife who had various lovers, but refused him her sexual favors because she didn't like him. Therefore, one day the man took his wife alone into the jungle and killed her. Then he cut her to pieces and smoked her, put the pieces into a basket, and returned to the village. Near the village he put the basket down and spat several times in wide circles. Then he went to the village and told his mother-in-law that her daughter would soon come, too. The old woman went out of the village and called her daughter in a loud voice, but instead of the dead, the spittle answered, once from one direction, then from the other. The woman followed the calls and wandered around in the jungle for a long time. Finally she discovered the basket and found out what had happened to her daughter. She ran back to the village and informed the others. The brothers-in-law grabbed their weapons and pursued the man, who climbed on a rock, using a liana. When he arrived on top, he cut the liana and sang a song in which he described his wife as smoked meat of a howler monkey. He remained on top of the rock forever.

Tale 6

Some kingfishers lay in their hammocks and rocked back and forth by pushing themselves with a stick [a reference to their long beaks]. They sang, "Itshurekwa is hunting without worry while his wife makes love to Kanakanani." Because Itshurekwa heard their song from far away, he came over and told the kingfishers to repeat the song. When they refused, he broke their sticks, whereupon they sang the song again. Then Itshurekwa wanted to see for himself that his wife had a lover. He climbed a tree on the riverbank. Soon his wife came to the river and struck the water with a gourd bowl, whereupon the water began to subside, and the water demon Kanakanani appeared in the shape of a handsome man. As he began to make love to the woman on a sandbank, Itshurekwa sent a gadfly against Kanakanani, and it killed him. The demon rolled off the woman, who ran back to the house. Itshurekwa went to the water, cut off Kanakanani's penis, and wrapped it up in leaves. Then he returned to the house, where his wife was just about to prepare manioc cakes, and put the package on the roasting plate. The wife assumed that her husband was roasting a big larva and began to eat a piece of it together with manioc. When he hinted to her what she was chewing, she ran to the water and vomited. The bits of the penis changed into *sabaleta* fish, the bits of manioc into thornbacks. Itshurekwa ran after his wife and slew her with the pole used for stretching the *tipiti*. She changed into a dolphin and the pole into an electric eel.

Tale 7

A girl was abducted by an *iwo* [the ghost of a dead person]. Her father looked for her all over and finally learned from a shaman where to find her. Several of her relatives went to look for her and discovered her in a clearing of the jungle, where she was rocking in a hammock. Her child, whom she had begotten with the *iwo*, was with her, but the *iwo* was out hunting. The people surrounded the girl and then caught her suddenly. When the girl had recovered from the shock of the attack, she told her relatives, "I am satisfied with my life here." "You have already become a beast," the relatives reproached her. The girl did not object to being brought back to the village, but declared that she loved the father of her child, because he had treated her well. The people went back and took the young woman with them without waiting for the arrival of the *iwo*. When they came to a brook, the mother of the young woman said, "I want to bathe my grandchild here." At a convenient moment she pushed the child under water and drowned him. All grieved over the death, but except for the young

Iwo mask

woman, they were only feigning. After the *iwo* returned to find the girl missing he followed her to the village. When he arrived there, he looked like a normal human being. All ate of the partridge eggs he had brought with him, and from then on he slept in the hammock of the girl. But the *iwo* played tricks on his brothers-in-law. For example, he made an armadillo out of a spiny plant and let it walk on the floor. When the others tried to catch it, they grasped the spines. "Hihihi," the *iwo* laughed at them. One day the brothers-in-law and the *iwo* were hunting peccaries, which took refuge in a cave. The people made the *iwo* go in and he fetched one animal after the other. Finally the men said to him, "Go and see whether there really aren't any more peccaries in the cave." When he looked in, they closed the cave with a stone, so that he was locked up and died in the cave some time after.

CARIJONA IDEOLOGY

Binary oppositions play an important role in human thought. If one is investigating the ideologies of various ethnic groups, one sees again and again how a broad range of phenomena are subsumed under a convenient pair of opposed terms. Considerable differences in meaning exist between the various paired concepts, as seen in such oppositions as "body and spirit," "cosmos and chaos," "nature and culture," "Yin and Yang," and "good and bad."

A basic opposition in the ideology of the Carijona is designated by the terms *karihona* and *manakïnï*. The notion *karihona* obviously refers to the members of the "we-group." In the speech of today it may also be applied to Creoles and members of other tribes. But in the folktales (where the world is still in order), the term *karihona* refers only to members of the tribe. On the other hand, the semantic extension of the word *manakïnï* (a term that is frequently heard) can only be explained with the help of an enumeration. *Manakïnï* has the following usages: (1) animals in the zoological sense; (2) most of the beings we would call supernatural; (3) human beings who are not Carijona; (4) as an epithet, Carijona individuals who are asocial persons or fools.

When speaking Spanish, informants used the word *animal* to translate the native word *manakïnï*, in reference to beings that I would have classed as monsters, demons, or spirits. However, this gloss is not completely satisfactory; the German word *Tier* cannot be applied to such beings, any more than can the English word *animal*. The semantic extension of *manakïnï* comprises what we would designate as supernatural as well as natural beings.

Evans-Pritchard, among others, has called attention to the fact that the opposition "natural-supernatural" may in certain cases inhibit an understanding of non-Western beliefs. He states: "We use the word 'supernatural' when speaking of some native belief, because that is what it would mean to us, but far from increasing our understanding of it, we are likely by the use of the word to misunderstand it" (1965: 109ff). One has to understand that both the notions "natural" and "supernatural" derive from our own ideology and that they contain a statement about reality that cannot be proven empirically.

During the course of my fieldwork it was repeatedly demonstrated how little help the notion "supernatural" is in trying to understand the world view of the Carijona. For example, one of the older men explained that during the mask performances it was the task of the shamans to keep away the dangerous *manakïnï*, such as jaguars, poisonous snakes, *ikoimï*, and the *itutarï* (demon of the jungle). The Carijona use the word *ikoimï* in reference to both the boa constrictor and the anaconda, known to us as natural species. However, the word *ikoimï* is also applied to the giant snake of Tale 3, who in one moment is able to devour an entire man and in whose belly the hero of the story remains for some time; this giant snake can be only a supernatural monster for us. In the Carijona language all these beings are included in the category *ikoimï* (as all dogs are dogs for us, regardless of their breed), without making distinctions that are of basic importance for us. Similarly, when describing a jaguar, the Carijona endow it with capacities that we do not. Speaking in terms of our culture, one might say that the Carijona ascribe to this animal "supernatural powers." Yet to put it this way would hardly be helpful for understanding their conceptualization of the jaguar.

The signification of the term *manakïnï* thus seems to come closest to that of the British English term "beast." Both words often imply a certain contempt on the part of the speaker. However, "beast" is not an exact equivalent translation of *manakïnï,* and the meaning of this word must therefore be understood according to the above-mentioned qualifications.

According to Carijona ideology, there should be a definite separation between Carijona and beasts. Whereas in the mythology of other South American tribes (such as the Mundurucú) human beings may change suddenly and without difficulty into animals, and later change back again into human beings—almost as if changing a suit of clothes—the Carijona situation is very different. Here, transformation into a beast is never so simple; it always points toward a problem and is closely correlated with dying. In various cases the transformation precedes death; elsewhere it is a substitute for it, as in Tale 6, in which the woman does not die from a blow, but changes into a dolphin. In Tale 7, the mother of the young woman kills her grandchild on the way back to the village. This is no useless cruelty, but a necessity. The child was begotten by an *iwo* and is a bond between the beast and the young Carijona woman; this bond has to be destroyed as soon as possible and the gulf between Carijona and beast again enforced. Therefore, the woman has to drown her grandchild, and this must be done before the group's arrival in the village, for reasons that will be explained below.

Many folktales of the Carijona tell about events that in some way remove the barrier between Carijona and beasts. The order of the world has been disturbed. In order to restore it, the Carijona cannot hope for help from anybody. There are no "superior beings" who accomplish the separation for them; the Carijona themselves have to accomplish the task. Two kinds of beast play important roles in the life of the Carijona: the *manakïnï tanaemï,* edible beasts that are killed during hunting or fishing, and the *manakïnï inïtono,* the man-eating beasts. The latter are dangerous beings that repeatedly attack the Carijona; they play a part in most of the folktales presented in this paper. Their offenses are the following:

Tale 1: The *itutarï* kills the older sister and wants to kill the younger as well.
Tale 2: The *itutarï* tries to club the man.
Tale 3: The giant snake has been devouring Carijona.
Tale 4: The water demon drags the older girl with him into the water and tries to do the same to the younger.
Tale 7: The ghost abducts a girl.

In Tale 6, Kanakanani's making love to the wife of Itshurekwa is also a demonic offense, in the opinion of Carijona.

Beasts and Men

The folktales presented here contain various kinds of information about the general character of men and women and about the nature of beasts. Whereas men are able to fight beasts and in certain circumstances to defeat them, women are defenseless as soon as a beast lays hands on them. When encountering a dangerous beast, women at best succeed in escaping it, but never in killing it. Therefore, men are obliged to intervene when a woman has any contact with a beast. All the beasts in these folktales are endowed with more vigor than the men who finally defeat them. The *itutarï* is a jungle demon whose blow with a club can kill anyone. Shortly before dying, the *iwo* demonstrates his vigor by carrying one peccary after the other out of the cave. The giant serpent also displays considerable strength. Nevertheless, the Carijona heroes are victorious over these beasts, because they do not measure their strength against them but instead employ astute stratagems. The *itutarï* in Tale 1 is served overspiced food, and the hot pepper forces him to place himself in a helpless position, drinking from a brook. The *itutarï* of Tale 2 does not realize how he is trapped; he lies down readily and is crushed by the cluster of fruits. The *iwo* of Tale 7 allows himself to be sent back into the cave to check whether there is really no peccary left inside, and suddenly he is trapped inside. The giant serpent of Tale 3 takes the puppet for a man and devours it, only to become maddened by the noise coming out of its belly. Kanakanani might have proven a dangerous opponent, but there is no personal confrontation with him.

If in a Carijona tale a man encounters a beast in the jungle during the daytime, it is anticipated that, by using astuteness, he will be able to kill it. One man is sufficient to complete the task, and usually he is confronted with only one beast as an opponent—except in humorous tales. The situation immediately changes the moment it is dark or the beast enters the village. A beast in a village signals extreme danger, and at night it is utterly invincible. It is necessary to wait for the next day, and even then in several cases the ensuing extermination is not the deed of a single person; the inhabitants of a neighboring village have to assist in slaying the beast.

The man who kills a beast in the jungle during the day is not distinguished by being named, probably because he is only doing what is expected of a man. Only those who deviate positively or negatively from the average human are given names in the tales; these men are either shamans, who have more capabilities than usual, or inept or comical persons. The one who excels is named —and in a humorous story both extremes may meet and the fool be turned into a shaman.

In Tale 6 the woman's husband has a name, and in the initial episode, Itshurekwa's ability to communicate with beasts is indicated by the fact that kingfishers inform him about the escapades of his wife. This message that Itshurekwa is not an ordinary man is emphasized by the fact that he sends an insect against Kanakanani, who is killed by the sting. This proves that the man is an extraordinary person with special knowledge, for traditionally among the Carijona, only shamans were able to communicate with beasts. Even though Itshurekwa is not specifically identified as a shaman, capabilities similar to those of a shaman are ascribed to him. Moreover, in Carijona tales, shamans cannot be called to account for their deeds by ordinary Carijona. This may help to explain why retaliation against Itshurekwa is not even considered. Finally, Itshurekwa's trespass is minimized at the end; the woman does not die, but changes into a dolphin. As mentioned above, the transformation from Carijona to beast has a strong correlation with death. In this case, however, an advantage is taken of the belief that death and transformation—despite their close correlation—are not identical.

In Tale 3, with the help of the basketry figure and the drum, the man succeeds in killing the giant serpent but has to pay with his life, because the worms from the serpent's belly eat him up. Why should this be? The answer may be as follows: even though the man killed the giant serpent according to the rules—by his astuteness—he violated another principle, which I would like to call the opposition of distance and intimacy. Too much intimacy with beasts is hazardous to human life. In order to successfully eliminate a beast, it is best to keep a certain distance. A vertical distance promises the greatest advantage—that is, one should kill the beast from an elevated position. For example, the man who crushes the *itutarï* with the clusters of palm fruit is acting from the height of a tree. Likewise, Itshurekwa is up in a tree when he shoots his opponent with the sting of an insect. In Tale 1, the man hides in the roof and kills the beast as soon as it lies down on the ground. However, the man in Tale 3 was violating these rules: he managed to get inside

the giant serpent and consequently was eaten by the worms from the monster's belly. According to Carijona ideology, women are not capable of killing—in the correct way, that is: from a distance, as the Carijona men do when hunting game in daily life. This is the reason women cannot do much against beasts, as mentioned earlier.

The capability for killing that men possess by no means conveys only positive connotations, since in the tales the victims are not only opponents of Carijona but also some Carijona themselves. Nevertheless, there are restrictions on the ways in which one Carijona kills another. No tale is known in which this is done within the village. The man who intends to kill his unfaithful wife takes her into the jungle, and Itshurekwa slays his wife near the water.

In Tale 7, when the *iwo* does not find his wife, he follows her trail. Two details are important for the action that follows. First, he does not catch up with her on the way back to the village, but arrives in the village itself later on. Second, he introduces himself into the community by means of a gift, the bird's eggs, which are accepted and eaten by the Carijona; this makes him a member of the village, and he is protected by a truce that is always in effect among all such members.

If one man is sufficient to liquidate a beast in the jungle during the day (as mentioned above), why then do the brothers join forces to lock the *iwo* in the cave? To answer this question we have to find out in which other situations an ordinary human being is confronted by several other persons. The human opponent appears in Tale 5, in which several people persecute the man who has killed and smoked his wife. In both cases a distinct rule is observed: one person alone must not execute retaliation against another inhabitant of a village.

In the second part of Tale 7, the *iwo* is constantly pestering the Carijona with his pranks. Yet it is only his social relationship with Carijona that provides the chance to liquidate the monster. Once having become a member of the community, he cannot be killed either within the village or by one person alone. The killing has to take place outside the village and has to be done by a group of men; consequently the *iwo* has to be led into a deadly trap. (Similarly, his child has to be killed on the way back, before entering the village.) Therefore, the plot had to be constructed in such a way that the *iwo* does not catch up with the group bringing home his wife, but joins them only after their arrival in the village.

Itutarï, Edible Plants, and Manioc

In another paper I have dealt extensively with the tales of the *itutarï* (Schindler 1973); here I shall briefly review some of the results presented there. Many useful plants originate from the body of the dead *itutarï*, but not bitter manioc, which, according to one Carijona tale, was originally discovered growing on a tree (this motif has a wide distribution in South America [Zerries 1969]). The *itutarï* cannot be killed by weapons, but only by a blow with a soft plant, which the Carijona call *warumaimï*. Why should this be? B. J. Hoff (1973: personal communication) has called my attention to the possibility that this might be understood by analogy with certain characteristics of Kurupi, the forest monster of the Kariña. In some ways, Kurupi is the opposite of human beings: he uses serpents as plates and as ropes, but is afraid of the sting of lianas; his bows and arrows look like toys but are very effective (see also Hoff 1968: 290ff).

However, this does not explain precisely why the *warumaimï* plant is able to kill the *itutarï*. The following might serve as an explanation. The word *warumaimï* consists of the word *waruma* and the postposition *-imï*, which Koch-Grünberg (1908: 962) translated as "bigness"; this meaning certainly holds true in many cases. The equivalent in Kariña, the postposition *-imo*, might best be translated as "dangerous" and "similar," according to B. J. Hoff (1973: personal communication). *Waruma*, like *warumaimï*, is a reedlike plant (*Ischnosiphon* sp., belonging to the *Marantaceae*), and outer strips of the stems are used for making utensils by numerous tribes of the tropical forest of South America. If one asks a Carijona what *waruma* is good for, he will point to the *tipití*, with which the juice is pressed out of the grated manioc roots, and to various other utensils, most of them likewise used for the preparation of manioc. After harvesting, manioc may be carried home in a basket made out of *waruma* strips. Before the manioc pulp is

roasted, the larger woody pieces are removed with a sieve, whose surface is plaited out of *waruma* strips.

The manioc is finally served in a round pannier plaited of *waruma* strips, and a similar basket is used for washing the starch out of the manioc pulp. *Warumaimï* can be used to manufacture the same utensils as are made from *waruma*, but *warumaimï* is rarely used because it is less durable. I would suggest that there is an association made between *warumaimï*, *waruma*, and manioc, and that these plants stand in opposition to the plants grown out of the *itutarï*. In the tales this opposition is translated into the idea that a blow by the *warumaimï* is deadly for the *itutarï*.

It is still unclear, however, why the *itutarï* of Tale 2 scoops water into the man's boat; perhaps this serves only to indicate that the beast is an aggressor. The *itutarï* asks for *peraman* because this is one of his favorite dishes. The big testicles are evidence of the *itutarï*'s fertility, which is later manifested in the origin of edible plants.

Beasts and Women

The tales define the character of women rather negatively. In various cases women are not able to distinguish monsters from Carijona. This is most clearly expressed in Tale 4, in which the older girl takes the monster for her brother despite the warnings of her younger sister, who alone saves herself. In Tales 6 and 7 the women have monstrous beings as sexual partners. Tales 5 and 6 point to a related characteristic of women, which is referred to by Carijona men both in their stories and in daily conversations—namely, their sexual appetite.

Carijona woman

If the ideology states that women possess a strong sexual appetite which repeatedly leads to escapades, then the same ideology should maintain that husbands accept cuckoldry with nonchalance. But if a man must react with jealousy to the escapades of his wife, then the ideology contains a contradiction that is the source of continuous conflict in everyday life. This is precisely the situation among the Carijona. In their reports about daily life my male informants repeatedly talked about the extramarital relations of women and the jealousy of men. Through uxorilocal residence, wives were protected by their relatives. Murder of wives, I learned, did not occur. In the tales, however, such killings are mentioned; Benedict (1935: xix) appropriately labeled similar occurrences as daydreams. Two of the tales involve men who slay their unfaithful wives, but the details of the two stories vary considerably. In Tale 5 the woman deceives her husband with Carijona men. After murdering her the man has to escape to a high rock, pursued by his brothers-in-law. He is not killed (probably because he has the sympathy of the male listeners to the story), but he commits social suicide and remains outlawed. On the rock he sings a mocking song about his wife, whom he smoked like a howler monkey. He had thereby marked her as a beast. In Tale 6 there is a significant difference. Here the woman's lover is not a Carijona but a beast, and her aberration is therefore greater. She crosses a border that all Carijona should strive to maintain.

In the folktales the typical occupation of a righteous woman is the processing of manioc. To do this work, women remain most of the time in the village, leaving only to dig roots in the gardens. When it is casually men-tioned (as in Tale 2) that the woman is preparing manioc cakes, this indicates that she is acting properly, that she is innocent. Of course, this activity provides an opportunity for the wife to mislead the husband: she can pretend to fulfill her duties, but as soon as her husband turns his back, she visits her lover. Similarly, after the water demon is killed, Itshurekwa's wife runs back to the house in order to roast manioc cakes, thus pretending to be innocent.

The uxorilocality of the Carijona is reflected in the behavior of men towards their sisters. It is the brothers' role to be the protectors and the revengers of their sisters. After the *itutarï* has tickled the older girl to death (Tale 1), the brothers prepare for the killing of the beast, and one of them finally kills the *itutarï* near the water. In Tale 5, after killing his wife, the husband is pursued by her brothers until he reaches the rock where he takes refuge.

Even though the kidnapping of the girl by the *iwo* in Tale 7 no doubt represents an offense against the Carijona, in the first part of the story the killing of the beast is not a goal. Only the worst abuses have to be remedied. The girl has to be brought back from the jungle to the community of the Carijona; because she is not able to recognize her aberration herself, her relatives have to fetch her. (Since a woman does not oppose men directly, this might be the reason the girl allows herself to be brought back to the village without resisting.) Finally, the child has to be killed since it represents living evidence of the ignominious union between a Carijona woman and a beast.

REFERENCES

Benedict, Ruth
1935   *Zuñi Mythology,* vol. 1. New York: Columbia Univ. Press.

Coudreau, Henri A.
1887   *La France équinoxiale.* Vol. II: *Voyage à travers les Guayanes et l'Amazonie.* Paris.

Cuervo, Antonio B.
1894   *Colección de documentos inéditos sobre la geografía y la historia de Colombia,* vol. 4. Bogota.

Durbin, Marshall, and Haydée Seijas
1973   Proto Hianacoto: Guaque-Carijona-Hianacoto Umaua. *International Journal of American Linguistics* 39: 22–31.

Evans-Pritchard, E. E.
1965   *Theories of Primitive Religion.* Oxford: Oxford Univ. Press.

Friede, Juan
1948   Algunos apuntes sobre los Karijona-Huaque del Caqueta. In *Actes du XXVIIIe Congrès International des Américanistes* (Paris, 1947), pp. 255–63.

Hahn, Robert A.
1973   Understanding Beliefs: An Essay on the Methodology of the Statement and Analysis of Belief Systems. *Current Anthropology* 14: 207–24.

Hoff, B. J.
1968   *The Carib Language.* The Hague: Martinus Nijhoff. *Verhandelingen van het Koninklijk Instituut voor Taal-, Land- en Volkenkunde* 55.

Jacopin, Pierre-Yves
1970   Mission chez les Indiens Yukuna de la région du Miritiparaná, Amazonie Colombienne. *Journal de la Société des Américanistes* 59: 155–63.

Koch-Grünberg, Theodor
1908   Die Hianakoto-Umáua. *Anthropos* 3: 1–112.

1910   *Zwei Jahre unter den Indianern: Reisen in Nordwest-Brasilien,* vol. 2. Berlin: Ernst Wasmuth.

Marcoy, Paul
1869   *Voyage à travers l'Amérique du Sud de l'Océan Pacifique à l'Océan Atlantique,* vol. 2. Paris.

1875   *Travels in South America from the Pacific Ocean to the Atlantic Ocean,* vol. 2. London.

Martius, Karl Friedrich Philipp von
1867   *Beiträge zur Ethnographie und Sprachenkunde Amerikas, zumal Brasiliens,* vol. 1. Leipzig.

Pérez, Felipe
1862   *Jeografía física y política de los Estados Unidos de Colombia,* vol. 1. Bogota.

Schindler, Helmut
1973   Warum kann man den Itutari mit dem Gwaruma erschlagen? *Zeitschrift für Ethnologie* 98 (2): 246–76.

1974   Die Stellung der Carijona im Kulturareal Nordwestomazonien. In *Atti de XL Congresso Internazionale degli Americanisti* (Rome–Genoa, 1972), vol. 2: 457–67.

Sebag, Lucien
1964   *Marxisme et structuralisme.* Paris: Payot.

Zerries, Otto
1969   Entstehung oder Erwerb der Kulturpflanzen und Beginn des Bodenbaues im Mythos der Indianer Sudamerikas. *Paideuma* 15: 64–124 (Wiesbaden).

6. ON BEING CARIB

Lee Drummond
Department of Anthropology, University of Montana

This paper has to do with the social history of a word, the way in which a designation acquires new meaning and importance, and, finally, the process through which people attach labels and evaluations to themselves and others.

In South American ethnography, "Carib" has generally been used as a generic term in referring to groups of Amerindians that are or were scattered throughout the islands and the mainland north of the Amazon (Steward and Faron 1959: 289). For the most part, the classification is based on linguistic criteria. Carib-speaking groups need have no traceable affinity in space or time; it is enough that their languages are identifiable as belonging to a common linguistic stock. A Kalapalo is unconscious even of the existence of his linguistic brethren in French Guiana and Dominica and, if enlightened, would not identify himself as a member of a social group embracing those remote individuals—just as I would find little sense in identifying myself as a citizen of the world or as a member of the class of adult males over five feet tall.

In the Guiana region the presence of several Carib-speaking groups has created a complex situation in that the existence of these separate groups, all with unique "tribal" names, has occasioned some confusion in the process of matching the label "Carib" with particular individuals and groups. While it may seem an easy matter to keep linguistic criteria separate from the identification of social groups, there is a correspondingly natural inclination—even for professionals—to believe that a Carib Indian has something Carib about him.

Almost a century ago im Thurn made a confusion of this sort the basis of a theory of pre-Columbian migration in the Guianas[1] (1883: 171–73). On the premise that

---

1. Im Thurn's discussion of Guyana's Amerindians is couched within a general taxonomic system of hemispheric proportions. The system is based on a suspicious linguistic analogy and derives its force from an evolutionary assumption. Thus, all Amerindians are members of a single *race* as evidenced by the fact that they all speak polysynthetic languages. The Amerindian race is composed of numerous *branches* according to similarity in linguistic "structure" (im Thurn does not elaborate on this term, and his comparative linguistic analysis consists of brief word lists from vocabularies of the various Guyanese Amerindian languages). He recognized four branches among the Guyanese groups: Arawak, Carib, Warrau (Warao), and "Wapiana" (the Wapishana, who inhabit the southern Rupununi savanna, in fact speak an Arawakan language whose lexicon is very different from that of the coastal Arawak tongue). Each branch in turn is represented by one or more *tribes.* The tribe is, for im Thurn, the nexus between linguistic and social structures. In his taxonomy the tribe is the first unit in which social interaction takes precedence over linguistic classification. In the case of the Arawak and Warrau, each branch is represented within the borders of Guyana by only one tribe, whereas the Carib and Wapiana branches have six and three, respectively (two Wapiana-branch tribes were almost absorbed or extinct at the time im Thurn's book was published, and today they no longer exist). The smallest unit in his taxonomy is the *family,* a term he invested with the rather special meaning of "clan" because of his experience with the coastal Arawak matrilineal nonlocalized clan organization. A family that became large and isolated from its tribe could, through cumulative dialect changes, become a tribe in its own right, and by extension a tribe could become a branch.

The taxonomy accomplishes little, but I find it highly significant as a testimony to the absence of neat, self-evident social divisions among Guyana's Amerindian groups and to the consequent need for the ethnographer to supply some kind of theoretical distinctions that identify individuals as belonging to A, B, or C. Im Thurn's attempt was a necessary first step in exploring the difficult concept of ethnicity.

people who speak similar languages must have had a common origin, im Thurn speculated about the origins of several Carib groups in what was then British Guiana—now Guyana. (I have opted to use the latter name throughout this paper, despite the occasional anachronism involved, and have retained the customary term "the Guianas" when referring to the geographic region between the mouths of the Amazon and Orinoco rivers.)[2] For im Thurn, a common origin, of course, meant a specific place or region—the fount of Carib culture—and he found the obvious solution to this Genesis puzzle in the Lesser Antilles, home of the island Carib. Having fixed on a spot, he was saddled with the consequence of every evolutionary solution: the very considerable problem of accounting for the diverse geographical locations and customs of peoples reputed to have had a common origin. Im Thurn met this challenge with alacrity, setting forth hypotheses as to the order of migration and even the probable routes followed by the several Carib groups in Guyana (1883: 173–74). Thus the Makusi, savanna dwellers on Guyana's borders with Brazil and Venezuela, were featured as some of the earliest emigrants from the islands via the Orinoco River. The Makusi did not stay long on the Orinoco, im Thurn argued, because a later wave of Arekuna emigrants forced them to the headwaters and, eventually, overland to their present savanna habitat. To tribes inhabiting the mountainous forests nearer the coast, like the Akawaio and Patamona, im Thurn assigned a different migratory route. He supposed that these Carib groups originally landed on the Guiana coast and, unable to displace the Arawak they found living there, traveled up the rivers to settle in the mountainous interior. In this way im Thurn worked his way to the coast, equating space with time and assuming all the

while that there was something significant in the fact that these various Amerindian groups were all "Carib."

It was at this point in his evolutionary narrative that im Thurn encountered the problem of how to classify the coastal Carib groups such as those living on the Pomeroon River, where he wrote the preface to *Among the Indians of Guiana*. These groups not only spoke a Carib language but called themselves Carib, or by names that got translated into that term by Europeans who wrote about them. The coastal groups, that is, were not Makusi Carib or Waiwai Carib or Arekuna Carib, but Carib Carib. Led to this redundancy by his first premise concerning the relationship of language to group identity, im Thurn coined the term "True Caribs" to distinguish the coastal and island groups from the interior tribes (1883: 163).

Like the true American and the true believer, the True Carib is an inherently improbable and, one suspects, contradictory being. The island Carib, and even the Orinoco Carib, provide a poor model for im Thurn's portrait of a cohesive, stable society or "people." An examination of Roth's lengthy compendia of Guiana's tribes and their customs and manufactures (1915, 1924) provides convincing testimony to the fractionated nature of social organization in that part of the world—where myriad groups are scattered along a tangle of waterways, each group identified by a separate (tribal?) name and tied to other groups in the area by tenuous and sporadic encounters.

Both im Thurn and Roth relied heavily on their experiences on the Pomeroon River of Guyana for their information regarding coastal Carib groups, and yet at the time they wrote the Pomeroon Carib had undergone generations of a refugee-like existence in the bush. The population of Pomeroon Carib in the period 1880–1920

2. Since this paper is about the significance of a name, I shall mention some of the complexities involved in writing about Guyana. When the colony of British Guiana became independent in 1966, it became officially the nation of Guyana. The orthographic change was accompanied by a change in pronunciation, with the initial vowel (sounded as the *e* in *e*vent) of Guiana becoming the diphthong *ai* in Guyana. The new orthography, although not the pronunciation, is close to the Venezuelan Spanish, *Guayana*. These seemingly minor changes may nevertheless be invested with considerable affect by some contemporary Guyanese; a person using the old pronunciation (even though unconsciously) may be branded a conservative, whereas a government official delivering a political address may be especially careful to sound the diphthong.

The matter becomes more complicated in referring to events with any time depth. Thus, did im Thurn write about the "Indians of Guiana" (the title of his book) or about Guyanese Amerindians? Should I refer to him as an "observer of the Guyanese scene" when he never saw a day break on the new nation? North American writers

have to strain to grasp the political sensibilities involved in these nuances of meaning. We write from a long history of political independence and have long since become inured to the nice distinctions of freedom and servitude contained in some of our apparently unassuming proper nouns. A writer on the subject of North American Indian history would feel himself needlessly criticized for neglecting to refer to the early Iroquois as "British colonial Indians" or some such epithet rather than "American Indians," yet two centuries ago political relations between European powers, American colonies, and the Indian tribes made such distinctions quite pertinent.

As I write, Guyana is involved in a border dispute with Venezuela over the territory where I did my fieldwork, so that the parallels between the American colonial and Guyanese situations are quite close. There is the remote possibility that Guyanese Indians who were formerly Guianese Indians may, if Venezuela carries the day, become Guayanese Indians. Given this tenuous state of affairs, Guyanese officials are understandably a bit touchy about the lexicon of foreign writers.

consisted of those who had survived the depredations of smallpox, measles, influenza, and pneumonia. These survivors were themselves descendants of Carib who had fled from Spanish soldiers in Venezuela or from emancipated slaves in other parts of Guyana. This calamitous heritage left the Pomeroon Carib with only vestiges of whatever indigenous social structure they had once possessed. By 1970 Creole English was the household language in a majority of Carib homes, most Carib were baptized members of the Anglican Church, and the one Carib settlement of any size on the upper Pomeroon (St. Monica, or *turu rab*) was the site of a school staffed by Creole teachers. With this kind of social history, the "True Carib" might be better called the "ex-Carib," for he is truly a chimerical figure. Yet the historical process that so thoroughly "deculturated" the Carib in the Guianas and the Caribbean also created a vivid image or ethnic stereotype of the Carib that has had considerable appeal to the popular imagination. In this respect the Carib is like the Plains Indian, for both captured the imagination of Europeans and white Americans as they were being nearly exterminated by them. We can see in our mind's eye the Carib in the prow of his war canoe, just as we can see the Plains Indian on a buffalo hunt, but the images we conjure up are so vivid only because those life-styles were dramatically curtailed by the expansion of Western settlement.

Im Thurn was led to the creation of the fictional being, the True Carib, in what must be one of anthropology's earliest attempts to define differences between social units, ethnic groups, and tribes. The problems he encountered in delineating groups of people and in attempting to reconcile their linguistic differences with their social affinities are highly complex and still provide subjects for anthropological discussion; im Thurn's reading of Guyanese ethnography cannot be dismissed as a piece of linguistic naïveté.

I think it is worth while to ask why a long-term observer of the Guyanese scene like im Thurn should have felt compelled to characterize the Carib groups of interior and coastal Guyana as a type, disregarding differences in region, habitat, and custom to lump together a number of tribes that share something recognizable only to a trained linguist. I believe the answer is fairly obvious: he used a term that was in wide circulation and that seemed to have a certain intellectual closure. A scholar resident in the Caribbean for extended periods, or simply conversant with Caribbean literature, could not have avoided being exposed to the stereotypical notion of the Carib Indian that had its roots in the first voyage of Columbus (see, for example, Sauer 1966: 31). The European experience in the Caribbean and the Guianas was not with such groups as the Oyana, Taino, Wapishana, or Trio, but with one of two kinds of Indians, as different in the colonists' eyes as night and day: the Arawak and the Carib. The Carib were distinguish-

able as a people by their warlike nature; they, or their ancestors, had pillaged and cannibalized throughout the Lesser Antilles and along the "Wild Coast" of the Guianas. The Arawak, in contrast, were notable for their "pacific disposition" (as *Webster's New International Dictionary*, second edition, summed up the consensus of travelers' wisdom). They submitted to extermination with admirable grace and, where a few survived, settled down peacefully in villages near colonial settlements.

In contemporary Guyana, representatives of the Carib "race" (I use the word that occurred in a number of interviews I have had with Amerindian and non-Amerindian Guyanese) are frequently characterized on the basis of sentiment rather than social structure. In most cases it is not as important for a Pomeroon Creole farmer to know of a particular Carib that he belongs to such and such a community and is the son or daughter of so and so as it is for him to know that the individual has a belligerent streak in him, is proud, and holds himself apart from other men, Indian and non-Indian alike. Again like the Plains Indian, the Carib is a notion to conjure with; the word calls forth strong associations, vivid images, and, eventually, professional opinions in which the Carib is featured as a member of a canoe-bound master race that spread itself over a respectable portion of the continent. Im Thurn was himself immersed in the historical tradition that gave rise to the stereotype and was consequently inclined to regard the presence of Carib-speaking groups in widely scattered areas of Guyana as evidence of a concerted migration, rather than as a demonstration of the conservative nature of language and as the residue of a centuries-old colonizing process.

Sentiment, with its origins in history and prejudice, takes precedence over social structural features of Arawak and Carib life primarily because there is little in the physical appearance or speech of individual Caribs to distinguish them from other coastal Amerindians, notably the Arawak and Warao. On the Pomeroon River, for instance, the upriver area is occupied by two Amerindian groups, the Arawak and Carib, living contiguously and exhibiting few immediately perceptible differences. Members of both groups speak Creole English fluently, and it is the language of choice for most Arawak and Carib. Rather more Carib than Arawak remain fluent in their indigenous tongue, but this is a difference that may be noted only in the privacy of individual households. When members of the two groups travel downriver to the market town, or when Arawak and Carib delegations journey to Georgetown, their dress and demeanor make tribal distinctions all but impossible for anyone not personally acquainted with the individuals. Nor is there a clear distinction between Arawak and Carib on the level of social organization. The residence pattern on the upper Pomeroon does not consist in isolated villages of Arawak and Carib, but primarily in individual households or small household clusters dispersed over several hundred miles of rivers and creeks (see Map 6.1). While there is an Arawak settlement of thirteen households, and a Carib settlement of nine households, the most significant units in the residence system are actually Arawak and Carib *sections* of the river. The Arawak section is downriver from the Carib section and contains about 100 households, not all of which are Arawak. The Carib section occupies the most remote settled part of the Pomeroon and its tributaries, and it contains more than 60 households, almost all of which are Carib. The two sections of the river shade almost imperceptibly into one another, although there is an official boundary for administrative purposes.

The absence of sharp distinctions in the language and social organization of the Arawak and Carib groups makes it tempting to speculate that it is precisely this lack of differentiation on the sociological level that encourages the Arawak and Carib to maintain an ideology of tribal identity. Regardless of the possible dialectic between idea and act here, however, the fact remains that an ideology of tribal identity does exist on the upper Pomeroon and it does enter into local politics, marriage choices, legends, and economic life. This ideology is equally a product of the colonial experience and a contributing factor in contemporary social relations, not only between Arawak and Carib but between them and Pomeroon Creole farmers and Georgetown officials. To understand what being Carib entails, at least in the Pomeroon context, both Guyanese history and Pomeroon social life must be examined. Let us first consider the historical background.

The stereotype of the Carib that originated with Columbus was strengthened by early developments in the colonial history of Guyana. When the Dutch established trading forts on Guyanese rivers in the 17th century, they discovered that some Indians were anxious to settle near them while others kept to their forest haunts and occasionally proved troublesome if enlisted by a privateer for the purpose of raiding (Rodway 1894: 13). The sedentary Indians were predominantly Arawak with a sprinkling of Warao, and they chose to live near the foreign white men for a very good reason. Their villages were being raided by the coastal Carib, who, unlike their island cousins, had not been decimated by hostile encounters with Europeans. When Carib groups did establish peaceful relations with a Dutch settlement, they tended to preserve their autonomy to a greater extent than did the Arawak. The demographic scheme in which a colonial settlement has attached to it an Arawak village, with a few Carib households at a further remove, is a feature of Guyanese social structure that has persisted for centuries.

The historical origins of Arawak and Carib stereotypes are, so far as I know, not mentioned by travelers and missionaries to Guyana such as im Thurn and the Reverend Brett, although these writers dwell on the stereotypical contrast between the peaceful Arawak and the warlike Carib. However, the Arawak's greater familiarity with European ways must have been no mystery to the early Dutch traders, as Rodway makes clear in his matter-of-fact account of conditions at Kyk-over-all, the major Dutch settlement in 17th-century Guyana:

The vicinity of the fort and the paths for traffic, were therefore centres around which the weaker Arawacks congregated, as the Caribs hardly dared to provoke their friend the Commandeur. Indian villages were then scattered all along the banks of the rivers, not as at present, only in the interior, but from the fort downwards as well. There was even a tendency to an increase of the native population in the lower districts, from the encouragement given to the production of the various articles which then formed the only exports of the settlement. [Rodway 1894: 13]

When the trading forts became the nuclei of plantations and the slave trade deposited thousands of Africans to work in the new sugar fields, the roles of Arawak and Carib were reinforced. Guyana is peculiar in having had a mercantile administrator, Laurens Storm van 's Gravesande of the Dutch West India Company, who had enough political acumen to conceive and implement a policy of divide and rule: he utilized the plantation Indians as a bush police force to terrify the burgeoning slave population (Rodway 1894: 197, 208, 219, 226; Storm van 's Gravesande 1911: 206–7). The Blacks' fear of their Indian wardens was heightened by stories of their uncanny and supernatural powers—especially the *kenaima* (a kind of vendetta murderer with unhuman abilities)—and by reports of the barbecued hands of slaves who had escaped only to be hunted down by the Indians for bounties of rum, guns, knives, and cloth. At one time, Storm van 's Gravesande had under his command 400 Arawak and 800 Carib, a truly formidable force in an era when the arrival or nonarrival of a couple of hundred soldiers could mean the difference between keeping a colony and losing it to another European power. In the scant historical references to these Indian soldiers (Rodway 1894: 197–200), there is evidence of a differentiation between Carib and Arawak. Although fewer in number, the Arawak slave fighters were better armed and more skilled in the use of firearms than their Carib counterparts. This difference suggests the arrangement already remarked on: the Arawak lived closer to the whites than did the Carib and learned more of their habits and skills.

Whatever the indigenous circumstances of Arawak and Carib groups may have been, the historical circumstances of contact and colonization created, or redefined, differences between them. For a variety of reasons, including local differences in the emigrant society into which Arawak and Carib merged, the effects of contact

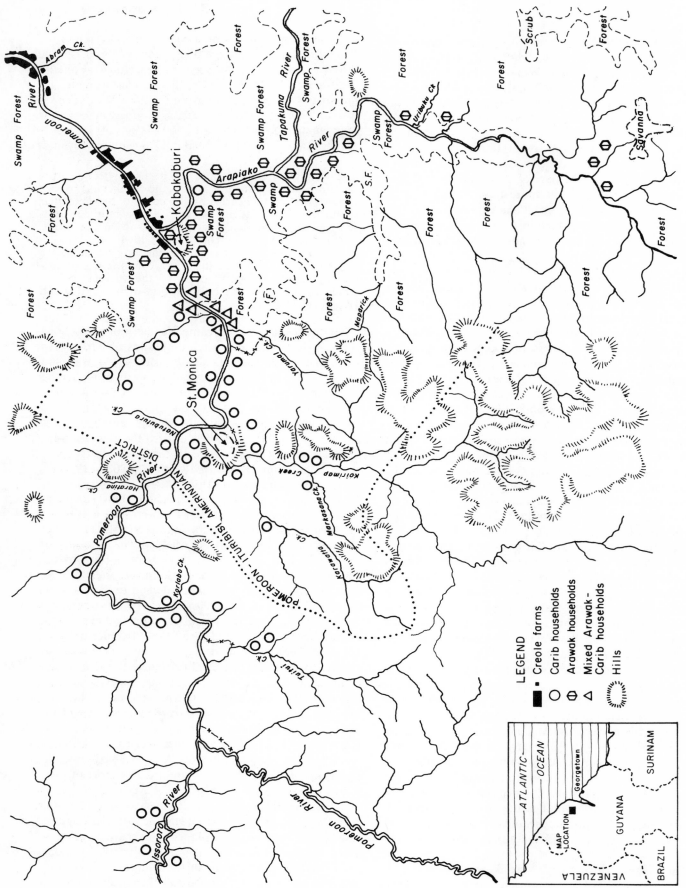

Map 6.1. The upper Pomeroon River system, showing tribal settlement patterns and Creole farms

LEGEND

- Creole farms
○ Carib households
⬡ Arawak households
△ Mixed Arawak-
   Carib households
⬤ Hills

Swamp Forest
Abram Ck.
Pomeroon River
Forest
Swamp Forest
Swamp Forest
Forest
Tapakuma River
Swamp Forest
Forest
Arapiako
Arapiako River
Swamp Forest
Swamp Forest
Kabakaburi
Forest
S.F.
Uriubuku Ck.
Swamp Forest
Forest
Scrub
Forest
Forest
Forest
Savanna
Forest
Forest
Forest
Maparick
Forest
St. Monica
Forest
Koit'imap Ck.
Narhubui'u Ck.
Yarumai R.
Kotawatta Ck.
Markasana Ck.
Harataha Ck.
Pomeroon River
POMEROON-TURIBISI AMERINDIAN DISTRICT
Kariabo Ck.
Turai Ck.
Pomeroon River
Issororo River

VENEZUELA
GUYANA
SURINAM
BRAZIL
ATLANTIC OCEAN
Georgetown
MAP LOCATION

and assimilation differed for the two tribal groups. Actual Carib hostility was reinforced by the colonists' preconceived stereotypes of Carib aggressiveness and social reticence, while the martial inferiority of the Arawak and their consequent dependence on colonial settlements was interpreted by the colonists as evidence of Arawak sociability and sophistication. This mutual interaction of act and perception has shaped the historical process through which contemporary Arawak and Carib groups have become what they are. If anything, the perceptions, or ethnic stereotypes, have had a greater impact on contemporary social organization than have original differences in the indigenous social structures of the Arawak and Carib. For today the indigenous social structures of the coastal groups, and even the historical circumstances under which they altered, are largely unknown to most Guyanese—Amerindian and non-Amerindian alike. Still, Guyanese who have frequent contact with individuals of the two tribal groups observe certain differences that they continue to attribute to antithetical personality types and tribal characteristics.

The Arawak and Carib themselves are anything but immune from this sort of ethnic type-casting: the popular stereotypes of Arawak and Carib accepted by neighboring Guyanese Creoles are believed by the Amerindians themselves. The Arawak makes the claim, acknowledged by Pomeroon dwellers, that he is more sophisticated than the Carib, has a better command of English, and—the paramount colonial virtue—is more English generally in his dress and daily life, in the type of house he builds, and in the kind of boat he owns. The Carib does not pretend to have the Arawak's civilized ways; he admits that his style of life is rougher than the Arawak's and confesses to a basic shyness and fear of outsiders that make him far more comfortable in isolated households than in a riverside village. Yet being Carib is far from bearing a stigmatized identity, for while the Carib recognizes a certain Arawak cultural superiority, he sees it at the same time as a kind of decadence. The Arawak is soft; like a woman or child he needs the shelter of a warm, dry house and provisions that can be had only in shops. The Carib, however, can bear up under privation; in fact, his whole existence is predicated on it. Nor do the Carib forget their very considerable military prowess of days gone by, when Arawak and Warao hid their households in swamps and at the heads of tiny creeks to escape detection by Carib war canoes.

The area where I did my fieldwork, on the Pomeroon River in the Essequibo District of Guyana, has a long history of settlement by both tribal groups and is consequently an excellent source of material on the subject of Carib identity. Members of both groups tell anecdotal stories about one another that illustrate their attitudes

A timber crew on its way to a work camp on the Pomeroon River. The man in the foreground is Carib; the driver of the boat is a mixed Arawak from Kabakaburi.

toward ethnicity and the extent to which predominant tribal stereotypes shape their thinking.

As noted earlier, the upper reaches of the Pomeroon are inhabited by Carib, while the Arawak, true to popular form, live downriver nearer the Creole shops and coastal road. The local attitude toward Carib privation and Arawak plenty is nicely represented by the following vignette. On a trip I made to one of the most remote Carib households on the river, I was accompanied by an elderly Arawak man, a valuable informant. He used the occasion of our visit to remark on a poignant difference between himself and our hosts. The Carib family, he pointed out, lives two days by dugout canoe from his own Arawak village, where the last shop on the river is located. They travel downriver every month or so, depending on when they have a supply of smoked bush meat, fish poison, or logs to trade with the shop owner for provisions. My informant described the situation in the Creole English of the river: "The coffee finish, the sugar finish, the kero [kerosene] finish, and still they remain at home. When the matches about finish, then they does leave. That is the real Carib way. If it was Arawak now, the coffee finish and he again back at the shop!" My companion's amused self-criticism is an indication of how widespread and commonplace the tribal stereotypes have become. These stereotypes recur in every aspect of Amerindian life on the Pomeroon and affect the relationships established between the Arawak and the Carib, as well as between members of both tribal groups and Guyanese Creoles living outside the Amerindian District.

Before exploring these stereotypes in more detail, let us take stock of where we are in this explication of Carib identity. I began by suggesting that im Thurn was influenced by the popular notions of his day when he elaborated a theory emphasizing the affinity of the several Carib-speaking groups in Guyana. Yet it now appears from my last remarks above that tribal stereotypes are a very real factor in the lives of Guyanese Arawak and Carib themselves. If these stereotypes cannot be dismissed as unfounded prejudice that unfortunately surfaced in the work of a creditable scholar, what then is one to make of them? In my opinion, stereotypes of ethnic identity that affect social relationships to the degree seen in the Guyanese case must be considered part of the social fabric of everyday life and treated as an aspect of the objectifiable world. We have learned, under the masterful tutelage of Lévi-Strauss, to regard myths as something other than fabulous stories that either ignore or confirm in a trivial fashion the empirical realities of social organization; it is time to begin thinking of the concept of ethnicity in the same way. The analogy I am trying to make between the study of myth and the study of ethnicity may be seen if we take Lévi-Strauss's eloquent statement on the sociological level of the Asdiwal myth and apply it to the Guyanese tribal stereotypes we have been discussing:

When we move on to the sociological aspects, there is a much greater freedom of interpretation. It is not a question of an accurate documentary picture of the reality of native life, but a sort of counterpoint which seems sometimes to be in harmony with this reality, and sometimes to part from it in order to rejoin it again. [1967: 10]

The stereotypes that the Arawak and Carib nourish about themselves and about each other form part of a larger myth of ethnicity that constitutes the most important element in the ideological life of Guyana, the multiracial emigrant society par excellence.

There is here an ironic vindication of im Thurn's interest in the True Carib, the reservation being that the True Carib is not a figure in an evolutionary adventure story but an image of a life-style—a set of ethnic touchstones—that occupies a prominent place in the imagination of many Guyanese. (This image is most prominent among Amerindians and among those non-Amerindians who live near Amerindian Districts in that peripheral zone separating "bush" from "country." Guyanese who live in Georgetown or on the coast are generally unaware of the Arawak-Carib distinction and speak instead of Amerindians, a term that they invest with considerable ethnic significance and that carries its own stereotypical connotations. In fact, coastal Guyanese often use the term "buckmen" rather than "Amerindian"; the word derives from the Dutch and is explicitly derogatory.) The stereotypical Carib is part of real life, but not in the way im Thurn imagined—for to un-

derstand the significance of tribal stereotypes one must ignore possible affinities between geographically distant Carib groups and look instead at the social relationships members of a particular Carib group have with non-Carib living around them.

On the Pomeroon River, the Carib and Arawak have been living in immediate proximity to one another since at least 1840 (Brett 1868: 121–5; 163–5). The two groups have been exposed to Western influence—through contacts with traders, missionaries, soldiers, timberworkers, rubber collectors, and sugar planters—for an even longer period, so that the process of what is sometimes called creolization has completely altered the indigenous social structures. Nevertheless, the long period of contiguous residence and acculturation has not produced a homogeneous social or cultural order: the acculturation of the two tribal groups has been differential, not parallel.

The most evident difference between the Arawak and Carib is their choice of residence, which in turn has a pervasive effect on their education, economy, family structure, and political organization. As noted earlier, the Arawak inhabit an area of the Pomeroon and its tributaries that is closer to and in greater contact with areas of Essequibo where Black, East Indian, and Portuguese Creole farmers constitute the bulk of the population. In their choice of the actual building sites for their homes, the Arawak also make themselves more accessible to outside contact than do the Carib. Arawak families build their homes on the wet clay banks of the Pomeroon and on the banks of the Arapiako, while Carib families are most frequently found living well up tributary creeks where the land is high and sandy. The implications of these residential modes are extensive.

In building on the riverbank, Arawak families abandon the traditional habitat where manioc agriculture is practiced—the sand hills at the creekheads—and opt instead for a location that offers easier access to the shops, school, church, medical aid, and social functions of the river's largest Amerindian settlement, the Arawak village of Kabakaburi (see Map 6.1). A move to the main river lessens transportation problems to and from the village. Arawak children consequently attend school more faithfully than the sons and daughters of Carib families and are correspondingly more familiar with and competent in the ways of the wider Creole society. At the time of my fieldwork, in 1969–1971, truancy at the school in Kabakaburi (where a number of Carib children from upriver and Creole children from downriver also attend school) rarely reached 25 percent. In contrast, the school at the Carib settlement seven miles upriver not uncommonly operated with more than half its students absent; this was particularly true in May and early June, when many Carib families paddled 60 miles and more down to the ocean to collect and feast on the crabs that swarmed onto the beaches at that time. The Arawak children's routine school attendance and the Carib children's casualness are reflected in the numbers of each who pass their school exams. The remnants of the British colonial system of education are still sufficiently present to maintain a sharp distinction between children who have passed a particular exam and those who have not. While civil service, managerial, and professional careers are unrealistic goals for most Arawak students on the upper Pomeroon, they are impossible ones for all but a tiny handful of Carib students. The different residential choices of Arawak and Carib families are consequently reinforced by their children's successes and failures at school. Arawak children who attend school regularly and pass their exams may well find jobs outside the District and thereby become more assimilated into Guyanese society. For the Carib children who fail because of slack attendance, life in an isolated household on a sparsely populated creek may be their only real choice.

Because the relatively populous riverbank is a poor place to hunt or fish, and because few Arawak have yet geared themselves to the type of farming necessary to cultivate riparian land, Arawak families are extensively involved in a cash economy—someone has to earn the money to purchase provisions at the shop, to outfit the children with clothes and school supplies, and to provide for some entertaining at home. The necessity for earning money involves Arawak men in transactions with Creole outsiders, who frequently employ the English-speaking and "creolized" Arawak in timber and rubber operations in Guyana's interior. Such experience broadens the Arawak's social horizons; he becomes more knowledgeable about his country's geography, economy, and customs—or, in the abbreviated language of the stereotype, more sophisticated than the Carib. The Carib, in contrast, is more often involved in direct extractive labor, such as cutting logs or making shingles in the deep bush and bringing them out to sell at a river shop every month or so. This economic differentiation between Arawak and Carib has important implications for family structure, which I can only touch on here.

Being committed to a cash economy, the Arawak family members often find themselves uprooted and at cross-purposes. The family lives on the riverbank so the children can attend school regularly, yet this means that the woman must paddle several miles to her manioc plot on a creekhead sand hill while the man absents himself from the household for weeks or sometimes months at a time to work timber upriver or to labor outside the Amerindian District. In its domestic predicament, the Arawak family seems more like the Guyanese Negro family as described by R. T. Smith (1956) than an indigenous institution. There is, however, an important difference between Arawak and Guyanese Negro family structure: the Arawak family often accommodates itself to conflicting demands by having a dual residence, or at least an extra shelter in the bush where its members can spend the months of June, July, and August farming, hunting, and fishing.

Most Carib families do not depend on a steady influx of cash and are consequently more sedentary than their downriver Arawak neighbors. Because educational goals and economic pressures are not so important among the upriver Carib, kinship plays an important role in determining residence choices. Like some of the older Arawak, most Carib have a particular creek they consider a "home place," where a number of their family members still reside. On a large tributary creek in the Carib section of the Pomeroon, there are usually two or three major family groups represented (see Map 6.1). Each family group occupies a particular part of the creek, where several households (rarely more than three or four) are clumped to form a tiny nucleated settlement that is all but invisible from the water. There is no discernible residence rule underlying this Carib practice, in the sense of, say, uxorilocal rather than virilocal residence. A son is about as likely as a daughter to establish a separate household beside the parental home. Whether children continue to live near their home after marriage or drift away seems to depend primarily on the stability of the parental union and on the economic status of the parents. A mature Carib couple that has provided well for its children and that encourages them to remain nearby may well find itself the center of a small settlement consisting of a son or two, a daughter or two, their families, and perhaps an odd relative here and there. Conjugal unions are often rather impermanent affairs among Pomeroon Amerindians, so that a couple that is still together after raising a family is likely to attract others to it.

The two or three family groups that inhabit a particular creek often provide spouses for one another, giving rise to a principle that might be called "creek endogamy," for want of a better term. In this the Carib differ again from the Arawak, whose residential choices, educational backgrounds, and jobs often expose them to a much wider range of potential conjugal partners, including in many cases Creole men from downriver. One of the most striking trends I noted during my fieldwork on the Pomeroon was that Carib men and women rarely mate with Creoles, while Arawak frequently do, especially Arawak women. There is a good deal of evidence to support the view that the upper Pomeroon is the scene of a system of ethnic hypergamy in which Creole men frequently mate with Arawak women while Arawak men often look to the upriver Carib for casual, and sometimes not so casual, affairs (see Table 6.1).

A Carib family at home on the Issororo River. Hammocks are slung over the crossbeams of the house, out of the way during the day. The cooking area is at the rear of the house. The "house master" sits on a chair of local "bush rope"; the man standing is an Arawak visitor.

Young woman of the household shown in photograph at left.

From the preceding it is clear that Arawak and Carib exhibit diverse behaviors and perspectives in a number of important areas of social life, and that many differences between them are tied to their respective modes of residence. The contrasts between life in the creekheads and life on the riverbank predicate differences in family structure, economic activities, and marriage preferences; and these differences in turn are expressed and amplified through the ideological idiom of ethnicity. The features of tribal stereotypes that distinguish Arawak from Carib leap into prominence when contact between Arawak and Carib is made or contemplated. How do members of the two groups interact, and what attitudes do they have about their interaction? In turning to a consideration of intertribal social relations, it is important to remember that, for all their acculturation, the two groups are characteristic of tropical forest peoples in two respects: their numbers are few and the land they inhabit is sparsely settled. At the time of my fieldwork (1969–1971), the total Amerindian population of the upper Pomeroon Amerindian District was around 1,350, with Arawak slightly outnumbering Carib.[3] Most of this population is distributed along a 20-mile stretch of the Pomeroon, along the Arapiako, a

tributary river that flows into the Pomeroon just below the Arawak village, and along tributary creeks of the Pomeroon and Arapiako (see Map 6.1). Given the small size of the two tribal groups, their stability with respect to migration, their isolation from the coast (the Arawak village is 17 miles by river from the nearest road), and the fact that both groups live with their backs literally against a wall of uninhabited tropical forest, it is not surprising that the Arawak and Carib see a good deal of one another. What is surprising is that the two groups have managed to maintain ethnic boundaries—or what in some instances might more precisely be called fictions of ethnic boundaries. Social relationships between the Arawak and Carib are ultimately based on a physical separation of the tribal groups: the Carib live upriver in the bush; the Arawak live downriver on the riverbank. The form interaction takes consequently depends on who goes where to do what.

In the economic sphere, as noted earlier, Arawak men find it necessary to travel upriver into the traditional Carib area to cut logs, hunt, and fish (since there is little game, fish, or marketable timber to be found in the more populous Arawak area of the river). Given the traditional animosity between the two groups, it occurred to me to inquire about possible conflicts sparked by such travel. Arawak informants found this an irrelevant if not amusing question, for they regarded their use of upriver Carib territory as natural, proper, and inoffensive. In fact, as I later determined, Arawak men enjoy something of a master-client relationship in their economic affairs among the Carib. An Arawak man will sometimes organize a timber party consisting of three or four Carib men, provision them, and arrange for the transportation and sale of the logs cut by the Carib workers. Similarly, an Arawak loaned a Carib man his

3. Any statistics of this sort must be hedged with the qualifier that, as I want to emphasize, it is by no means an easy matter to distinguish an Arawak from a Carib in some cases or, on another level, to distinguish an Amerindian from a Creole. Guyanese society is replete with niceties of ethnic distinction, which shade imperceptibly one into another. The whole question is to know what circumstances entail a person's wearing one ethnic label over another.

shotgun (a precious article under the stringent restrictions of Guyana's Security Act) on the condition that he receive a portion of game killed with the gun. Similar transactions involving the use of outboard motors and large plank boats (the Carib possess mostly dugout canoes) go on all the time and set the pattern for the stereotype already described: Arawak have material assets unavailable to most Carib and, moreover, some Arawak have access to coastal businessmen and marketplaces that enable them to become entrepreneurs in their own right among the Carib.

The upriver Carib find themselves similarly imposed upon on those occasions when they see Arawak for purely recreational purposes. Birthdays, weddings, baptismal celebrations, and even a simple abundance of manioc provide opportunities for intertribal socializing, which invariably takes the form of a "spree," as it is known in the Creole dialect. All sprees have four activities in common, although they vary a great deal according to how intensively people pursue one or another of these activities. Dancing, sexual assignations, drinking, and fighting combine to make the Amerindian spree a distinct social, if not ceremonial, occasion. I was told by several informants that a decade or two ago, when feelings between Arawak and Carib were reportedly stronger than today, sprees at which both groups were present invariably involved some fighting along tribal lines. The institution of the fistfight assumes a benign form among Guyanese Amerindians. The combatants do not come to grips until both have drunk enough to be well past the ability of doing one another serious harm.

The fight, rather than being a form of aggravated conflict, is simply the terminal phase of the spree, ending perhaps in the departure of one party and a lapse into unconsciousness of the other. Amerindian brawls are usually in sharp contrast to drunken fighting among Creoles, where rum and a machete (called a "cutlass") make a lethal combination that results in the mutilation or occasional murder of one of the antagonists. (It is intriguing to make a comparison between Pomeroon Amerindian pushing matches and the stylized fighting practiced by other tropical forest people, such as the Yanomamö, but there is really no way of establishing a connection.)

While Carib and Arawak sprees are similar in the activities that occur, they differ in terms of who feels free to attend the functions. Carib do not ordinarily attend sprees at Arawak homes unless they are well upriver from the Arawak settlement. When they do put in an appearance, it is usually as a family unit attending at the special invitation of the Arawak host, with whom they happen to enjoy a close relationship. Arawak are not so reserved in the matter of attending Carib sprees. It is not uncommon to find a few Arawak youths enjoying the hospitality of a Carib family miles upriver from the last Arawak household. These occasions are sometimes volatile and give the Amerindian spree its reputation for quarrelsomeness. The Arawak youths enjoy both drink and dancing partners, and this almost invariably irritates their Carib counterparts and results in a tumultuous expulsion of the interlopers. Yet such events have well-established precedents; they are part of the course of

TABLE 6.1
Parental Ethnic Affiliation and Legitimacy of 100 Children Born on Upper Pomeroon River, 1969–70

"Race" or Tribe		Legal	Nonlegal	Total
Father	Mother	Births	Births	Births
Arawak	Arawak	15	0	15
Carib	Carib	16	22	38
Arawak-Carib*	Arawak-Carib*	3	5	8
Creole	Creole	5	2	7
Creole	Arawak	2	12	14
Arawak	Creole	3	2	5
Creole	Mixed Arawak-Carib	2	3	5
Creole	Carib	0	0	0
Arawak	Warao	1	0	1
Carib	Warao	0	1	1
Unknown	Arawak	0	4	4
Unknown	Carib	0	1	1
Unknown	Mixed Creole-Warao	0	1	1
Total		47	53	100

*One or both parents are mixed Arawak and Carib, or one parent is Arawak and the other Carib.

events in everyday life. Arawak habitually encroach while Carib maintain their reserve and propriety.

Interestingly, the Arawak reconcile this hypergamous situation, in which they are the wife takers, with the Carib tribal stereotype they cultivate, even though that stereotype portrays the Carib as a strong and aggressive people. Historically, of course, the Carib were notorious for slaying entire islands of Arawak men and incorporating Arawak women into their society on a wholesale basis. The Arawak seem to resolve the contradiction by stressing Carib shyness and reclusiveness (marked by dwelling in the forest) when they discuss intertribal sexual episodes; as one Arawak informant expressed it, "Nobody know where the Carib come from. They just grow in the bush." This idea also finds expression in a myth the Arawak tell of Carib origins. According to this myth, the Carib originated when an Arawak woman was expelled from her family and went to live in the bush. There she spontaneously conceived a number of children and taught them to hate and make war on the Arawak. Because the Carib were born as a result of a kind of spontaneous generation, elderly Arawak occasionally refer to them as the "worm people." The myth cannot be fully interpreted here, but it is cited for the light it sheds on Arawak-Carib relations.

Meetings at dances, at school, and in the marketplace provide opportunities for Arawak and Carib men and women to bridge the tribal barrier in a seemingly definitive way by forming unions (legalized and nonlegalized) and producing offspring who are neither Arawak nor Carib. Such events occur, and indeed it would be curious if they did not. What is intriguing about these intertribal unions is the way the resultant households are fitted into the downriver and upriver spheres of Arawak and Carib respectively (see Map 6.1). In a sample survey I made of 100 births recorded for the upper Pomeroon during 1969 and most of 1970 (see Table 6.1), I determined that 8 were the result of mixed Arawak and Carib unions, as compared with 15 births to Arawak parents and 38 to Carib parents (the remainder resulted from unions between Amerindians and persons of other ethnic groups). Most of these mixed Arawak-Carib births occurred in households situated on the river midway between the main Arawak and Carib settlements. As Map 6.1 illustrates, this section of the river is laid out like a social chromatograph. Arawak households extend to a certain point, after which one finds a band of households in which one conjugal partner is Arawak and the other Carib, or in which one partner is a comparatively full-blooded member of one tribal group and the other a mixed Arawak-Carib. Further upriver, households are composed almost exclusively of Carib. The existence of intertribal unions should contradict established tribal

stereotypes, for it would appear that there can be nothing distinctive about being Arawak or Carib when there are a fair number of persons who are both. However, the settlement pattern that has emerged maintains the tribal stereotypes intact by spatially isolating intertribal households and hence assuring the existence of tribally homogeneous communities. Incidentally, some of the most interesting material I gathered on the subjects of ethnic identity and political organization came from informants who lived in the transitional zone.[4]

My search for im Thurn's "True Carib" has become a complicated one. From the preceding it appears that the fellow does not exist, although his stereotype does and is persuasive enough to overshadow the fact that real flesh-and-blood Arawak and Carib sometimes marry and give birth to children whose lives would seem to belie the stereotypes. The dialectic between tribal stereotype and actual social relations is an intimate one. I have noted that individuals in mixed Arawak-Carib unions, whose offspring are a living contradiction of tribal stereotypes, are often spatially segregated in the local settlement pattern. I would now like to conclude by presenting a few details from the life history of a "real Carib," as one Arawak informant referred to him—or a "True Carib," as im Thurn would have it.

Randolph is an older man who has lived all his life far up a large creek, upriver from the Carib settlement discussed above. The location of his household, on an isolated sand hill, is distinctly Carib, as is its physical appearance—rough palm log structures, thatched, with open sides save for a few rough boards lashed together to form well-ventilated sleeping quarters. Randolph and his Carib wife are the nucleus of what is, for Pomeroon Amerindians, an extensive household group: two daughters and a son have set up housekeeping on the same hill. As noted earlier, the extended family residence pattern is itself a Carib trait; for several reasons Arawak tend toward a much more atomistic family life. One of Randolph's daughters lives with a Carib man from the same creek, while the other lives with an Akawaio who came from a now defunct Akawaio enclave near the

---

4. After I returned to the U.S. I learned by letter that a recent election for "captain," or political head, of the Arawak village had resulted in the installation of a mixed Arawak-Carib from this area of the river. The event involves more than the local political scene, for national politics figured prominently in the election. It is likely that new-nation politics will here lend fuel to a local factional dispute between mixed Arawak-Creoles on one side and mixed Carib-Arawaks and Caribs on the other.

headwaters of the Pomeroon. There are several children by these two unions, and Randolph's household is regarded as a strong and vital one by his Carib neighbors on the creek.

Randolph's son is not so typical a case, however. The youth worked for a time on the Corentyne River, which forms Guyana's border with Surinam. There he met and married an Arawak woman from the Amerindian settlement of Orealla, and later he returned to his native sand hill to start his family. The Corentyne has a popular image among Guyanese, including Amerindians, as the home of powerful *obeah* men and sorcerers.[5] The wife of Randolph's son was now isolated from her kinspeople and, because of her Corentyne origins, became the object of suspicion and rumor on the part of some local Caribs. Living deep within Carib territory, she has little occasion to interact with the Arawaks downriver, and even in case of contact she would have little basis for establishing close relations with any of them. She is now a member of a Carib household. Her children will grow up among the Carib and will attend a school where the Carib make up the student body almost to a pupil (an unusual circumstance in multiracial Guyana); they may well take Carib mates, and they will, in short, be Carib.

Now let me backtrack a little. I have portrayed Randolph as a model of Carib manhood: a man who has had the resolve and strength of character to stick it out on his remote hilltop farm, eschewing the easy comforts of the village and, most important, managing to keep his children near him after they have married. I deliberately withheld one piece of information that might have prejudiced this image: Randolph's father was Arawak. The father came to the creek, as do many Arawak men, for a few weeks of timber cutting. While there he met Randolph's mother, a Carib girl living in her parents' home. Their brief affair ended with the Arawak's return to the civilization of his downriver settlement. The child of that union, Randolph, remained in his mother's care and grew up a member of her Carib household. His mother, however, did give him his father's surname. It is because of this practice that today on the river one meets Carib, Arawak, and Creoles with the same surname and some

genealogical connection. (For an example pertinent here, I have documented three other fertile unions involving Randolph's father, all with Arawak women living near the Arawak settlement or downriver from it.)

Like the children many Pomeroon Amerindian women bear, Randolph is a social cuckoo, deposited in a domestic world not consistent with his tribal or racial origins. Yet Randolph, the child of an itinerant Arawak, has attained the status of a Carib man of affairs, and he has now received grandchildren from his son, by an Arawak woman who was uprooted from her origins and required to live within a wholly Carib environment. These children possess the key to the complexities of being Carib in Guyana today. Although more Arawak than Carib in their parental inheritance, they may well remain on the sand-hill farm, acquire Carib mates, and perpetuate Randolph's Carib life style. On the other hand, it is possible that one or two of them may find their way to Georgetown, perhaps receive an education, and marry Creole women who will bear children that are not Carib, or even Amerindian, but Guyanese. In such an event, the grandchildren of Randolph, the "True Carib," will themselves cease being Arawak or Carib and will assume the identity of Amerindians in the multiracial society.

The case of Randolph is unusual only in that it brings the contradictions of Pomeroon ethnicity full circle. Randolph and his son's Arawak wife are essential to perpetuating a sense of Carib identity precisely because they are outcasts, abandoned by Arawak in one case, isolated from them in the other. Had Randolph's Arawak father remained with the Carib woman, it is unlikely that Randolph would have grown up and remained on the remote sand hill that is his present home. Similarly, Randolph's Arawak daughter-in-law relinquished her Arawak home and kin to produce Carib children.

It seems that being Carib is defined always as a negative state. The Pomeroon Carib appear to be succeeding in maintaining themselves as a group, unlike the Pomeroon Akawaio, who are now defunct. If they are successful, it will be because they regularly incorporate non-Carib into their ranks. An indication of this process occurring is to be found in Table 6.1, where as many as 15 of the 53 births (28%) to Carib or part-Carib parents result from interethnic unions. A considerable number of these children, like Randolph, have an Arawak father. While maintaining their discreteness as a group, the Carib are becoming more extensively intermixed with the Arawak, who in turn maintain a sense of being Arawak while mixing with downriver Creoles. Yet while Arawak men perpetuate this phenomenon among their Carib neighbors, Arawak women are the recipients of similar attentions from Creole men living outside the

---

5. The Corentyne derives this reputation from its proximity to Surinam, whose Bush Negro settlements have the reputation among superstitious Guyanese as a kind of witchdoctor's Mecca. That Pomeroon Amerindians are familiar with this reputation was dramatically confirmed in a conversation I had with a local Carib *piai,* or sorcerer. He related to me a fantastic story of how he was once magically transported to the sorcerers' land in the east and there witnessed many bizarre and terrible acts performed by the local doctors.

Amerindian District. The absent father is a fundamental theme in Amerindian social organization.

The process I have described has been in full swing for more than a century on the Pomeroon and will doubtless continue. And while sociological and linguistic distinctions between Arawak and Carib become less meaningful, the tribal stereotypes originally based on those distinctions take up the slack so that ethnicity becomes primarily an ideological posture. The pervasiveness of ethnic categories in Guyanese thought almost insures that being Carib will be a tenacious status for some time to come. Unfortunately, there is the unattractive corollary that maintaining a Carib identity in contemporary Guyana will be accompanied by a sense of being something unreal—of bearing not so much a stigmatized identity as a nonidentity. It would be unrealistic to ignore this negative aspect of being Carib and concentrate exclusively on features of Carib social life considered as parts of a cultural isolate, for the Pomeroon Carib are at once the product and the remnant of a historical cataclysm of unprecedented magnitude: the Conquest of the New World. For centuries their social organization has been based on the principles of retreat and accommodation, and that is how they have come to be, in Johannes Wilbert's telling phrase, the "survivors of El Dorado."

REFERENCES

Brett, Rev. William H.
    1868   *The Indian Tribes of Guiana.* London: Bell and Daldy.

im Thurn, E. F.
    1883   *Among the Indians of Guiana.* London: Kegan Paul, Trench.

Lévi-Strauss, Claude
    1967   The Story of Asdiwal. In *The Structural Study of Myth and Totemism,* ed. E. R. Leach, pp. 1–47. *Association of Social Anthropologists Monograph* 5. London: Tavistock Publications.

Rodway, James
    1894   *History of British Guiana, From the Year 1668 to the Present Time.* 3 vols. Georgetown, Demerara.

Roth, Walter E.
    1915   An Inquiry into the Animism and Folk-lore of the Guiana Indians. *U.S. Bureau of American Ethnology, 30th Annual Report (1908–1909),* pp. 103–386. Washington: Government Printing Office.

    1924   An Introductory Study of the Arts, Crafts and Customs of the Guiana Indians. *U.S. Bureau of American Ethnology, 38th Annual Report (1916–1917).* Washington: Government Printing Office.

Sauer, Carl O.
    1966   *The Early Spanish Main.* Berkeley: Univ. of California Press.

Smith, R. T.
    1956   *The Negro Family in British Guiana.* London: Routledge and Kegan Paul.

Steward, Julian, and Louis Faron
    1959   *Native Peoples of South America.* New York: McGraw-Hill.

Storm van 's Gravesande, Laurens
    1911   *The Rise of British Guiana,* vol. 1. London: Hakluyt Society.

Wilbert, Johannes
    1972   *Survivors of Eldorado.* New York: Praeger.

7. FROM DOGS TO STARS: THE PHATIC FUNCTION OF NAMING AMONG THE PANARE

Jean-Paul Dumont
Department of Anthropology, University of Washington

What is named in a given society (and how it is named) illustrates the way in which members of that society think of themselves, as well as the way in which they think of other "beings" in relation to themselves. To name is already to express a judgment on oneself and on others. It is a way to establish communication. Although it addresses somebody, it is not always clear that some thing about the person is addressed; hence what often seems to be emphasized in the use of names is their phatic function—specifically, that of initiating and maintaining communication. In this paper I shall tentatively analyze the system of proper names among the Panare Indians of Venezuelan Guiana from this perspective.

Briefly, the territory of the Panare corresponds to the northwestern part of the Cedeño district of Bolivar State. Roughly triangular in shape, this area is delimited on the northwest by the right bank of the Orinoco, on the south by the basin of the Rio Suapure, and on the east by the basin of the upper and middle Cuchivero. There are approximately 2,500 Panare today scattered in local groups that are known in the area as "tribes." Each local group has a variable number of inhabitants that does not go below 10 or above 60. Although the history of the Panare is obviously extremely shallow, my informants were well aware of the fact that their parents had scattered from the upper Cuchivero area to occupy their present territory. Such a demographic expansion was still going on at the time of my fieldwork (1967–69),[1] as I witnessed the first establishment of a longhouse and gardens on the right bank of the Suapure.

The most striking feature of the naming system among the Panare is undoubtedly the restriction of its extension. For example, geographical features can be designated only by means of a specification of relevant local human interrelationships. The Panare refer to their settlements by the names in use among the rural Creole population. When some doubt arises about context, the Panare can be more precise—"at the house of headman X," or "at the house of my parent Y headed by Z." They may also use the Creole name—for example, *turiwapo,* which means "at Turiba." Some ambiguity may still remain because several headmen have the same name and Creole names are not always used with precision. For instance, "El Tigre" may refer to the settlement of that name, or, more elliptically, to "the settlement in the area of El Tigre, you know where I mean." Should any doubt remain in the mind of the listener, a Panare could specify more precisely by using the name of a kinsman. Confusing as this may seem (and indeed was, for the investigator), there never appears to be any difficulty for the Panare themselves. Just as their settlements have no precise names, neither do topographic features such as rivers or hills receive a designation. The only "beings" or "entities" to receive names in Panare culture are human beings, dogs (the only domesticated animals), and certain celestial bodies.

Collecting names was the most excruciating ethnographic "must" I was confronted with in the field. One of the first things I learned was the fact that there are two types of people, "We the Indians" *(otñepa)* and "you the Creoles" *(tatto).* I was immediately classified, yet anonymous, since I was addressed by the latter categorical term.

As I pressed my informants for individual names *(tsunka aiče,* "What is your name?"), I got rather puzzling answers: "Marco," "Felipe," "Manuel," and so forth. As I inquired about women, the answer was *aišpwi,* "She has no name." I spent another few weeks asking, imploring, begging for names in vain, before an informant asked me to his garden and revealed several

---

1. My field research among the Panare Indians was conducted between the summer of 1967 and the summer of 1969. Financial support was received from the Wenner-Gren Foundation for Anthropological Research (New York), the U.C.L.A. Latin American Center (Los Angeles), the Fundación Creole (Caracas), and an Andrew W. Mellon Predoctoral Fellowship (Pittsburgh).

A Panare man building a house.

"true" names of his fellow villagers, while stoutly refusing to reveal his own. I paid generously and came back to the longhouse only to discover the shocking "truth": I had been given obscene names in the grand style.

A decisive turn came when I agreed to show snapshots of members of my family. I had chosen to exhibit only women and bearded men, in an attempt to be differentiated from the Creoles, who shave more or less closely. From that moment on I was referred to as *taŋtsipoto*, "the bearded one." I had lost my anonymity. I belonged to a subclass of *tatto* who were all *taŋtsipoto*. Being thus categorized I could be identified with no problem; more facetious than serious, one Panare called me *yim*, "father," and a few minutes later somebody called me *puka*, which is a man's name.

Collecting the names of each inhabitant of the settlement had now become all but a game. What had happened was that I had been neither rejected nor adopted, but merely accepted. However, that acceptance could only come after an identification—that is, as a member of a class. Since I was neither Indian (obviously) nor Creole (I did not look nor did I behave like them), I was a disgraceful "no-one man from a nowhere land." The exhibition of family photos had suddenly given me social depth, as shown by the fact that when I gave the French names of those pictured, they were renamed in Panare fashion by my listeners. I had acquired a classificatory valence that eclipsed, at least momentarily, the logical scandal of my own presence in Panare land. The joke of my adoption had been played in order to *defuse*, to *dedramatize* such a presence.

Communication was thus established when we had respectively identified ourselves in opposition to each other as well as to the Creoles. As long as I had remained an unexplained and intruding presence, I was dangerous, being someone who could not be named. I was therefore present, but I did not exist. In a way I had a pure proper name, as my body was a sign without reference. After I had lost my sanctity by showing family pictures, my categorization became permissible, and the complicity of naming had begun when I stooped to my profane dimension.

Such naming was strictly phatic, for it was the unique guarantee that communication had been established. Communication demands a preliminary classification of the involved locutors into categories compatible with that communication. Lévi-Strauss is therefore correct in his statement that:

Le choix . . . n'est qu'entre identifier l'autre en l'assignant à une classe, ou, sous couvert de lui donner un nom, de s'identifier soi-même à travers lui. On ne nomme donc jamais; on classe l'autre, si le nom qu'on lui donne est fonction des caractères qu'il a, ou on se classe soi-même si, se croyant dispensé de suivre une règle, on nomme l'autre "librement": c'est-à-dire en fonction des caractères qu'on a. Et, le plus souvent, on fait les deux choses à la fois. [1962: 240]

A further illustration of this statement can be found as we examine what other entities, besides people, are named. Let us begin with celestial bodies. Among the many visible celestial bodies (an unnamed category including stars, planets, and certain atmospheric phenomena), only a few are named: stars in general *(tyakun);* moon *(wono);* sun *(ečexkun);* Orion's belt *(peška);* the Pleiades *(yoroo);* Antares *(totseŋpitomuno);* and the Milky Way *(toëpinkomune),* each star of which anonymously represents a dead Panare soul that is burning away. All stars are supernatural beings (see Dumont 1972a: 162ff). The named stars are marked stars that are individualized within the unifying category of *tyakun.* Therefore, among all *tyakun* there are: first, individuals (Antares, Orion's belt, and so on) that were cast out of culture from the beginning of time; second, the souls of the dead that glow in the Milky Way, an undifferentiated class of individuals who have been cast out of culture by their death; and third, those stars that are neither named nor located within the Milky Way and have little conceptual value. We shall come back later to the souls of the dead. It is noteworthy that the individualizing names of stars are less true names than a sort of serial registration (with a specific reference) of those *tyakun* that are relevant for the conceptual needs of Panare symbolic thought.

We may wonder whether stars are perhaps named because they represent the perceptible part of supernature—in other words, whether their naming may not consist of a conceptual manipulation in order to tame supernature (I use "supernature" rather than "supernatural world" because the form parallels that of the words "nature" and "culture"). Among all supernatural beings, stars are unique in being currently perceptible—unlike spirits, for instance, who roam in the forest and who are not named. Hence, would not stars be a

hinge between culture and supernature? To answer this question it will be sufficient to look in the opposite direction and wonder whether there are named beings whose position is the reverse of that of the stars. Such seems to be the case with the dogs.

Within the class *krinapoŋ,* "dog," only Panare dogs receive names. To the best of my knowledge, no meaning can be found for any dog name: *ačowa, aupi, ču, katire, makuro, matamu, oŋtapwi, orotsame, potsorumu, roro, rumu, ryo, tsirumu, tapuru, torauxku, tupi, tyomiŋ, yaroko.* Dogs are bought from the Creoles by Panare men. The name, which is given by the new owner, is independent of the sex of the dog. Although this naming follows a sort of fad, so that some names like *tyomiŋ* were positively "in" at the time of my fieldwork, the list of dog names remains open. Within the same settlement several dogs may have the same name, but two dogs belonging to the same man must have two different names. In this respect, the naming of the dogs is like the naming of stars: the function of the name is individualizing. However, the classifications are used differently. Dogs' names are used only by their owners, who act as if they do not know the names of their neighbors' dogs. One may beat or chase away another man's dog; one may not call or use somebody else's dog. Thus, while dog names, like star names, belong to a definite class, and while each dog, like each star, is classified—that is, individualized by a given name—the names of stars are a public classification, the names of dogs a private one.

As we have seen, dogs and stars are the only beings, apart from humans, that receive names. In contraposi-

Panare man collecting honey, an exclusively male activity that occurs at the end of the dry season

tion to stars, dogs constitute a hinge between nature and culture. Dogs as animals are natural, but as domesticated animals they are already cultural. Dogs are in contact with men, they live beside men; stars are far away from men, they are above men. While stars are cultural beings who have been forced into supernature, dogs are cultural beings who have been forced in from nature. Dogs are almost but not quite members of human society. Dogs and stars are both outside of culture, the former on the side of nature through inherent defect, the latter on the side of supernature through symbolic excess; yet both are quite close, dogs spatially and empirically, stars temporally and conceptually, to culture. Dogs and stars are cultural hinges that constitute a pair of oppositions among named "beings"—as if the cultural order protected its integrity, defending its fringes against the intrusion of nature and supernature, by means of exorcism: the naming of ambiguous beings, dogs and stars. Naming is different for dogs and for stars, however, because there is a progression from nature through culture to supernature. While for the Panare it is an individual concern to deal successfully with one's own bit of nature, death is a public identifying future for all. Hence the phatic function of naming again appears, but in its maximally extended form. To name dogs and to name stars is to ensure that communication is established from one end of culture to the other in such a way that communication does not escape cultural control.

Since we are in need of confirmation of the preceding structural sketch, we now turn to Panare personal names for human beings. We shall begin with a negative aspect, the fact that infants have no personal names. Until a baby is weaned, he (she) is referred to and addressed as *nyamča*. Even a fetus is referred to by this word. The word *nyamča* thus categorizes an individual from conception to weaning. This categorization is minimal, since it identifies someone only as a permutable member of an age class. Indeed, although *nyamča* as a term of address leads to hardly any confusion because of the context in which it is enunciated, such is not the case when it is used as a term of reference. Risks of confusion in situations of reference are reduced rather than eliminated (we shall see below why it is necessary to be circumspect with such an assertion) by using what might be called the reverse of a teknonym—the form "so-and-so's child." (Tylor [1889: 248] coined the term "teknonym" for the formula in which an individual is addressed as "so-and-so's parent.") In addition, the terms *yawoŋ* ("son") and *yintseŋ* ("daughter"), which are practically never used in Panare, are replaced by the term *yuŋkiŋ* ("child"), used for both male and female. Sex differentiation is made only through the teknonymous principle of "sex-linked mixed descent" (Gillin 1948: 433), by which a male *nyamča* is linked with his father (as in *puka-ŋkiŋ*, "child of [a man named] Puka")

and a female *nyamča* is linked with her mother (as in *mato-ŋkiŋ*, "child of [a woman named] Mato"). It is noteworthy that this use of a reverse teknonymy is congruent with the Panare usage when referring to settlements, which might be called "reverse geononymy" (the term "geononymy" has been proposed by Lee and Harvey "for the practice of using place names as qualifiers for kinship terms" [1973: 41]). As we have seen above, the Panare use kinship terms and headmen's names as qualifiers for settlements, which seems to indicate that they conceive of themselves as coextensive with the category of space.[2] In any case, teknonyms as well as geononyms are by definition descriptive and not equivalent to personal names.

As far as the *nyamča* are concerned, the use of a reverse teknonym to refer to them seems only to emphasize their social nonexistence. Fetus or infant, a *nyamča* is no more than a would-be human being, as yet undifferentiated. This brings us back to the opposite end of the life cycle where the dead, soon forgotten, become undifferentiated. Although there is no taboo on using the names of the dead, it was extremely difficult for me to collect these names. Some individuals could not even remember the name of their father and justified their lack of memory by saying that death had happened a long time ago. To go up two generations above *Ego* in genealogies was nearly impossible. When I asked about such ancestors, I was often given the answer, "Never mind, he (she) is dead." Panare social organization does not emphasize any descent principle, so there is no pressure to memorize the names of the dead, whose souls glow in the anonymity of the Milky Way. On the other hand, in contrast to societies in which names belong to clans, lineages, or similar groupings, Panare society has no need to place these names at the disposal of newcomers. The result is this intermediary formula in which names are kept by the dead but are forgotten by the living.

Such social amnesia fosters what I see as a correlation and opposition between the dead and infants. While any infant is still a *nyamča*, any dead person is already an *ičin*. Infants do not yet speak, while the dead speak no more. The former, still close to nature, are yet to be encultured, while the latter are segregated from culture and expelled into supernature, where they will be identified as permutable stars in the Milky Way. Through this process, they are de-individualized and recategorized into a general class: the dead. The only effect is to classify infants as *not yet* with us, and the dead as *no longer* with us.

2. For a more extended discussion of the ways in which the Panare conceive of themselves in terms of spatial relationships, see Dumont 1972b.

Panare women preparing food in a dry-season camp

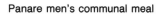

Panare men's communal meal

We can now understand why there is a differential treatment of the celestial bodies as far as their naming is concerned. The Panare segregate the Milky Way from other, named stars; the former identifies the dead in general, while the latter individualize mythical beings. In addition, the two hinges (nature-culture, and culture-supernature) are in a relationship of reversed symmetry. Already or still within culture, the infants and the dead are reduced to the zero degree of classification—designated simply as members of a class. Not yet or no longer within culture, dogs and mythical celestial bodies are individualized. It can be easily seen that there is an opposition, *identification-individualization,* which corresponds to a certain viewpoint. The individualization of stars and dogs is used as a reference point for the supernatural and natural orders, which are outside the cultural order.

Dogs, like stars, are only metaphorically close to culture. However, the identification of infants and the dead represents a sort of inherent logic: infants and the dead (respectively close to nature and close to supernature) are limiting markers of the cultural continuum, within which discontinuities are perceived. This, of course, represents the exact reverse of the conceptualization of dogs and named stars, whose discontinuities in relation to culture are conceptually suppressed. In the former case, culture introduces fictive discontinuities within an actual continuum; in the latter case, culture introduces a fictive homogeneity between "entities" that are by definition heterogeneous.

What remains important is that the two conceptualizations are marked differently, the former by identification, the latter by individualization. From a semantic viewpoint, the assignation of the terms of the opposition *identification-individualization* could have been reversed without affecting the system, provided that the outermost pair of terms remained marked in opposition to their innermost counterparts. In each case of naming, culture is concerned with the establishment of communication; however, communication is minimized *de jure* where it exists *de facto,* and maximized *de jure* where it is denied *de facto.* Hence the phatic function of naming appears in its two extreme aspects, since in one case culture ensures itself that communication does not extend beyond the minimum while in the other case it ensures itself that at least this minimum is reached.

In this structural setting of denomination, how can we integrate the names of those individuals who are weaned and still alive, cultural individuals *par excellence?* Turning to the examination of their names, we shall see that they are equally opposed to identification and to individualization, in order to bring into play another principle that I shall call *individuation. Individuation* refers here to the principles governing an *existential* relationship between a set of names and its equivalent set of name bearers.

We now have to give account of four sets of human names. After their weaning, children are given, temporarily and quite informally, a name by either or both parents. These names are to be chosen from one of two sets. Those for males include *čikoxpwo, čiporoŋ, etana, ikureŋ, kopwo, meñakari, tsimoŋ,* and *tukari.* Those for females include *arawa, atsipa, čiruwa, etsara, kaiñam, karapwi, karime, komutsin, kučono, maara, makuiŋ, meštetu, pemo, tikiri, tuporeŋ,* and *wamo.* I have found no meaning to any name on these lists, which are finite and closed.

When boys are initiated and when girls have their first menses, these names are replaced by permanent names, given by the members of the settlement who are of the same sex as the child. There are only six permanent names for males *(mañaŋ, naxto, puka, tona, totse, uñey),* and four permanent names for females *(ačim, atoŋ, into, mato).* I have not been able to discover a precise meaning for any of these names either, except for *ačim,* which means "crayfish" and is perhaps a case of homonymy. However, these sets do have a more general meaning, in that they commemorate the names of the very first Panare who came out from ten caves in the upper Cuchivero Basin after their creation by the demiurge *Manatači.*

In all four cases, a name may be "freely" chosen for an individual from one of the categories—male child, female child, male adult, female adult—and the choice is not submitted to any other determination. Since the Panare have no social units other than the residential group, the names are neither the property of a group nor transmitted by inheritance.

The identifying function of such names is immediately obvious, since the mere enunciation of a name is indicative of the social status of its bearer: the individual is either a male or a female, either initiated or not. Such an identification is absolute. However, it is noteworthy that the two "adult" sets are to be further dichotomized following a socially contextual (relative) categorization. In effect, the Panare particle *čaŋ* "connotes the idea of return, of reciprocity with an idea of positive value" (Dumont 1972: 145). In a naming context, the use of this particle connotes an affinal relationship between two individuals, while its absence connotes a consanguineal relationship. Before addressing somebody with his (her) name, the speaker therefore has to know what kind of relationship already exists between himself and the person named. Of course, one can also manipulate an existing relationship by the use of a *čaŋ*-modified name that would not normally be used. At any rate, identification in this case is a relative categorization, since the use of either *totse* or *totse-čaŋ,* for example, informs a

Panare man painting blowgun darts with curare

Panare listener about alter's social status *vis-à-vis* the speaker.

I have shown above the identifying function of Panare personal names. It is clear that this is not their only function, for if it were, there would be no need to have several available names within each of the four sets. Nevertheless, it appears that these names do not secure to their bearers any individualization. These names only generalize about sex and age grade. Thus (to the observer) these names favor rather than avoid confusion. Although parents tend to choose names for their initiated children from those that are available after the elder ones have been named, this is only a tendency and certainly not a necessity. Furthermore, if a couple has five daughters, two of them must inevitably have the same name. Even worse, because of sororal polygyny a man may have two wives bearing the same name. Under these conditions, genealogical investigation becomes an uncanny puzzle.

Personal names do more than identify and they do less than individualize. Yet we can see that names are neither freely distributed nor automatically attributed. The question is, then, what is their function? In effect, we have a problem with Lévi-Strauss's statement on denomination quoted above. The difficulty seems to come from the fact that Panare personal names come close to being pure proper names. They have no reference. They are meaningful only contextually, and they create an existential relation with their bearer: their meaning comes through their use. Furthermore, such names do not convey concepts of individuals, for any one of them can be used to designate many persons: a Panare man may have the same name as his father or two of his brothers. Under these conditions, using names is simply a way of perceiving others by apprehending the existential relation between a given name and a given individual.

However, there is no reason to wonder why there is so

little confusion with these names in daily practice. Individualization can be created by other means such as the use of a kinship term or a periphrastic turn, or the context of the utterance. In fact, the phatic function of these names and their individuating aspect are intimately connected. In conversation, a name may be used to individualize somebody. However, in order to do so it has to be used in combination with something else. Furthermore, the name is used to establish communication between the individuals within an actual group—for instance, in conversation during a meal or from one hut to another. The name in this case is mainly phatic because its enunciation aims at establishing a conversation. Hence, I call a person *into,* and she then calls me *puka* in return. By means that are paralinguistic (such as the sound of her voice, the distance from which she speaks), I am assured that communication is established with the desired individual.

Such a phatic function is enhanced by the way in which personal names are used in everyday life. Obviously, the personal names of the Panare constitute only one element in their system of reference and address. Since personal names do not individualize "enough," it becomes understandable that they have a limited use as terms of reference. And indeed, unless the context remains unequivocal, it is rare to hear somebody refer to *puka* without individualizing him "further" by means of a kinship term or a periphrase; or both. No avoidance pattern whatsoever is involved here; it is simply a matter of clarity. The problem is somehow different if we consider the use of names as terms of address. In the course of conversation with a certain *maŋan,* my use of his name had been called "dumb" *(tinčakye-iškye,* which can be translated literally by the English word "ignorant" but is often used to mean "dumb," "crazy," or "stupid"). However, to turn then to the use of a kinship term did not make it sound better. It was not a matter of prohibition, as *mañaŋ's* comment made clear: "Why should you call me, since I am already talking with you?" A proper use of his name would have been possible only if I had wanted to establish the conversation with him. Such an incident illustrates the fact that a name is used mostly, if not exclusively, as a way of calling the attention of its bearer to the speaker, and that the common use of names is thus decidedly phatic.

We can now understand that Panare personal names do nothing but establish an intracultural communication, in relation to sex, age, and consanguinity. It becomes clear that there is no need for a taboo on the names of the dead, since these names have never individualized their bearers. Conversely, there is no need even to individuate the infants, since they will never be individualized by name in any case. However, a practice similar to the avoidance of dead persons' names appears

upon initiation. When the child name has been abandoned for an adult name, the enunciation of the former is strictly forbidden, as if it had individualized its bearer. This can easily be explained in structural terms. In effect, the four sets of personal names are located at the very center of cultural space and not at its margins. Since there are more temporary names than permanent names, and although both individuate, the temporary names are rather on the side of individualization, while the permanent names are on the side of identification. This usage reproduces within culture what the Panare perceive to happen outside of it. For we remember that dogs and named celestial bodies (beings most distant from the cultural order) were individualized, while the infants and the dead (beings closest to culture) were identified. Thus, the greater availability of temporary names as compared to the lesser availability of permanent names indicates that there is progression within culture itself and that children are less cultural individuals than are adults. On the other hand, the taboo on temporary (child) names that have been replaced by permanent (adult) names is in opposition to the social amnesia concerning the names of the dead and to the namelessness of the infants. For the discontinuity that is introduced by the changing of name is a strictly cultural sanction; it is entirely artificial, in contrast to weaning (which is the end of natural behavior) and in contrast to death (which is the end of a cultural behavior). Under these conditions, it is understandable that the taboo stresses an aspect of human development that is not immediately perceptible. It merely asserts a change of status that comes from a cultural decision, whatever may be the pretext for changing the name. In the case of women the pretext is the first menses, which are a natural function, like weaning. (I have shown elsewhere [Dumont 1972a] that children are conceived of as culturally inferior to women, who in turn are considered inferior to men.) In contrast, in the case of men the pretext is supernatural, since initiation is conceived of as a manipulation of the supernatural by which the children are symbolically killed and are then reborn as adults. Death itself is conceived of as the shocking intervention of supernature into culture. Hence in any given dry season (when boys are initiated) two symbolically opposed rituals (that of death and that of initiation) cannot both take place because they are mutually exclusive. This establishes perfectly, in the naming process, the correlation *female : male : : children : adults : : life : death : : nature : supernature.*

To sum up, we have seen that Panare names have mainly a phatic function, which consists in ensuring that communication is installed within the cultural order. In addition, the names are used to delimit the frontiers of such a cultural order. Therefore, what culture is doing in the naming process is to assert itself as such in opposition to nature and supernature. Through naming rules, it asserts itself as the very domain of communication in order to prevent, symbolically at least, intrusion into its core by nature and supernature. In other words, culture establishes not only that it "makes sense" but that it alone has the property of making sense. Doubtless Panare names do categorize, but their main function seems to be that of guaranteeing the limits of a certain order that is coextensive with Panare culture, beyond which begins non-sense: the non-sense of the Creoles, and the non-sense of the anthropologist.

REFERENCES

Dumont, Jean-Paul
  1972a   Under the Rainbow: A Structural Analysis of the Concepts of Nature, Culture and Supernature Among the Panare Indians. Ph.D. dissertation, University of Pittsburgh.
  1972b   Espacements et déplacements dans l'habitat Panare. *Journal de la Société des Américanistes* 61: 2–30.

Gillin, J. P.
  1948   *The Ways of Men.* New York: Appleton-Century-Crofts.

Lee, K. K., and Y. K. Harvey
  1973   Teknonymy and Geononymy in Korean Kinship Terminology. *Ethnology* 12: 31–46.

Lévi-Strauss, Claude
  1962   *La pensée sauvage.* Paris: Plon.

Tylor, E. B.
  1889   On a Method of Investigating the Development of Institutions. *Journal of the Royal Anthropological Institute* 18: 245–69.

8. THE KALAPALO DIETARY SYSTEM

Ellen B. Basso
Department of Anthropology, University of Arizona

In unusual contrast with other tropical lowland tribes of South America, members of Upper Xingu society in central Brazil customarily reject most species of land animals as food. Although visitors to the area have not failed to comment upon the peculiar dietary practices of the inhabitants, published accounts are limited to brief descriptions or lists of the kinds of food eaten by members of particular village groups (see, for example, Carneiro 1956–57; Galvão 1949; Murphy and Quain 1955; Schultz and Chiara 1971; von den Steinen 1894; Villas Boas and Villas Boas 1970). To my knowledge, there has been no detailed presentation of the dietary as a system, especially with respect to the adherents' own statements about what should and should not be eaten, and why. The purpose of this paper, then, is to clarify the specific practice of rejecting certain animal species, by placing it within the context of the total dietary system as understood by the Kalapalo, a Carib-speaking group who are members of Upper Xingu society. In addition to describing the significant features of the Kalapalo dietary, I shall explain the logic of that system in terms of their taxonomy of "living things," and discuss its importance as a moral code that elucidates Kalapalo cosmology.

In general the Kalapalo are quite explicit about the rules that constitute their dietary. The rules are important because adherence to the dietary is one symbol of the uniqueness of members of Upper Xingu society *(kuge)* as a whole and of the distinctiveness of Kalapalo *(aifa otomo)* in particular. The other primary symbol of this uniqueness is *ifutisu* behavior. *Ifutisu*, a highly polysemous term, refers in this context to generosity and pacificity, which are the attributes of what the Kalapalo define generally as "good" *(atutu)* behavior. Together with their dietary rules, *ifutisu* is a means by which the Kalapalo differentiate themselves from other members of Upper Xingu society, and differentiate people of that society from other categories of human beings.

Because adherence to the peculiar dietary rules and to the ideal of *ifutisu* are each aspects of a general notion about how human beings should behave, they are used by the Kalapalo to express disapproval towards individuals or local groups with whom they are in an-

tagonistic relationships. For example, when individual Kalapalo wish to express hostility towards members of another village group who have accused them of witchcraft, they are able to assert their own humanitarian propensities by implying that only they (Kalapalo) eat the proper food and behave peacefully, whereas the accusers are known to eat anything and to be excessively violent like "fierce Indians" *(iñikogo)*. The latter class of human beings includes formerly hostile neighbors of the Kalapalo (Suya, Juruna, Txukahamae Kayapo, Shavante, Txicão) who were not members of Upper Xingu society and who were known to be unpredictably aggressive *(itsotu)* and to value meat in their diet.

The most significant aspect of the Kalapalo dietary system is the way in which "living things" are classified according to whether they are eaten or not eaten by people of Upper Xingu society. The Kalapalo recognize that many of the animals they reject are eaten by other human beings and that for this reason it would be inappropriate to suggest that the species in question are considered inedible. Rather, the Kalapalo say that these things are unfit for consumption by themselves and other Upper Xingu people. Coupled with this rejection is an explicit definition of other kinds of living things as "eaten by Upper Xingu people." To understand how these categories are distinguished, it will be useful to look briefly at the general principles underlying the Kalapalo system of classifying "living things."

SYSTEMS OF CLASSIFICATION OF "LIVING THINGS"

The Kalapalo classify certain things in their experience according to a set of categories that are arranged in a hierarchy, or in a sequence of more or less inclusive units (Table 8.1). Each category is defined and differentiated from other categories in terms of a few specific attributes that the Kalapalo consider distinctive. All the referents of these categories together are known as *ago*, or "living things."

At the most specific levels of their taxonomy, the Kalapalo make use of such empirical attributes as

TABLE 8.1

Partial Taxonomy of *ago*, Showing Classes of "Living Things" Important in the Kalapalo Dietary System

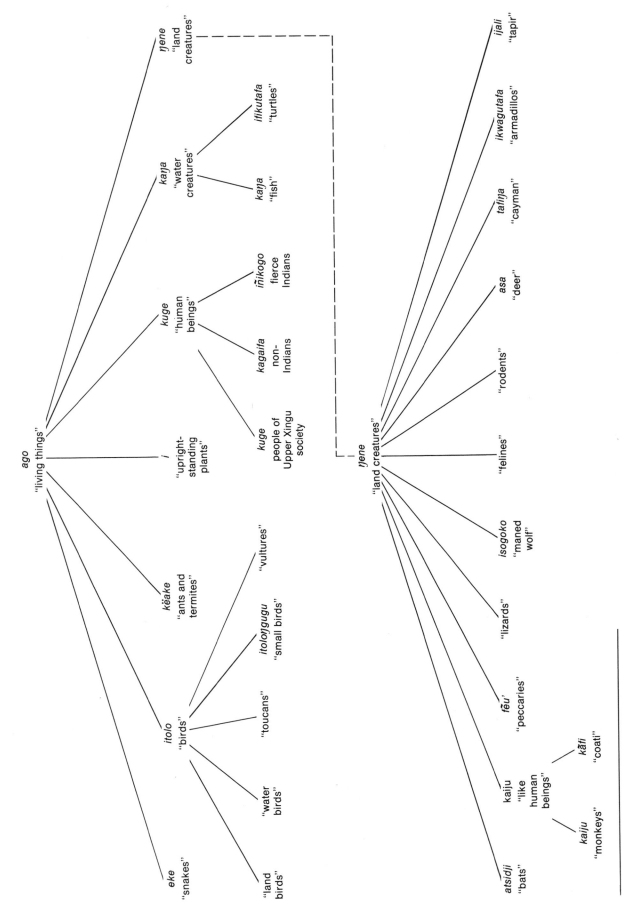

NOTE: Taxa showing no Kalapalo terms are unlabeled.

morphological characteristics, eating habits, and habitat to distinguish different kinds of natural species. The selection of one or another of these attributes often varies for pragmatic reasons. At more inclusive levels, however, some of the criteria used to differentiate categories of living things are nonobservable attributes.

The category "living things" is divided into several general subcategories. The most culturally significant are: *kuge,* "human beings"; *itolo,* "birds"; *ŋene,* "land creatures"; *kaŋa,* "water creatures"; *eke,* "snakes"; and *i,* "upright-standing plants." All of these groups are further differentiated into mid-level taxa, many of which do not have names. At the most specific level of the hierarchy are categories containing only one item—that is, referring mainly to particular natural species or varieties of plants and animals. (Sometimes these taxa include beings believed to be visible only to shamans, however.) Table 8.1 illustrates how these categories are ordered in a hierarchic relationship, and shows in some detail the internal differentiation of those classes of "living things" that are significant for an understanding of the Kalapalo dietary system.

The category *ŋene,* "land creatures," includes several more specific units, among them "felines," "deer," "peccaries," "rodents," "armadillos," "maned wolf," "tapir," "monkeys," "cayman," "molluscs," "lizards," and "bats." The Kalapalo and other Upper Xingu villagers regard virtually all *ŋene* as disgusting and refuse to eat them. The two exceptions are monkey and (sometimes) coati, which are classed together in a subcategory of *ŋene* called *kaiju.* (The problem of things that are "sometimes" eaten will be discussed shortly.)

In contrast, "things that live in the water" (called *kaŋa*) are highly prized as food. This group includes fish, turtles, the stingray, the Surinam toad (but no other frogs or toads), fresh water crabs, and (sometimes) the electric eel, giant catfish, and red piranha. Because of the value placed on *kaŋa,* fish alone account for nearly all the protein consumed by the Kalapalo.

Birds *(itolo)* are divided into several categories, only a few of which are defined as "eaten." The most important "eaten" birds are parrots and a group defined as "birds that walk on the land" (both taxa are unlabeled). The latter include doves, partridge-like species *(Tinamidae),* and the curassows *(Cracidae).* Hummingbirds, as a general class, may also be eaten, though the reason for this is unclear to me. All other kinds of birds, including water birds, owls and nightjars, vultures, birds of prey, toucans, and a multitude of small birds, are rejected. Duck *(kofoŋo)* is an exception, because it may sometimes be eaten, depending upon whether it is considered a "land bird" or a "water bird."

Except for plants (which seem to be of little interest to the Kalapalo during discussions of proper food), all the previously described categories of *ago* are also grouped by the Kalapalo into three categories that crosscut the general taxa discussed above:

1. "Things that no one eats" *(afïtï kugefeke teŋetakola). ŋene* is explicitly defined in this way, but the group also includes any other categories of *ago* that are not explicitly defined as "eaten," such as *eke* (snakes). This is a category of generally tabooed items, which are subject to the expletive *kïtsï,* connoting something disgusting (literally, "avoid it!").

2. "Things everyone eats" *(kugefeke teŋetako).* This group includes *kaŋa,* "land birds," parrots, and monkeys. Some informants called this group *kuge otu,* "people's food."

3. "Things some people eat" *(iñalu kotote teŋetako).* The few species in this group (electric eel, duck, coati, giant catfish, and red piranha) are those that are ambiguously classified, falling sometimes within a group that is eaten, and sometimes within a group that is not eaten. This ambiguity of classification is consistent, in that it is these same species that are continually subject to alternative assignment. There is no general agreement among the Kalapalo as to what these things "really" are; whether they are to be eaten or not is therefore questionable. Apparently, how any individual classes them is a matter of personal preference, based on whether it is necessary at the time to demonstrate one's "Kalapalo-ness." Kalapalo sometimes classify an item as "eaten" when they are hungry, but otherwise consider it unfit to eat. Ambiguous items are not eaten under any circumstances during ritual events, or when other groups are present and continually assessing the appropriateness of their hosts' behavior.

I noted above that those items in the group "things no one eats" can be considered objects of a general taboo—that is, they are never eaten. Those in the second group, "things everyone eats," are the subject of specific taboos—that is, they become temporarily prohibited for individuals in specific situations. For example, all birds that are normally eaten are prohibited for young men when they are wrestling during the time of their puberty seclusion. The prohibition is justified by a belief that this food will make their bones brittle. Similarly, the flesh of birds is also avoided by parents with young children who have not yet been weaned, for this kind of food is bad for the growth of the child's bones. Second, *kaŋa* (the "water creatures" that are eaten) are prohibited to persons in some kind of physical danger, especially "bleeders" (women after childbirth, menstruating women, boys whose ears have just been pierced), and to seriously ill individuals, their parents, siblings, and offspring. Third, monkey is prohibited to boys who have just undergone ear piercing. However, this prohibition is part of a general fast, during which their diet is exclusively vegetarian. After a period of eating manioc and fruit, monkey becomes the first non-vegetable food eaten by these boys.

The first category of tabooed items, birds, is prohibited as weakening for persons who are in critical periods of growth: adolescents and young children. This association may be considered "sympathetic," in that there is a direct association between the subject and object of the taboo: weak bones are caused by eating the flesh of brittle-boned birds. In the case of the second set of taboos, those focused on the eating of *kaŋa,* the association is a "negative" one between this category of living things and persons who are in physical danger. It is not clear, nor can the Kalapalo say, why there is such a correlation.

The third taboo, that concerned with monkey, appears on only one occasion, when it is part of a general fast. Thus, monkey can be considered the supremely edible item in the Kalapalo diet, a kind of food that is acceptable in all circumstances but one. A clue to why this is so lies in the Kalapalo justification for eating monkey in the first place, even though it belongs to the generally prohibited *ŋene* category. The Kalapalo say, "People of the Upper Xingu eat monkeys because they are like human beings." Some of the ways in which the Kalapalo speak of different kinds of "living things" help to explain this statement, and to these I shall now turn.

COSMOLOGICAL LABELS AND THEIR USE IN SPEECH

The category *ago,* "living things," can also be thought of as a member of a paradigmatic set[1] in which four categories are defined in terms of two intersecting dimensions. Each one of these categories, taken alone, represents a specific model consisting of several defining attributes. The use of a term labeling such a category signals how some thing in Kalapalo experience behaves toward, or is related to, a human being. These behavioral attributes and relationships contribute to conceptualizations of the possible relationships between humans and nonhumans, and thus they can be thought of as crucial features of a general model of "Xingu humanity" or "Xingu distinctiveness."

---

1. I use this term following Kay (1966). See his paper for a discussion of the formal properties of paradigmatic and taxonomic models.

Kalapalo men dancing with Kuikuru women in the latter's village

The Structure of the Paradigmatic Set

The four categories that compose the paradigmatic set (see Table 8.2) are ordered through the intersection of two dimensions: (a) what I have termed the "human metaphor" and (b) the suffix indicating "possession." The paradigmatic ordering of these categories is an analytic structure devised by the anthropologist, for the Kalapalo do not explicitly compare and contrast the categories with one another, nor can they make general statements about the two dimensions. The importance of these dimensions is demonstrated, however, by their continual and predictable appearance in speech.

TABLE 8.2
Paradigm of Kalapalo Cosmological Terms

"human metaphor"

	+	−
suffix /giʼ/ **+**	*itologu* "pets"	*iŋikogu* "possessions"
suffix /giʼ/ **−**	*ago* "living things"	*itseke* "monsters"

The phrase "human metaphor" subsumes a set of terms that refer to physiological and social phenomena and that are used when speaking about things called *ago,* "living things." Even though the terms are most often applied to human beings, they are acceptable for speaking about nonhumans as well. The following are examples of this human metaphor used by the Kalapalo.

1. Terms for physiological phenomena
   a. growth *(atukulu)* and death *(apïŋgulu)*
   b. offspring *(itijipïgï)* and parents *(oto)*
   c. names for parts of the body
2. Terms for "mental" states
   a. *ifutisu:* in the special sense of "retirement from public activities," used to refer to the behavior of an untamed animal (for example, a turtle withdrawn into its shell)
   b. *itsotu:* unpredictable anger or unreasonable rage (as when a dog bites people who enter its owner's house)
   c. *awïnda* ("speak falsely"): used when an animal, although undisturbed, makes loud noises of apparent protest, which are humorous to the Kalapalo (as when a pet macaw suddenly squawks inside a house)
3. Terms for social relationships (used in referring to many classes of *ago)*
   a. village representatives *(anetaw),* villages *(etu),* and followers *(otomo)* of *anetaw*
   b. wives *(efitsaw),* husbands *(iñoko),* and frequently kinship relationships as well (especially those marked for affinability)

The use of human metaphor is a means of explaining relationships between classes of things and thereby implying that all "living things" hold in common certain attributes. By speaking of nonhuman beings in terms normally associated with humans, the Kalapalo make the more general relationship between nonhumans and humans one of explicit closeness, admitting of possible intimacy. This potentially intimate association often becomes realized in mythological incidents, in which humans and nonhumans engage in sexual relations and produce offspring. Belief in the possession of common attributes is not only explicitly stated by Kalapalo; it is also evident in the similar treatment of human offspring and members of a wide variety of natural species, especially with respect to procedures for influencing growth and behavior.

The second dimension of the paradigm refers to the suffix /gï/ (allomorphs are /gï/, /gu/, /sï/, /su/), indicating a "thing or attribute that is possessed." It must be affixed to the term for any object or thing (for example, material objects, ceremonies) whose possession is indicated during the course of the utterance; it also occurs as an element in the structure of names for classes of things that can be considered "normally possessed"—for example, parts of the body.

To summarize, the paradigm formed by the dimensions "presence or absence of the human metaphor" and "presence or absence of the suffix indicating possession"

contains the categories *ago,* "living things," *iŋikogu,* "possessions," *itologu,* "pets," and *itseke,* "monsters." The Kalapalo conception of these four categories is discussed below.

Kalapalo Models of the Paradigmatic Categories

Ago, "living things." These are all spoken of in terms of the human metaphor, but they do not take the possession indicator. The term *ago* labels the highest-level taxon in the hierarchy discussed earlier, but as I suggest below, it also connotes features not made explicit in native definitions of that category.

Itologu, "pets." When speaking of "pets," the Kalapalo make use of the human metaphor, and they also attach the suffix indicating possession to the pets' taxonomic names. Birds, monkeys, and turtles are the only wildlife kept as pets. Other animals are occasionally captured and briefly held in the village until they die of maltreatment or lack of food; such animals are not referred to as *itologu,* except in jest. Dogs are considered "pets," but they were apparently introduced into the area relatively recently and only after Brazilian contacts were made. (Compare the Kalapalo word for dog, *katsawgo,* and the Brazilian *chachorro).*

Like their wild *ago* counterparts, "pets" are spoken about in terms of the human metaphor, but another set of symbols, having reference to the parent-child relationship among humans, establishes a deeper metaphorical relationship. The Kalapalo view the relationship between *itologu* and *oto* ("pet" and "owner") as being characterized on the human side by nurture and protection within a household, and on the animal side by lack of *ifutisu* (in the specific sense of shyness)—in other words, by being tame. This relationship is particularly interesting because the distinctive features are also those that define the filiative relationship—that between human parents and their children. Children and pets alike are supposed to be fed, reared, and kept protected within the confines of the house; they share an intimacy with their *oto* (this word means, among other things, both "parent" and "owner") that is characterized by informality and lack of restraint. Often pets are secluded like human adolescents "to make them grow beautiful," especially when the animal is a young bird able to provide its owner with valuable feathers as it reaches maturity.

Although *itologu* may be members of *ago* species generally defined as "eaten by Upper Xingu people," they themselves are never eaten, nor should they be killed. Ideally, such animals are supposed to be buried when they die, rather than be discarded or fed to another pet. Both unnamed children (such as stillbirths or infants who die during postpartum seclusion) and pets are buried near the hammock of the parent or owner. Pet birds are the only animals held to have a village of the dead. As men who die travel to the village of dead men located to the east where the sun rises, so dead pets go to their village of the dead located in the direction of the sunset. (It is perhaps for this reason that men are buried with heads facing east, pet birds with heads facing west.) Thus the *itologu-oto* relationship is conceived of as a special emotional tie between humans and nonhumans, and it takes on even greater meaning through association with symbols of vital importance in human life-crisis rituals.

Iŋikogu, "possessions." Human metaphor is not applied to items referred to by this term, but the possession indicator is always used. Included in this category are things that are normally possessed, such as items received as payment *(fipïgï),* water in a container, harvested crops, and material paraphernalia such as fish hooks, arrows, hammocks, baskets, ceramics, and feather ornaments. A person who is *oto* (owner) has usually acquired his possessions through some form of exchange—social prestation (such as widow remarriage payment, payment to a ceremonial performer, payment for grave digging), personal buying and selling, or the *uluki,* "trade ceremony." The transactions in all of these instances are legitimate means of exchanging wealth (see Dole 1956–57; 1956–58; 1966). Although different things appear in each kind of exchange, they are referred to generally as *fipïgï,* "payment." In addition, a person may of course manufacture something himself, or, as is usually the case with a "pet," he may capture it in the wild. In all of these situations, the resultant relationship is one of "property" to "owner."

Itseke, "monsters." Human metaphor is not applied by the Kalapalo to items referred to as *itseke,* nor is the possession indicator used. The category includes celestial phenomena (which are not included in the taxonomy of "living things") and items that are considered monstrous in some way. The Kalapalo consider *itseke* potentially malevolent beings, but this aspect of their nature is apparent only in discussions of the relationships between *itseke* and humans, and cannot be derived from the paradigmatic criteria. Because of their potential malevolence towards human beings, *itseke* are creatures that are both physically dangerous *(tekotiñï)* and violent *(itsotu).* They are believed to cause harm in several specific ways: (1) by projecting *kwifi,* or invisible darts, into a victim's body; (2) by capturing a person's shadow *(akuagï);* and (3) by merely presenting themselves to the sight of a human being.

Itseke are also characterized by their unusual and shocking appearance. Some *itseke* are known for their ability to transform themselves, while others are considered monstrous because they suddenly and inexplicably appear to be different from normal phenomena. *Itseke* may appear monstrous because they combine morphological attributes from different categories of "living things," or simply because they are abnormally large in size (compare *tsekegï,* "[having the property of] large size," and *itseke,* "monster"). Thus the names of many *itseke* take the form: (1) name for some ordinary low-level taxon in the *ago* hierarchy, plus (2) the suffix /kuegï/, an augmentative with the implication of "potential malevolence," and thus of "monstrosity." Examples of *itseke* names are: Safundukuegï, "monstrous bass-fish"; Tifagikuegï, "monstrous stingray"; Tïtsahakuegï, "monstrous giant kiskadee"; Itaukuegï, "monstrous women" (water sirens).

Having now specified the Kalapalo models associated with each of the four categories, I would like to turn to specific examples of contextually varying classification, which demonstrate how these models are symbolized by use of the categories in Kalapalo speech.

Situational Variation in the Use of the Paradigmatic Concepts

The use of the four cosmological labels often appears contradictory, since, while they mark categories defined in terms of specific and mutually exclusive relationship attributes, different labels are often applied to the same specific things. This apparent anomaly is easily explained, for these attributes are meaningful only during specific situations in which some kind of relationship with or behavior towards a human being is indicated, and such a relationship or kind of behavior may change or cease to exist in some other situation.

As I noted earlier, the relationships between parent and child and between pet and owner are defined by the Kalapalo in terms of similar normative behaviors. These similarities are the basis for a metaphorical use of the term *itologu* to refer to a child who has come under the nurture and protection of a nonrelative. Although adoption (wherein a child is jurally considered offspring of someone other than its real parent) is unknown among the Kalapalo, fosterage is quite common. In the latter case, a child is raised by a relative of a deceased parent (usually a sibling), but in no way is this considered, or referred to as, a parent-child relationship. Because of *ifutisu,* the Kalapalo ideal of generosity, kinsmen of a deceased person have an obligation to care for orphaned children. However, when a nonkinsman takes charge of such a child for no apparent reason (that is, with no prior obligation based on *ifutisu),* the child is called *itologu* of the person supporting it. This special metaphorical use of the term indicates recognition of a behavioral relationship similar to that between owner and pet, since it includes nurture and protection of an immature being provided without any prior relationship or obligation. A child is of course also considered a "human being" (*kuge,* which is a category of "living thing") and is referred to as such when the speaker wishes the child to be distinguished from another living thing. The use of *itologu* in reference to a child is thus an example of contextually varying classification.

When a Kalapalo wants to specify an animal's identity as pet of some human being, the term *itologu* is used. This is often done when the speaker needs to stress the fact that the animal in question is not an ordinary *ago.* For example, if a person wants to kill and eat a bird or monkey he sees roaming the village, another can refer to it as *itologu* of a specific individual, thus denying the suitability of such an idea. In general, then, the use of the term *itologu* appears to be a special reference to a certain kind of social relationship that can exist between men and "living things" that are nonrelatives. The latter may or may not be human beings. As we saw earlier, however, when the Kalapalo want to emphasize the dimension of "ownership"—whether of an animal or any other possession—the term *iŋikogu* is applied.

The use of the term *itseke* appears to involve a situational denial of some of the same human-like attributes that are indicated for other categories by the use of human metaphor. For example, morphological-ly human heroic figures are mythically associated in human-like relationships and situations, and yet these beings are nonetheless referred to as *itseke.* In such instances, the term symbolizes the endowment of these characters with nonhuman attributes, which to the Kalapalo are truly "abnormal" and therefore awesome. Mythological characters (and the dead) have the ability to change their shape, engage in fearful destruction, and change or invent things.

As with *itologu,* items that are normally eaten are rejected if they are labeled *itseke.* For example, on one occasion a very tasty fish the Kalapalo call *wagiti* was rejected as appropriate food by some Kalapalo men because a water rat had been found in its stomach. When I asked them why they did not eat the fish, which they had thrown away during a period of extreme scarcity, they explained that the *wagiti* was not in fact food at all, since it was not *kaŋa* but rather *itseke* and therefore inedible. When I then suggested that fish occasionally were found to have such things inside them, the men assured me that only *itseke* would eat *ŋene,* "land creatures." The proper diet of fish was defined as other fish and various plant materials, according to the species. This incident illustrates how things normally classed as *ago* are considered *itseke* on the basis of attributes that are considered antithetical to those of human behavior. In this case, a decision was made to classify something normally considered "fish" as *itseke* on the basis of a dietary practice considered improper according to Kalapalo rules about eating.

Kalapalo women singing in the village plaza

Kalapalo women preparing *piqui* (a cultivated fruit) and manioc soup for a ceremonial food distribution

At this point, we may return to the question of why the Kalapalo justify their eating monkey by the phrase, "It is like human beings." The examples given above illustrate a generalization that can be made about Kalapalo cosmology. This system incorporates a morality according to which things in the universe that manifest human-like behavior (adhering to a diet similar to that of Upper Xingu people, and acting peacefully) are extolled and embraced, and things behaving otherwise (especially, having an indiscriminate diet and acting violently) are denigrated and avoided. Thus the Kalapalo dietary, by specifying indirectly that only human-like creatures are to be eaten, is a specific metaphorization of Kalapalo cosmology. Put differently, the consumption of food is given a uniquely Kalapalo meaning through symbols that constitute the Kalapalo world view.

REFERENCES

Carneiro, Robert
　1956–57 La cultura de los indios Kuikurus del Brasil central. I: La economia de subsistencia. *Runa* 8 (2): 169–85.

Dole, Gertrude
　1956–57 La cultura de los indios Kuikurus del Brasil central. II: La organizacion social. *Runa* 8 (2): 185–202.

　1956–58 Ownership and Exchange among the Kuikuru Indians of Mato Grosso. *Revista do Museu Paulista,* n.s. X: 125–33.

　1966 Anarchy Without Chaos: Alternatives to Political Authority among the Kuikuru. In *Political Anthropology,* ed. Marc Swartz et al., pp. 73–88. Chicago: Univ. of Chicago Press.

Galvão, Eduardo
　1949 Apontamentos sobre os índios Kamayura. In *Observações zoológicas e antropológicas na região dos formadores do Xingu,* by José C. M. Carvalho, Pedro E. de Lima, and Eduardo Galvão, pp. 31–48. *Publicações Avulsas* 5, Museu Nacional, Rio de Janeiro.

Kay, Paul
　1966 Comments on Colby. In *Cognitive Anthropology,* ed. Stephen Tyler, pp. 78–92. New York: Holt, Rinehart and Winston.

Murphy, Robert M., and Buell Quain
　1955 The Trumaí Indians of Central Brazil. *American Ethnological Society Monograph* 24. Seattle: Univ. of Washington Press.

Schultz, Harald, and Vilma Chiara
　1971 Informações etnográficas dos Indios Waurá. In *Verhandlungen des XXXVIII. Internationalen Amerikanistenkongresses* (Stuttgart–Munich, 1968), vol. 3, pp. 285–308.

Steinen, Karl von den
　1894 *Unter den Naturvölkern Zentral-Brasiliens.* Berlin: Geographische Verlagsbuch Handlung von Dietrich Reimer.

Villas Boas, Orlando, and Claudio Villas Boas
　1970 *Xingu: Os indios, seus mitos.* Rio de Janeiro: Zahar Editores.

9. A STUDY OF THE PROCESS OF VILLAGE FORMATION IN YE'CUANA SOCIETY

Nelly Arvelo-Jimenez
Department of Anthropology, Instituto Venezolano de
Investigaciones Cientificas, Caracas

In Ye'cuana society the village is the structural unit of the political system. For the individual the village embodies all meaningful sociopolitical relations. Hence it is important to discern under what conditions villages come to life, disappear, and give way to new villages. Furthermore, villages are the institutionalization of a stage, the last one, in the overall process of group formation. To understand this final stage and its development, one has to delve into the preceding stages and elucidate their ruling principles. In this paper, emphasis is placed upon internal migration (a recurrent event in Ye'cuana sociopolitical life) because it governs the formation, disintegration, and reconstitution of groups and villages. In addition, migration is itself the key to an understanding of the functioning of three important structural principles. These are:

1. The rule of postmarital residence by which uxorilocality and local endogamy should prevail. Departures from this rule (as well as from others to be mentioned) foster social frictions, which in turn provoke cleavages between groups, village splits, and migrations.

2. The preference for marriage between bilateral cross-cousins and between persons classified as grandparents and grandchildren. (The cross-cousin category includes several subtypes classified by degrees of collaterality or degrees of consanguinity; the marriage norm defines first-degree cross-cousins as the most desirable, and this desirability decreases with collateral distance.) The function of this preference is to achieve the localization of a compact group of close kin. In practice, marriage with a cross-cousin does not necessarily fulfill the postmarital residence rule. Nor does it necessarily involve individuals who fall into the preferred cross-cousin subtypes.

3. The rule of bilateral descent by which kin ties on either side can be stressed. The elasticity implicit in this rule is widely used in recruiting new members to consolidate groups and villages. This form of recruitment, while in compliance with one jural rule, obviously contradicts others.

THE LIFE CYCLE OF GROUPS

Recruitment into sociopolitical groups—the nuclear family, the extended family, and the village—is based on kinship and regulated through marriage. Recruitment at the village level is basically political and thus transcends kinship principles.

The Nuclear Family

A marriage alliance undergoes a process of development with successive phases of increasing independence. The initial phase of a marriage is the time of greatest dependence on older kinsmen. The union has to survive manipulations by persons directly or indirectly related to the marriage partners. It is generally true that in this phase the stability of the marriage is in the hands of the relevant members of the senior generation and independent of the will of the spouses. In its procreative phase a marriage becomes a nuclear family and starts to achieve independence. Generally several years pass before a marriage falls into this phase. Time (which allows for the assimilation of the inmarrying spouse) and the arrival of children consolidate the procreative phase. A marriage enters into its mature phase when the family of procreation becomes an incipient extended family.

Marriages that are locally endogamous and monogamous, have, from the outset, a better chance to become stabilized. Partners in this type of marriage must still counteract several forces in order to stabilize their alliance. One such force is the pressure placed on spouses to divorce and marry a relative who, besides fitting into the preferred category of cross-cousin, shares a closer degree of consanguinity. In the case of polygynous unions, these pressures are placed on the husband by the parents of other wives he may have within the same village. In the case where the wives are not full sisters, the husband has several different sets of in-laws. Each set tries to monopolize the political loyalty and the economic contribution of the man. Finally, the husband may find himself urged by one or more groups of affines to fully assimilate with them. At this level, full assimilation means that in political and economic spheres a married

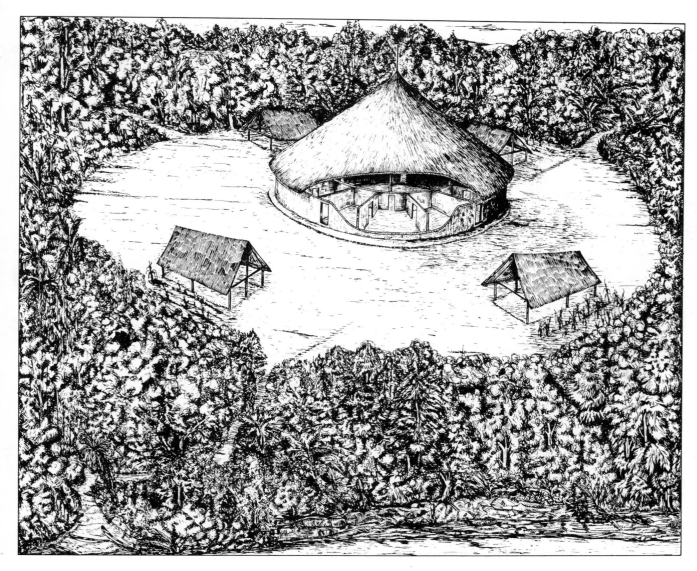

Sketch of a Ye'cuana village

man should prove beyond doubt that his first loyalties are with a particular wife's family.

Locally exogamous marriages have additional problems, such as: (a) achievement by the husband of unchallenged membership in a wife's village, which means he must be regarded as a villager, not as a foreigner; (b) resisting the pressures put on a husband by his family of orientation and village of origin to return to them; and (c) keeping under control conflicting demands from different sets of in-laws when the man is married into more than one village.

Marriages outside the preferred categories have stronger forces working against their stability. Nevertheless, they do not, comparatively, show greater instability. These marriages are the result of a personal commitment from both partners to defy the rules of their society. This fact may explain their relatively greater endurance in the face of negative pressures.

Several forces coming from different levels of sociopolitical action (the extended family, the village, and the intervillage levels) work against the stability of the nuclear family. However, those forces permeate the whole social system and operate at all levels in a generalized struggle involving the allocation and reallocation of people.

The Extended Family

The extended family is a unit that comprises three to four generations. It grows gradually with the marriage of its female members, the household thus formed showing a tendency toward matrifocality. Senior persons of both

The *wöwä*, a basket woven by Ye'cuana women for use in carrying manioc and other crops

sexes make decisions regarding social, economic, and religious events within this social micro-universe. For intravillage affairs the extended family has one representative in the senior male circle of the village.

Social frictions involving a whole extended family may spring from the same pressures that threaten the stability of the nuclear family. They may also originate in a defective assimilation into a host village in the case where the extended family is an absorbed group. However, pressures coming from outside the extended family do not fragment it. When such pressures prove unbearable, the extended family leaves the village *en bloc*. The community's political strength is then affected.

The extended family plays a very crucial role in the political life of a village. However, success in this role as a pressure group in the political arena is attained only when the extended family lacks internal divisiveness and therefore behaves as a highly cohesive unit. The solidarity of this group may be affected by its vertical growth to three- to four-generation membership. From a four-generation family, a smaller one can split off and eventually achieve political autonomy. This type of cleavage (coming from within the extended family) is common only in large and politically mature villages.

The Village

A circular clearing amidst the tropical forest indicates the presence of a village. In the center of the clearing stands the large round communal house, with a capacity of approximately 60 people or four to six extended families. The constituent sociopolitical unit within the village is the extended family. Accordingly, in less acculturated areas, the round communal house is internally partitioned into "households" for each extended family. In more acculturated areas, the number of extended families is equivalent to the number of houses within the community.

The extended families of a village belong to a local kin group that consists of members of the kindred of an older person or of a group of siblings who have founded a particular village. However, as we shall see below, not all members of a local kin group are directly related to the central sibling group. Any modification in the composition of the extended families of a community is bound to affect three different levels of relations—the extended family, the kindred, and the village.

Villages usually split along extended family lines, and those splitting groups become the core founding groups of new villages. Hence villages may be founded by a group that has split from a mature village, by a group seceding from a nonmature village, or by a group that has migrated from a disintegrated village. (I exclude old village groups that migrate as a unit to a new site, in search of better hunting grounds or healthier environments.)

One of the most useful criteria for ascertaining the degree of autonomy of a village is the size of its population. The population of incipient villages may range from 8 to 27 persons. A village in the process of achieving stability as an autonomous community has approximately doubled its original population to about 30 to 40 persons. The population of consolidated or mature villages may range from 50 to 70 persons.

In its incipient stage a village is composed of one extended family. To succeed as a village, this core founding group must attract and assimilate new members. Failure in this endeavor entails realignment of the group; the incipient village has to become attached to another that has a better chance of achieving political maturity, or it has to join a politically autonomous village.

There are five ways of acquiring village membership, but only birth can guarantee full enjoyment of political and social rights. The other means are marriage, adoption, invitation, and use of the subterfuge of extended paternity. Though all four are not unusual, they are considered artificial means of acquiring village membership.

Membership by birth. In a society with no inheritable, material property and hence no goods to capitalize on, an individual's only wealth is (a) his membership in an autonomous social unit—that is, a politically mature village; (b) his membership in a locally compact and numerically strong group of close relatives; and (c) his ritual skills, which are unrelated to kinship. To be a member of a village means that one can suggest, approve, or veto actions and decisions concerning village affairs at the meetings of the senior men's circle. One cannot exercise these rights in any other village. This is the basis for the desirability of continued membership in one's own natal village. Village membership also gives an individual a political identity in relation to the rest of the Ye'cuana nation.

Marriage. A marriage, especially a locally exogamous one, is likely to produce a chain reaction in the respective household groups of the spouses, in their villages, and even in other villages. It implies the reallocation of a member who might be wanted by more than one group of close relatives or by more than one village. Marriages, then, are not outside the field of forces that create new groups, realign them, fuse them, or split them apart. Marriages are useful means of consolidating some groups at the political and social expense of others.

Adoption. Adoption is intimately related to kinship in Ye'cuana society. Only consanguineal relatives have rights in the adoption of an orphan or a child of divorced parents. The only problem that may arise concerning such children is that they may be reclaimed by close relatives of the other parent.

Invitation. Invitations to join a village are extended for political reasons. They are made either to groups or to individuals by the headman or another member of the recipient village. Invitations are extended to seceding groups or to groups from disintegrated villages. Invitations to individuals are always accompanied by the offer of a local girl in marriage. If both the immigrants and the hosts manage to overcome the social and political disadvantages that go with the status of outsider, the two groups eventually provide benefits for one another. The marriages that take place between immigrant and indigenous kinship groups are the most effective means of leveling the differences between them. However, the process is never fast or smooth. For example, one may find communities that are numerically and chronologically mature, but are still maintaining a precarious balance between core members and absorbed groups and individuals. Balance among the component kin groups of a village, and most especially in relation to the absorbed groups, is always a matter of degree and is never absolutely attained.

Extended paternity. Ye'cuana believe that each copulation contributes to conception. The fashioning of a child is alleged to be a process induced by repeated copulation. The seminal fluid gradually and increasingly accumulates in a woman's womb until it is completely filled up; at that point conception has reached its zenith and the woman is pregnant. Therefore, Ye'cuana reason, every man who is identified as having had sexual access to a woman between pregnancies is genitor and pater of her next child. As a result, some people consider more than one man their genitor and pater. This belief is used to justify the creation of additional kin ties between certain children, their putative fathers, and the respective families of these children.

MANAGEMENT OF VILLAGE LIFE

Kinship principles are the foundation of Ye'cuana group structure. However, there are no statuses ascribed by the kinship system for handling groups, other than the respect for seniority that gives seniors managerial authority over juniors. Even in group formation the elasticity of the cognatic principle allows for versatile combinations in the composition of Ye'cuana social groupings. Such elasticity makes it possible for each of several family groups to have equally rightful claims over a relative. Such claims and counterclaims on common relatives are elements in the process of group formation, and they foster the confrontation of centrifugal and centripetal forces each village has to undergo in its struggle for autonomy as an independent unit. As it increases its own membership, each village depletes the population of others. Time balances out the gains and losses, but people in each village speak and behave as if gains were permanent and lawful accretions to a community of exclusive membership, and as if losses were both unlawful encroachments on their own community's population and superfluous additions to other communities.

At the level of intravillage relations, management of political life is the shared responsibility of the headman and the senior men's circle. Headmen come to office either through having been the leaders of splitting groups and thus founders of new villages, or through having uniquely strong personalities, in which wisdom in handling people (by way of example, persuasion, courage, generosity, and technical skills) is combined with greater ritual proficiency than commoners have. A headman's duties are the prevention of social disruption (meaning open confrontation) and leadership in executing the policies agreed upon at the meetings of the senior men's circle. A headman is the person authorized to establish communication among the different household groups and to lead them into reaching decisions.

The senior men's circle is made up mostly of household heads. At most meetings the members do not discuss politics. However, the circle functions as an ad hoc council and becomes political upon the headman's initiative. At such times the discussions mainly concern communal labor and hence the mobilization of individuals from all extended families, and each member of the circle is pressed to exercise his political rights. Decisions are reached by consensus and then executed by the headman.

Matters such as friction or conflict between individuals of different extended families, or between the community and one of its extended families, are not the province of the senior men's circle. Discussion and resolution of those issues would require judicial and penal powers that neither the senior men nor the headman have.

There are no formal Ye'cuana courts, but there are redressing mechanisms whose function is to check the rise of factional struggles, and thus to prevent or at least delay a division of the village community. These mechanisms are manipulated by the aggrieved individual with the support of his extended family. The intervention of this group is of great political consequence at various levels. First, the individual is affected because his or her extended family is the only supporting unit in confrontations with other members of the community. Second, the family's functions go beyond a solidary support for its members; the family is also protecting its own public image and political status. Third, and most important, the intervention of the extended family affects the social equilibrium within the community; if a conflict remains unresolved, village solidarity undergoes progressive deterioration and eventually a village split takes place.

Offenses are settled in different ways according to the degree of criminality involved. Most minor problems tend to be solved through mechanisms such as gossip, indirect complaints, and temporary self-isolation of aggrieved persons. However, slander, unreasonable gossip, and intentional troublemaking—in other words, extreme use of these sanctions—are the utmost social offenses and provoke village splits.

The forces of the gossip circle are put to work by spreading the alleged offense among the women. The asocial act is scrutinized, its motives hypothesized and censured. As a given complaint goes around two, three, or more rounds of the gossip circle, additional evidence accumulates to bring out the truth. This procedure takes the place of the cross-examination technique used in formal courts. Moreover, in this way the wrongdoer is warned and society's values are indirectly reasserted. The offended person may also state his grievances in a monologue at dawn when his fellow villagers are still in their common sleeping quarters. With this procedure as well, personal confrontation is avoided, the wrongdoer is warned, and the community is informed and spurred to give a verdict.

A temporary withdrawal from village life carried out by individuals or by nuclear families also avoids open confrontation and is a means of opening a way to the restoration of social equilibrium. However, a well-integrated extended family that is repeatedly aggrieved slowly detaches itself from village affairs until it definitely

Ye'cuana man dressed up for a festival

breaks off. In some cases, an absorbed extended family that is poorly integrated into the village may find pressures upon it unbearable and decide to drop membership in the village quickly and permanently. Thus, secession of a household group from a village, although an extreme measure, is another mode of settling disputes. These splits may occur in both mature and nonmature villages, and they may occur as a result of the political crisis that follows a headman's death. A severe crisis of the latter type may cause the disintegration of a village into extended and even nuclear families.

INTERVILLAGE RELATIONS

I have discussed the formation of groups of increasing numerical and social complexity as well as the integration of the smaller ones into those that embody more diversified sociopolitical relations. In so doing I described the principles that rule them as well as the multiple interpretations of these principles that are expressed in Ye'cuana social groupings. Furthermore, I showed that there are contradictions between some of those principles, a fact that rules out adherence to all of them by all groups at the same point in Ye'cuana history.

The internal differentiation of these groups was examined, and it was shown how each represents a distinct level of sociopolitical structure and of social cohesiveness—a cohesiveness that is better understood by sequentially opposing each level with one of greater sociopolitical complexity. Thus, as we have seen, in intravillage affairs the extended family is the social unit that defends the political rights of its individual members against encroachments by members of the local kindred and other fellow villagers. In turn, the local kindred protects the indigenous kin groups' rights against encroachments by members of immigrant, absorbed groups. In intervillage affairs each village behaves as one whole corporate unit that provides political support and gives political identity to each of its individual members.

Nonvillagers are considered foreigners. A foreigner is not entitled to political rights, and he is allowed only the privilege of enjoying the hospitality of a host village. Hospitality is the responsibility of the village headman as representative of his local community. Religious beliefs explain disease, misfortune, and death as caused by manipulation of supernatural forces from outside —that is, from other villages and regions. "Foreigners," according to cultural dogma, are malicious and unreliable.

Despite the fact that groups at each level are interfered with by the more complex ones, smaller units depend on larger ones in recruiting members and in becoming mature working social units. The result is an interdependent web of sociopolitical relations involving the whole society. Ye'cuana are conscious that this network of relations has no tangible boundaries at the village or pan-societal levels, yet every Ye'cuana village tries zealously to keep its political autonomy. To this end its members establish arbitrary limits by manipulating whatever social, spatial, and religious mechanisms they can to increase its political distance from other villages.

Six specific mechanisms that stress separateness at the village level are present in Ye'cuana society. First is the political sovereignty of the village, with its concomitant that full political rights can be exercised only in one's own natal village. The second is the postmarital residence rule, which prescribes locally endogamous marriages and forbids locally exogamous ones. The third is the value given to relationships with kinsmen who are localized; in some cases this produces structural amnesia in persons who fail to reckon their kin ties with relatives settled elsewhere. Fourth is the belief in the ill will of nonvillagers and in their ability to manipulate supernatural powers in order to undermine one's health and well-being. Fifth is the spatial and structural arrangement within the round house, which fits with and symbolizes the structure of the universe as it is understood and visualized by the Ye'cuana. A Ye'cuana village is interpreted as a small replica of the universe; this belief obviously reinforces the model of village autonomy. The sixth mechanism is the widely scattered settlement pattern and economic independence of the villages, which also augments political distance.

All this fits into a model of independent, self-sufficient social units. However, in reality all Ye'cuana villages belong to a socially interdependent whole. Conflicts that arise from violations of the norm of village solidarity are interpreted by the Ye'cuana as deepening the cleavages between local groups and their constituent social units. But it is through conflict that interdependence is attained, because forced departures from the norms— however deplored by the Ye'cuana—reinforce the necessary interchange among all units.

Most Ye'cuana groups have, during the course of their history, shown a sequence of change. They have conformed to the ideal model of relations, have violated the norms, and finally have achieved or attempted to achieve a reversion to the guiding structural principles. The latter have proved their enduring relevance in shaping Ye'cuana sociopolitical behavior over the last 200 years.

Ye'cuana woman weaving a bead apron

10. THE AKURIYO WAY OF DEATH

Peter Kloos
Institute of Social and Cultural Studies, University of Leiden

Akuriyo is the name now generally used for a small population of hunters and gatherers living in the tropical forest of southeastern Surinam and neighboring parts of Brazil (see Map 10.1). At the time of their rediscovery in 1968 their number was about 80. *Akuriyo* is the name the Trio of Surinam use for these nomads; they are called *Wayarikure* by the Wayana, and *Wama* by an early European observer (Ahlbrinck 1956). The Akuriyo represent a degree of sociocultural isolation that is extremely rare today. Although the existence of an Amerindian population called Akuriyo or Acooreo is known from the early 17th century onwards (they were, of course, not necessarily the ancestors of today's Akuriyo), European contact came late.

In 1937 members of a border expedition met a small group of Amerindians on the Oelemari River. After a couple of hours these Amerindians, who possessed stone axes and apparently did not use iron tools, again disappeared into the forest (Meuldijk 1939). As a result of this contact, the government decided to send the missionary Father W. Ahlbrinck, well known for his studies on coastal Carib culture, to the Oelemari River in 1938. Ahlbrinck met the same group in the same area, and kept contact for a day and a half. The Wama, as he called them, were afraid and hostile, and they left the contact site early in the morning of the third day (Ahlbrinck 1956). It took 30 years before a third documented contact was established. In the meantime, there were rumors about Bush Negroes (Djuka) who went fishing and hunting in the Oelemari basin and saw "Wild Indians" or who never came back, presumably having been killed by those Indians. We know now that the Akuriyo occasionally did kill Bush Negro intruders into their territory.

In 1953 the Surinam government again organized an expedition to the Oelemari headwaters. Although trails and even footprints of Amerindians were found by members of the expedition, the people who made them did not allow themselves to be seen (Felhoen Kraal 1957; J. Michels 1972: personal communication). From 1965 on, members of the American West Indies Mission, who had been working since 1961 among the Trio and Wayana in southern Surinam, organized a number of expeditions with the purpose of bringing the gospel to these elusive Amerindians. The missionaries also found enough signs to warrant the assumption that nomadic Amerindians still lived in the forests of southeast Surinam. In 1968, actual contact was established by accident. A number of Wayana Indians came drifting down the Waremapan, a tributary of the Litani. Hearing some noise on the left bank and believing it to be a herd of peccaries, they disembarked and walked into a small band of hunting Akuriyo men—much to the surprise of both groups. The Wayana paid a visit to Akuriyo camps, left their hosts after a couple of hours, and subsequently reported what they had found to the American missionary at Kawemhakan on the Lawa.

Between 1968 and 1970, the missionaries (aided initially by Wayana, Trio, and Bush Negroes, and later mainly by Trio and by the Akuriyo themselves) established and maintained contact with all but one of the Akuriyo bands. In 1970 and 1971 the majority of the Akuriyo were brought to two Trio villages, Alalaparu and Përëru Tëpu. During the period of my fieldwork (January-August 1973, in Përëru Tëpu) the situation was as follows: 35 Akuriyo were living a more or less sedentary life in Tëpu; one Akuriyo, married to a Trio woman, lived in Alalaparu; and a group of about 10 was at that time probably in Brazil, just south of the border with Surinam. There may also have been a small group of perhaps 5 individuals still roaming somewhere south of the Tapanahony, in the Oranje Mountains. This group has never been contacted, but the names of several of the group (consisting of an elderly couple with three children) are known. The group itself may have died out, and its present existence is doubtful.[1] At the most, there are 50 living Akuriyo.

NOTE: Fieldwork in Përëru Tëpu, for six months in 1973, was made possible by the Netherlands Foundation for the Advancement of Tropical Research (Wotro). For information concerning the Akuriyo I am indebted to Claude Leavitt, Jan van Mazijk, Ivan Schoen, and Art Yohner.

1. In 1974 this band was finally located.

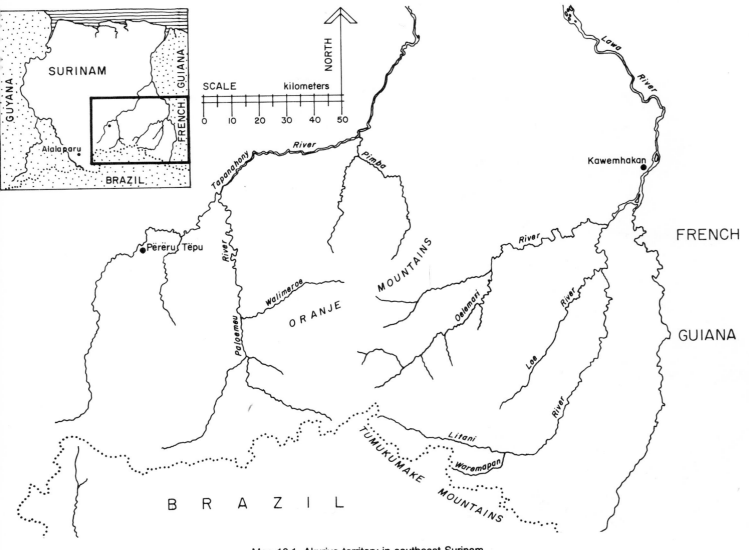

Map 10.1. Akuriyo territory in southeast Surinam

Until 1970 all Akuriyo were hunters and gatherers, but there are enough indications for us to assume that their ancestors were not. To summarize the available data, it may be stated that the Akuriyo in the first part of the 19th century were shifting cultivators in whose subsistence hunting, fishing, and gathering all played important roles. Their society and culture were very similar to and perhaps even identical with Trio society and culture at that time. In fact, de Goeje (1906: 2) was of the opinion that "Akuriyo" was just another name for the Trio (the people we today call Trio are an agglomeration of various populations that differ or formerly differed in minor aspects of culture). The ancestors of the Akuriyo left their villages, situated on the Oelemari River (*Maraoni,* in their language), probably during or following intervillage conflicts. They and their descendants managed to survive by adapting their society and its culture to a nomadic way of life, avoiding the big rivers and trekking along hardly visible trails in a habitat that was for the most part heavily forested.

By the time the displaced villagers took to the forest trails, they had already been in indirect contact with the outside world, probably with other Amerindians as mediators. For example, they made use of iron tools and already had terms such as *kamiča* (a fiber loincloth) and *pusa* (gun), which indicate contact and trade in earlier days. Therefore, the nomadic Akuriyo of the 20th century cannot be regarded as a last remnant of the ancient Amerindian migrants who populated the continent as hunters and gatherers before the invention of cultivation in the Western Hemisphere. Rather, they represent a case of *devolution,* having reverted from a semipermanent, agricultural village existence to a nomadic hunting and gathering way of life. Furthermore, they reverted from a life in which artifacts not locally produced had begun to take a place, to one of complete dependence on

Meke'ne (4 years old), an Akuriyo
wiri'i, or "girl"

what could be contrived and made from raw materials in the habitat. It is in the latter respect that the Akuriyo represent an extreme form of isolation: they avoided contact with other human beings, and managed to survive with nothing but their own resources.

While the Akuriyo as a distinct, isolated population survived, Akuriyo individuals perished. Group survival and individual death are closely related phenomena everywhere, and certainly so among the Akuriyo. My genealogy of the population comprises 154 individuals. Only about 33 percent of these were alive when the genealogy was collected. How did the other 66 percent die, and how is the Akuriyo way of death related to their way of life? It is my purpose here to arrive at a preliminary answer to these questions. First, I shall present my data on the causes of death. Then I shall try to show how the causes of death are related to social, cultural, and ecological characteristics.

AKURIYO DEATH

During my fieldwork in Përëru Tëpu, I collected data that enabled me to place almost all Akuriyo into a single, though admittedly complicated, genealogy. When an individual was no longer living, I tried to find out his or her age, cause of death, and if possible, the circumstance of death. The results of this part of my investigation are shown in Table 10.1. Although the table may give an impression of considerable precision and reliability, this is more apparent than real. Before continuing I shall examine the data in order to show to what extent they are unreliable.

The first source of unreliability lies in the genealogy itself. With the Akuriyo, genealogical research is the only possible way to study their demography. It is a truism to state that no genealogy is very reliable, but in the Akuriyo case the situation is even worse. Before about 1971 the Akuriyo lived in small bands, scattered over a vast territory. The bands irregularly met each other, but the interval between meetings was often several years. Furthermore, the Akuriyo are divided into two classes, the *tura ëka* and the more numerous *akuri ëka (ëka* means name, *tura* is a small brown monkey, and *akuri* is the agouti; there is a third class, the *pïnëkë ëka,* or "peccary name," but these people are usually classified with the *akuri ëka*). The two classes intermarry but are not exogamous. Children take the name of the father. There are slight dialect differences between *tura* and *akuri* and there are tensions between them; one of the bigger conflicts in the past was between these two groups. The origin of the classes is uncertain; perhaps they are a remnant of the past, representing ancient villages.

The distribution of Akuriyo among widely scattered bands and the *tura-akuri* division act together against the existence of a general body of genealogical knowledge. This meant that a genealogy had to be pieced together by using information from persons all over the genealogy. Even this was an inconclusive effort, however, for two reasons: (1) I never saw the group that was believed to be still in the forest, and (2) all older Akuriyo had died in the first year of resettlement in village life—my oldest informant was certainly not more than 40 years old. The link with the past was indeed thin. My main informants on the higher genealogical levels were an *akuri* (Marayaimë, about 35 years old) and a *tura* (Ënore, about 40 years old). Their knowledge overlapped by about 80–90 percent.

The weak spot lies especially in the number of children born to women who had died and whom I therefore could not interrogate. There is in my data a negative correlation between the number of children known to my informants and the genealogical distance between the informant and the mother in question. The

TABLE 10.1
Akuriyo Mortality and Causes of Death

Age Category	Causes of Death						Subtotal	Post-1970 Mortality Adjustment	Total
	Jaguar	*Fall from tree*	*Other violent death*	*Illness*	*Desertion*	*Unknown*			
Males									
infant	–	–	2	3	–	–	5	–	5
child	1	–	3	12	–	1	17	1	18
young adult	1	1	–	1	–	–	3	3	6
aged	4	4	1	2	3	7	21	2	23
Total	6	5	6	18	3	8	46	6	52
Females									
infant	–	–	–	1	–	–	1	–	1
child	1	–	1	17	–	1	20	2	22
young adult	1	–	–	2	–	–	3	2	5
aged	4	–	1	2	10	–	17	2	19
Total	6	–	2	22	10	1	41	6	47

implication is that infant mortality must be higher than Table 10.1 indicates. The mortality data for children are much less affected by this, and I believe that adult and aged mortality data are not affected at all.

The second source of unreliability lies in the age categories. Estimating the age of an Akuriyo is hazardous, and there are almost no known dates that can be used as guidelines. The missionaries estimated the ages of most of the living Akuriyo, and since most of them have lived for years among Amerindians, I think their estimates are not far from the truth. But this still leaves open the ages of Akuriyo never seen by any outsider. The Akuriyo themselves have a cultural classification of age, as shown in Table 10.2. The approximate age limits of the categories were found by comparing the estimates of the missionaries with the age classifications of the Akuriyo for the same individuals. An infant is a *pi'okoko* until it begins to walk. I never saw an Akuriyo child around that age, but I believe that the usual age for walking is less than one year, perhaps about 10 months. This implies that *pi'okoko* mortality is not the same as infant mortality in the technical sense. The consequence for the interpretation of Table 10.1 is that infant mortali-

ty appears somewhat higher and child mortality somewhat lower than it actually was. The transition between *tawi'në* and *pëito* as well as between *wiri'i* and *aru'ma* is not very sharp. Akuriyo girls marry before menarche, after which they are called *aru'ma*. Akuriyo boys marry somewhat later but are *pëito* when they have become self-sufficient, somewhere around 12 years of age. The category "aged" begins when the Akuriyo can be grandparents. Within the category some distinction can be made by differences in pronunciation: *tamutupë* is an old man, and *taaamutupë*, with long, stressed /a/, is a very old man; however, I suspect that this is a question not only of age but also of physical and spiritual condition. One of the Akuriyo women in Përëru Tëpu was often classified as *notëpë*, although she was certainly younger than 30 years old. She was a rather absentminded person, having a difficult time in adjusting to village life, and it was probably her activities and her appearance that caused the Akuriyo to see her as older than she was. The differences between the categories "young adult" and "aged" in Table 10.1 are thus relative and should not be taken too seriously. Finally, it should be emphasized that most of the individuals classified as "aged" are not more than 40 to 45 years old.

The third source of unreliability in the data lies in the causes of death as stated by my informants: this is entirely unverified information. However, the Akuriyo themselves are quite confident about their statements and also quite consistent with each other. The categories used in Table 10.1 are not Akuriyo categories and in a sense they are inconsistent. "Killings by jaguar" *(wïrï)* are in three forms, according to the Akuriyo: merely grabbed and killed by a jaguar; killed and eaten by a jaguar; and *wïrïkaimo,* "jaguar killing" in which an Akuriyo shaman

TABLE 10.2
Akuriyo Age Classification

English Gloss	Approximate Age	Male	Female
"Infant"	0–1	*pi'okoko*	*pi'okoko*
"Child"	1–12	*tawi'në*	*wiri'i*
"Young Adult"	12–30	*pëito*	*aru'ma*
"Aged"	30 and older	*tamutupë*	*notëpë*

has sent a spirit in the shape of a jaguar to kill another man or woman. For my purposes, the distinctions were collapsed. "Illness" is a category very difficult to assess. In more than 90 percent of the cases defined as "illness" the Akuriyo refer to stomach and intestinal troubles, such as diarrhea. They explain this sometimes in terms of food eaten by the individual in question, sometimes in terms of food eaten by parents (the father of a newborn child, for instance, is not allowed to eat certain kinds of honey). But even in these latter cases the child dies from a disease. Another problem with the category "illness" is its relation to the category "left behind." A sick person, an old and weak one, or a small baby whose mother has died is given up by the Akuriyo: no food is supplied, and such individuals are left behind as soon as they can no longer follow the group on the move. For this reason, a number of cases in the category "illness" might belong under "left behind," and vice versa. Usually, leaving behind is explained by general weakness due to old age. I believe, therefore, that the distribution of cases within the two categories closely reflects reality.

In Table 10.1 I have made a distinction between mortality in the forest and mortality in the village (12 individuals) because the circumstances were completely different. Another distinction might be made but is more difficult. This is the difference between mortality occurring before contact in 1968 and mortality occurring after contact but before resettlement in 1970 and 1971. The expeditions certainly did bring illness and death to the Akuriyo, but it is difficult to say either how many died in that period, or how many of these died as a result of imported disease (see Kloos: in press).

It should be clear, after the preceding remarks, that the contents of Table 10.1 cannot be used without qualifications. Unfortunately, the sources of unreliability cannot be quantified. Taking the data from Table 1 as a point of departure and taking into account the direction and magnitude of error, the following statements can be regarded as relatively reliable. I would say that among the Akuriyo:

1. Infant mortality is relatively low. Expressed as a percentage of the number of births, it is perhaps about 10 percent.

2. Child mortality is fairly high and can be attributed to intestinal and stomach trouble, as a rule.

3. Young adult mortality is very low. Apparently the weaker individuals have died before reaching adulthood: about 50 percent never reach this age.

4. The aged males meet a violent death in half of the cases, being victims of jaguar attacks or having fallen from trees. A few aged males are left behind when they no longer have the strength to follow their group. Aged females are as often vic-

Towatowapo (24 years old), an Akuriyo *pëito*, or "young man"

tims of jaguars; however, the majority live longer than men, and they tend to be left behind when their strength wanes.

5. The mortality curve by age does not have the usual U-shape, but rather resembles a J, or even a sinusoid.

These statements I take as my point of departure for the next section: how is the Akuriyo way of death related to the Akuriyo way of life?

AKURIYO LIFE

The Akuriyo live in the forests of the headwaters of the Litani, Loe, and Oelemari Rivers (all tributaries of the Marowijne or Maroni) and of the Pimba and the Walimeroe (tributaries of the Tapanahony). Some years ago at least one band crossed the watershed near the sources of the Litani and wandered into Brazil, where they lived for some time in the forests of the Matawale River.

The area in which the Akuriyo live is rugged, especially around the Oranje Mountains. Steep and heavily forested hills, sometimes topped with rocky outcrops, are interspersed with small marshes and creeks. Although the Akuriyo come to the big rivers (especially the Oelemari) during the dry season in search of iguana eggs, they tend to hide themselves in the depths of the forests. They avoid the big rivers, do not make boats, and cannot swim. Rivers and creeks that cannot be forded are crossed by using fallen logs as footbridges. Often these logs are provided with a vine handrail, to prevent women and children from falling.

Since the Akuriyo do not have gardens, there is no necessity for them to stay in one place for any length of time. Furthermore, the distribution of food and other resources is such that a full nomadic way of life is probably the best adaptation conceivable. They hunt, fish, and gather in one place for only a couple of days (occasionally a couple of weeks) before moving on.

Kërëpakomo, "our food," has six classes:

1. *kotïkomo:* meat from all animals, birds, reptiles, and fish
2. *kïnapëkomo:* fruits and honey
3. *kurukomo:* tubers
4. *kïnamokomo:* meat and fish broth; a tuber porridge cooked with meat or fish
5. *kokïkomo:* beverage (water only)
6. *kïmeekomo:* palmnuts

Akuriyo hunters use only bow and arrow. The bow, more than a man's height, is made of letterwood. Compared with Trio and Wayana bows, the Akuriyo bow is extraordinarily strong and heavy. For hunting, three types of arrow are used. The type with a long lanceolate point of bamboo is used for big game, such as tapir, deer, and peccary. A second type is provided with a sharp bone shiver; having a barb, it is used for small game, such as agouti and large birds. The third hunting arrow has a detachable point of palmwood (painted with *urasi,* or curare) and is used for monkeys. A fourth type of arrow is used for fishing only. It has a detachable barbed arrowhead that is connected to the hunter by a long line. Big fish are lured to a palmleaf screen (behind which the hunter is hidden) by throwing the entrails of game into the water. Small fish are caught only by using fish poison (*ineku, Lonchocarpus* sp.).

Hunting and fishing provide the Akuriyo with protein and fats, which are prominent in their diet. Additional foods are honey, palmfruit and palmnut, and various tubers. The Akuriyo distinguish some 35 kinds of honey and they are constantly in search of nests. A hunter in the forest pays as much attention to bees flying among the tree trunks as to animal tracks. The majority of the bees have their nests high up in trees. The Akuriyo climb the trees and break open the nest with a stone axe. This is dangerous work, as Leavitt attests:

First they got a long pole, 20 feet or so, and this they tied crossways from the honey tree to another tree nearby. They tied it about 15 feet above the ground just high enough for Kananaman to stand on and cut the nest out. It took almost 1 hour to cut it out. He cut several holes in the tree, first below the nest, but found that he was not low enough, and then above the nest until he had exposed the entire nest. A palmboat (a honey container) was handed up to him and he inserted it below the honey comb and then proceeded to loosen the whole comb and let it drop into the container. There was plenty of honey and it filled the container to the brim. Then there was the problem of lowering the container that had no handle and that was too high up to reach from the ground. Finally Tiramu (another man) climbed up the tree and stopped just below Kananaman. Then Kananaman carefully placed the container, about 18 inches long, into his hand, carefully balancing it as he did so. Then Tiramu slid down to the ground with the container. [Leavitt n.d.]

In other cases the men go up 10 to 20 meters high into a tree, hanging on with one hand and cutting with the other. Their only device for climbing trees is a vine, which they tie around their feet. It is their fondness for honey that is fatal to many men (see Table 10.1; I know the names of several additional men who fell from a tree in the search for honey, and died, but these I could not insert in the genealogy). The Akuriyo are fully aware of the risks involved. Still, while they occasionally do cut a whole tree with their stone axes to get the honey, they prefer to climb it.

Vegetable foods consist of a variety of fruits and several tubers. Neither plays a preponderant role in the Akuriyo diet. Some fruits, such as those of the ite palm (*Mauritia* sp.), are eaten raw. Others, such as *mope (Spondias mombin L.)* and *kumu (Oenocarpus bacaba),* are processed into a drink. More important than these are palmnuts such as the kernels of the thornpalm fruits, *muru'muru (Astrocaryum sciophilum Pulle)* and *marakupi.* These nuts are cracked with a stone or a stone axe and eaten raw. Palmfruits are plentiful in the wet season (May and June), and for that reason people often stay in one place for several weeks.

The Akuriyo distinguish six edible tubers, all of which grow near granite outcrops. The tubers are dug out with the aid of a digging stick. Most of them are small (many of them not exceeding the size of a finger), and often a day of hard work is rewarded by not more than a pound of tiny tubers. Some of the tubers are roasted over a fire. Others are grated on a rough stone and cooked with meat broth.

The contributions of the various foodstuffs to the total diet—in percentages of weight or in calories—is not known. Possibly 70–80 percent of the diet consists of meat, palmnuts, and honey, with tubers and fruits constituting a minor element. It is certain that the Akuriyo have a very nutrient-specific diet, rich in fat and protein but poor in carbohydrates. About the reliability of resources no quantitative data are available. The Akuriyo certainly know days of hunger and periodic shortages of food (including the occasional absence of any food), but in general there is no shortage. The nomadic Akuriyo are well fed, in both a quantitative and a qualitative sense. However, getting enough food requires all their energy and most of their time. The majority of the adults of a group go in search of food almost every day. Only one or two women stay behind to take care of small children. On the days following an exceedingly rich catch the Akuriyo stay at home. Any amount of meat that they cannot cook in their earthenware pots is barbecued. It is usually consumed on the spot, but sometimes it is transported to the next camp. Times of consistent surplus are rare. The forests and rivers of the habitat contain many potential foods but never in great quantities, the only exception being palmnuts, which are plentiful in the wet season. For the rest of the year, the direct vicinity of a temporary Akuriyo camp is exhausted after a couple of days; thus the group is forced to move—and forced to leave behind anyone who can no longer follow the group.

The pattern of daily life adapted to these conditions is as follows. A band—ranging in size from one nuclear family to a group of 20–30 individuals—departs early in the morning. The women carry most of the possessions in their pack frames (katari), such as hammocks, pots, stones for grating and cracking, stone axes and axe heads, a few small utensils, a digging stick, and barbecued meat (see Kloos [in preparation] for an inventory of Akuriyo material culture). Some carry a baby on top of everything. All women carry fire; the Akuriyo are unable to make fire and have to carry it from camp to camp, never allowing it to die out. The women usually bring some dry wood with them and occasionally have to rekindle their fire on their way to the next camp. If the fire of a band goes out there are only two possibilities: to get fire from another band, or to die. "His fire has gone out" (nenkepï) is a euphemism for "he is dead." The men carry only their bow and arrows, a stone axe, and a small quiver with poisoned arrowheads. They are not only on their way to the next camp, they are hunting as well.

Early in the afternoon people decide where to camp. Both men and women busy themselves with the construction of simple shelters for the night: a couple of thin poles, partly lashed together with vines, and a number of palm leaves on top of this. A fire is built, hammocks are tied in the shelters, and the camping place is cleaned.

The next day the men leave to go hunting and looking for honey and fruits. The women go in search of tubers and fruits. Getting food is quite an individual affair: men often go all alone or accompanied only by a child, and women often do the same, sometimes returning to the campsite long after dusk. Men frequently spend a night away from their camp, making a small shelter and an improvised hammock from bark when it rains, or seeking cover between the roots of big trees when it is dry.

The Akuriyo practice of going out alone to hunt and gather probably explains the relatively high incidence of killings by jaguars. Among the Trio and Wayana such killings are extremely rare, but there are at least two differences: the Trio and Wayana go hunting with dogs (which the Akuriyo do not possess), and they hunt in small groups.

The preparation of food is women's work. The bulk of the food is collected by men: meat, honey, and many of the palmfruits. A man arriving at his camp dumps his load, puts away his bow and arrows, and retires to his hammock. There he busies himself with the making and—more often—repairing of arrows (arrow cane is scarce). It is the men who make hammocks from ite palm fiber and loincloths from wild pineapple fiber. In addition to preparing food, the women make clay pots and the small bead aprons that they wear. Both men and women make necklaces of beads (of the marayaimë palm) and monkey teeth.

A second or a third day is spent in the same manner, after which the band departs again, moving to a new camp that is usually not more than 8 to 10 kilometers away. The pattern of moving is determined not only by the fact that food resources become exhausted after a few days. In the movements of Akuriyo bands two levels can be distinguished. The first one is the level of day-to-day movement, from camp to camp, usually not exceeding 10 kilometers. The motive for these movements is almost certainly the search for and exhaustion of food in a restricted area. The second level is characterized by long-distance goals and purposes. The day-to-day movements of an Akuriyo band are not at all arbitrary or without plan, but in fact take place along routes to specific sites that will be reached only after traveling weeks or months or even longer. Some of these sites are visited because there is much game. The primary drive behind long-term movements, however, has to do not with food but with nonedible, yet nonetheless vital, materials. These are fiber for hammocks, fiber for string (used to make a variety of artifacts, such as arrows, axes, bowstrings, loincloths, necklaces), arrow cane, and stone for stone axes. All Akuriyo bands have their favorite ite fiber patches and wild pineapple fiber patches. There are in their habitat only three or four sites where arrow cane can be found, and there are only a few sites where stone suitable for an axe head may be found. These sites are widely distributed over the entire habitat, and some types of site are remote from each other. Sizable ite palm patches occur only in marshy areas. Wild pineapple grows on granite outcrops. Stones for axes are found in certain rapids. Arrow cane, growing at what are perhaps ancient village sites, can be found only on the upper Oelemari, on the Litani, and in one or two small creeks. The need for these resources is what forces the Akuriyo to make their long journeys.

These journeys follow quite definite trails, already in use for many years, even though a band may not use a trail for a year or more. The trails—chains of broken, bent, or twisted saplings, occasional axe cuts in the bark of a tree, emptied bee nests, and old camp sites—can easily be recognized by a practiced eye.

It is amazing how persistent the traces of human activity are. The Akuriyo on the move do not cut saplings but bend and partly break them. The sapling often recovers but remains twisted. Although the Akuriyo shelters are such that after two years or so very few remnants of the construction itself can be found, the site itself remains strikingly open because no big trees are cut down and thus no sunlight reaches the bottom of the forest. Triangles of three stones, used to steady the clay pots over the fire, mark the number and actual locations of the shelters and can easily be found even after 15 to 20 years.

More or less fixed trails are themselves probably an adaptation to a nomadic way of life in the forest. Although Akuriyo artifacts are ingenious enough, it is knowledge of the habitat more than skill in making and using artifacts that makes survival possible. In this case an advanced technology probably would not pay off (see Kloos [in preparation]). The Akuriyo bands do not have territories in the sense of bounded areas. Rather, they have trails that are more or less fixed. These trails, and a strip of forest along the trails, they know incredibly well. The areas *between* trails are relatively or completely unknown. For the Akuriyo a trail is not just a path, but a cultural phenomenon; not just a geographic feature, a line connecting more or less useful things, but an ongoing series of historically related *events*. A sample inventory of such events might run as follows:

Here Amana was bitten by a snake.

Here Marayaimë killed a curassow.

Here Towatowapo got honey, *ami'aikïrï* honey it was.

Here Posuwara and Marayaimë camped, we ate barbecued peccary, but we brought it here from the previous camp.

In this camp Nariyamo was born.

Here we left Napëkï'në, she was very old.

There we killed a tapir.

This was Irikinë's camp, I remember that he left an old pot behind, see, here it is.

Here Ariwë'në was killed by a jaguar.

This list is a construct: I never followed an Akuriyo on his own trails long enough to collect a true inventory. Situational memory of the Akuriyo containing information of this kind is extraordinarily rich and goes back at least 20 years. The mind of every adult Akuriyo must be crammed with this kind of information about his trails. Unfortunately this information cannot be tapped unless questions can be asked on the spot—that is what I mean by "situational memory."

The use of the term "band" may be misleading. It should be stated that, so far as is known, the Akuriyo never formed one band. They have always trekked in smaller groups, which vary both in size and in composition. There is no rule at all to account for the composition. In some societies the shifting composition of bands has been explained in terms of adjustment to available resources and their seasonal regional variation. This does not apply to the Akuriyo. One of the few guiding principles of group membership is that a man often seeks a wife (especially a first wife) in another group. But the marital relationship is very weak, and the frequency of divorce is extraordinarily high. The actual group composition—apart from the relationship between a mother and her young child—seems to be explicable only in terms of personal likes and dislikes and highly individual attachments. It should be added that the attachment between individuals is not strong: there is almost no emotional involvement among Akuriyo, whatever the relationship. I believe that here too, the Akuriyo way of life is directly connected with the Akuriyo way of death. Sick or old individuals who cannot move with the group are left behind. Such a harsh method has to do with the survival of the group, and it seems to me that the emotional aloofness shown by the Akuriyo is related to this necessity. A good example of the attitude of the Akuriyo is provided by the missionary Ivan Schoen, writing in an expedition report:

The Akoerios . . . told us [Schoen and some Trio Indians] that they had deserted an old lady far back in the mountains as she was dying. Upon hearing this news we set out on the trail to find her. The trail led us about 10 kilometers back up into the mountains. Along the way we met Sokwiwi. He told us that the woman was still alive, but dying, and that he too had deserted her. . . . We found her in a small camp. . . . She was huddled in her hammock over a smoldering fire; cold, hungry, and utterly without hope. . . . We carried her out over the trail . . . over mountains and through vast palm swamps . . . we arrived back in [the Akuriyo] camp with the woman alive and much improved in spirit. The Akoerios, on the other hand, laughed at us and said, "Why did you bring in those old bones?" [Schoen 1971: 8]

Indeed, many adult Akuriyo have at some time in their lives left behind children or parents, or both.

There are, of course, social relationships between bands. Most adults have close relatives in other bands, and a few individuals or nuclear families move from one band to another, being part-time members of both. Furthermore, whole bands occasionally plan to meet at intervals, though these meetings are probably fairly rare. On the other hand, there are no pan-tribal meetings of any kind; until their resettlement in 1970 and 1971, no Akuriyo had ever seen more than about 30 individuals at once.

Between certain groups, or perhaps between certain individuals, relations are tense. Trouble over women and suspicion of having caused death by wïrïkaimo ("jaguar killing" effected by a shaman) are the main reasons. A man's fear that another man may take his wife, or that his wife may prefer another man and leave him, is reason for avoiding other bands. Thus the Akuriyo not only isolate themselves from the outside world, but even tend to isolate themselves from other Akuriyo.

CONCLUSION: AKURIYO LIFE AND DEATH

To return to the main features of Akuriyo mortality, it is the unusual degree of social isolation, I believe, that is responsible for the relatively low infant mortality rate. A major factor in infant mortality the world over—namely, all kinds of contagious disease—is thus simply eliminated. Moreover, for infants there is no food problem at all, as long as their mother is alive. For *children,* however, there is a real food problem. Although there is sufficient food for all Akuriyo, the supply is irregular. If there is enough, the Akuriyo tend to eat all day long. On days of shortage they go with an empty stomach. Although the quality and variety of food is good enough, at least as seen over the course of the year, it may be limited and unvaried when seen over a shorter period. Finally, some food, especially barbecued meat, is eaten even when it begins to putrify. My hypothesis is that these factors largely explain child mortality among the Akuriyo. As a result of such mortality, those who survive childhood are a highly selected group, able to withstand the harshness of adult life and its continuous quest for survival. As a further consequence of the harshness of life, the Akuriyo age early, and during old age (which already begins between 30 and 40) probably more than half of the men meet a violent end during their search for food. Women live to be somewhat older than men, partly because they do not climb trees for honey, but they are left behind if they no longer have the strength to move when their group cannot afford to remain at a camp site. I believe that in many cases of desertion a group *could* stay for a couple of days, but in the case of weak, old people there is really no use in doing so. At any rate, the Akuriyo have developed an attitude of resignation in the face of approaching death and are not inclined to help anyone who is no longer able to help himself.

REFERENCES

Ahlbrinck, W.
   1956   *Op zoek naar de Indianen.* Amsterdam: Koninklijk Instituut voor de Tropen.

Felhoen Kraal, J.
   1957   Op zoek naar de Indianen. *West Indische Gids* 37: 223–6.

Goeje, Claudius H. de
   1906   Bijdrage tot de ethnographie der Surinaamsche Indianen. *Internationales Archiv für Ethnographie* 17 (supplement).

Kloos, Peter
   In Press *The Akuriyo of Surinam: A Case of Emergence From Isolation.* Copenhagen: International Work Group for Indigenous Affairs.
   In Prep. Akuriyo Artifacts: Stone Age Culture in the Tropical Forest.

Leavitt, C. W.
   n.d.   Expedition Report November–December 1969 [mimeographed report, West Indies Mission].

Meuldijk, K.
   1939   Reis op de nog onbekende Oelemari-rivier. *Tijdschrift Koninklijk Nederlands Aardrijkskundig Genootschap* 56: 872-6.

Schoen, I. L.
   1971   Report of the emergency trip made by the West Indies Mission to the Akoerio Indians, June 1971 [mimeographed report, West Indies Mission].